Fight Poverty - Not the Poor!

Allan C. Jones and Mikaya L. Gent Mills

Published by Allan Jones, 2023.

While every precaution has been taken in the preparation of this book, the publisher assumes no responsibility for errors or omissions, or for damages resulting from the use of the information contained herein.

FIGHT POVERTY - NOT THE POOR!

First edition. September 30, 2023.

ISBN: 979-8230021674

Written by Allan C. Jones and Mikaya L. Gent Mills.

Table of Contents

Preface

America used to be the global example for what a democracy could be. What happened? The simple answer is, "Poverty happened." While the short simple answer is true, it is not enough. Our goal in writing this book is to not only identify and raise awareness of the problem; we also want to energize, enable, and empower the readers to take action to fix the problem. Mexican poet and academic, Cesar A. Cruz is credited with saying, "Art should comfort the disturbed and disturb the comfortable." We hope the comfortable will be disturbed enough by this book to join our efforts to fix the problem, and the disturbed will see our efforts as a viable solution and be comforted by our efforts.

It is time to revive some democratic founding principles that have been lost. To do that, we must defeat poverty. Our American way of life is dependent on the economic prosperity of all our citizens, not just the few. Our prolonged active national neglect of fighting poverty in America is a relentless force that drives a very real threat to the longest running democracy in human history. Our neglect of the principles that made us great has enabled a number of unacceptable and dangerous conditions, including:

- Rise of nationalism, especially white nationalism.

- Support for authoritarianism.

- School and other mass shootings.

- Banning teaching/learning in school that is deemed "too woke" for the ear who doesn't want to listen, (creating an uproar from the minority community),

- Defying COVID precautions for political and profit reasons.

- Deliberately deepening poverty by denying Medicare dollars and Obamacare.

- Denying infrastructure spending that is needed in their economically struggling states.

- A weakened educational system

America's enemies, large and small, foreign and domestic, are rejoicing as they watch us allow ourselves to be divided, weakening our ability to unite behind our traditional democratic principles. As we look into these issues of what can be causing this lack of togetherness, it is our hope to not go back to our traditional ways, but to find modern solutions that can ensure satisfaction to everyone's ideal needs.

One of the fundamental foundations of a robust democracy is a well-informed electorate. Historically, America has had a strong, independent, and truthful collection of reliable media that provided our citizens with a broad assortment of sources of information. Technology has revolutionized the media landscape. We now have media sources whose full-time role is to evaluate and report on the veracity of media organizations. It is so bad that former military enemies have established disinformation as a major weapon. As we write this book, AI Chat bots like ChatGPT are emerging with the ability to develop and promote social media posts specifically designed to convince the reader that some spurious threat exists.

We have fallen short in responding to these issues because propagandized information is constantly on display from social media, television, and movies. Our nation is being gaslighted, divided, and weakened. Rational voices are not heard if they are speaking out against the dystopian way of life we have been led to believe exists. This raises a couple questions to think about as we dive deeper into the issues; "Have the traditional democratic principles always fallen short of delivering on the American dream for those who are in need? Has it only pushed certain agendas while allowing others to be overlooked?"

The reason that we neglect the poverty issue may be that people living in poverty have no political power. Most of them are too consumed with earning enough money to survive to be politically active. They do not have the time or resources to support causes that might force politicians to address their pain. The only political power or resource that most impoverished people have is exercising their right to vote. Sadly, in the current political climate, America's electoral process is under attack. Despite overwhelming evidence and many court cases to the contrary, as many as 40% of American voters believe the 2020 presidential election was stolen. Many voters have limited knowledge about which political side will work to help them achieve their needs. Politicians exacerbate the problem by going into targeted communities and feeding them specious information on how they will solve problems. After stealing the hearts of those who've been previously neglected, the politicians then disproportionately abandon those who actually need assistance. This has a compound impact. In the short term, the needs do not get met through governmental aid. In the long term, the citizens lose what little faith they may have had in the system.

In addition to our own intuitive observations, several reliable sources have told us our long-established democratic standards are under attack. If you have any doubts, read the references in the footnotes, or do your own research on the issue. Here are four respected sources.

- Protect Democracy is a nonpartisan, nonprofit organization dedicated to fighting efforts, at home and abroad, to undermine our right to free, fair, and fully informed elections. A year after Jan. 6th they warned us "Our democracy is in danger"[1]

- The Economist told us "How to think about the threat to American democracy" [2]

- The New York Times declared "Democracy Is at Risk"[3]

- NPR reported "6 in 10 Americans say U.S. democracy is in crisis"[4] as the 'Big Lie' takes root.

We don't need any outside experts to tell us democracy is under attack. Our democracy was already in danger when Obama took office in 2009. He created a push for "change". However, that change did not include long-term objectives that would save impoverished communities from being gentrified. Partisan bickering prevented passage of an infrastructure package. By rejecting large infrastructure projects,10 million Americans lost their homes between 2007- 2016 while dealing with a recession. During those times, and despite the good intentions for change, the same Americans continued to be homeless on the streets of their old communities.

---

1. https://protectdemocracy.org/the-threat

2. https://www.economist.com/leaders/2022/01/01/how-to-think-about-the-threat-to-american-democracy

3. https://www.nytimes.com/2022/01/05/opinion/letters/jan-6-capitol-hill-riot.html

4. https://www.npr.org/2022/01/03/1069764164/american-democracy-poll-jan-6

This book is an examination of what makes America the country we love, what is happening to it, and what we need to do to restore our moral, economic, industrial, and cultural position as an example for the rest of the world, not to mention making it a better place to live again.

It is like being the parent of a child who has shown great potential in the past but is evolving into a terrible teen. Hormones drive teenagers to become seemingly irrational, sometimes self-destructive, individuals who are not interested in self-improvement. For teenagers, hormonal change is the cause. For America, pervasive poverty is endangering its values. We still love the country, but exposure to harmful and dangerous conditions from poverty pose major threats. With this book, we are hoping to unite and motivate the voters and show everyone the value and importance of living up to our shared dreams and democracy's unlimited potential.

In November of 1863, President Lincoln reminded all Americans of our responsibility to preserve and defend our democracy. He was speaking on a battlefield following a deadly engagement pitting Americans fighting on both sides. We are in a frighteningly similar position today. Take a few minutes to refresh your memory of his inspirational words.

> *"Four score and seven years ago our fathers brought forth on this continent, a new nation, conceived in Liberty, and dedicated to the proposition that all men are created equal. [...] But, in a larger sense, we cannot dedicate—we cannot consecrate—we cannot hallow—this ground. The brave men, living and dead, who struggled here, have consecrated it, far above our poor power to add or detract. The world will little note, nor long remember what we say here, but it*

can never forget what they did here. It is for us the living, rather, to be dedicated here to the unfinished work which they who fought here have thus far so nobly advanced. It is rather for us to be here dedicated to the great task remaining before us—that from these honored dead we take increased devotion to that cause for which they gave the last full measure of devotion—that we here highly resolve that these dead shall not have died in vain—that this nation, under God, shall have a new birth of freedom—and that government of the people, by the people, for the people, shall not perish from the earth".

In 1863, slavery was the force driving a wedge between the divided parts of the country. Poverty, driven by greed, is the force driving today's wedge. Today's society has taken the essence of slavery and poverty and modernized it. Technological advances made possible with robotics, factory automation, and AI (artificial intelligence), enable companies to pay low wages to highly qualified citizens who are worth more. Failing schools and gaslighting media have weakened Americans' intelligence, judgment, and knowledge; leading to a new social dynamic that divides Americans into enraged mobs instead of uniting them into thoughtful communities.

By presenting America's problems through a partisan lens, recording the acts of violence that have become a trend, and providing no actual solution to combat these issues, citizens are deliberately influenced to perceive these social issues as dystopian conditions. Citizens are seen working high maintenance jobs, with long working hours receiving low pay, while inflation steadily increases. This opens a door for people to be without a home, food, and the resources needed to deal with their debt. Poverty is alive and well and threatening our democracy.

Lincoln was wrong when he said, "*The world will little note, nor long remember what we say here,*" but the rest of his words are as relevant today as they were in 1863. We must all unite to restore, defend, and preserve those fundamental democratic values. Since the Civil War, America has been involved in several military actions resulting in the maiming, death, and wounding of countless soldiers – all ostensibly fighting to defend our democratic way of life. We must ensure that those dead shall not have died in vain.

One last Lincoln quote. In June of 1858, Abraham Lincoln famously said, "*A house divided against itself cannot stand.*" America today is more divided than it has been in a long time. Unlike in Lincoln's time when slavery was the major divisive issue, today, numerous issues divide us, rendering the Congress hopelessly split along party lines and effectively gridlocked – unable to accomplish anything that significantly improves the living conditions of the average American citizen.

One of the most frightening aspects of this hyper-partisanship is the resulting gridlock and inability to collaborate, deliberate, and solve critical problems. The 2023 train wreck in East Palestine, Ohio is a great illustration. We'll present two scenarios. 1) what might have happened in a rational political environment. And 2) what actually happened as a result of petty partisan politics. These scenarios are based upon available reporting and press releases/conferences. We must assume that many dedicated people worked tirelessly to clean up this site and prevent further wrecks. While we saw some of that, we saw much more partisan bickering. We also have a meaningful bi-partisan bill.

1. National leader's non-partisan response.
    a. The wreck in Ohio was terrible. We need to know more about what happened and why.

        i. What immediate hazards must be mitigated?

            1. What needs to be done? Who will do it? Who will pay for it?

       ii. What warning signs were missed?

        i. How can we make sure that the citizens of the hit community are safe?

        i. Was this a unique event or is it part of a bigger problem?

        i. What is the larger extent of the damage?

           1. Environmental

           2. Supply chain

           3. Cost to the taxpayers, railroad company, consumers, environment, shippers, health, transportation system, etc.?

   b. What regulations and legislation can we pass and implement that will prevent future similar events?

   c. What is the most expeditious process for creating and passing the laws and rules needed?

1. National leaders' partisan response. (What actually occurred in this instance.)

   a. This would not have happened if they (the other party) had done their job.

   b. This happened because the other party did something.

   c. Whining that the leader of the party in power did not visit the site immediately.

       i. Disaster teams were on-site immediately.

To put the railroad issue in perspective, we have more than 1,000 derailments per year in the US – more than three per day. Looking at it another way, there are countless potential infrastructure jobs paying a living wage that would fix our rail safety problem while also reducing poverty. Infrastructure projects do more than directly provide jobs, they also use supplies and materials that create more jobs.

US intelligence agencies have proven that much of the social media fake news that promotes extreme positions on both sides of major political, cultural, and social issues is being generated and disseminated by Russia and other enemies in an attempt to destabilize our government and economy. They are using chatbots to harvest information from social media sites and then generate divisive posts on popular US social media platforms. Russia or any hostile foreign power wins when Americans become more divided! When we are literally the UNITED States, we are indomitable. There's no identifiable major contribution that will eradicate the state of poverty if we are not working together. As the old saying goes, "it takes a village to raise a child". It still applies to the poverty crisis we are facing today.

We have come full circle and are dangerously close to another civil war. The January 6th, 2021, attack on the US Capital was the proverbial 'shot across the bow', warning us that if we do not change course, we are sailing into dangerous waters. Both from their appearance and their rhetoric, we can infer that the participants in the 1/6 insurrection were not prosperous citizens. Poverty warped their sense of what America could and should be. Growing poverty is fueling threats to our democracy and freedoms. Both the left and right seem to have forgotten to value and ensure the wellbeing of all our citizens as our first principle.

A divided America is weakened and vulnerable to foreign attack. Attack is not limited to military action. Putin and other enemy leaders are smugly watching and propelling us as the US falls apart from within. Later in the book, we discuss the impact of 9/11 and how it impacted our democracy. We discuss several ways Al Qaeda won that interaction without firing a missile or dropping a bomb. Despite the President's claim of "Mission Accomplished!", it was not a military victory. Al Qaeda succeeded in significantly damaging our democracy by dividing us, causing us to give up some of our fundamental freedoms, and pitting the groups against each other instead of foreign enemies.

'Gaslighting' was a new term for me. From hearing it used in context, it seemed like just a big word for 'lying'. Turns out, it is a special type of lying. Gaslighting is loosely defined as making someone question their own reality. The Encyclopedia Britannica defines 'gaslighting' as, *"a technique of deception and psychological manipulation intended to make the victim dependent on the deceiver in thoughts or feelings."* The term may also be used to describe the actions of a person who presents a false narrative that leads their audience to doubt their perceptions and become misled, disoriented, or distressed.

For a current example, Putin is gaslighting to mislead his whole country into a war with Ukraine. Trump and his minions are gaslighting with their 'Big Lie' that the 2020 election was stolen. In this era of social media and politically biased 'news' channels, people can select their news sources and live in their bubble where they are subjected to extra-strength gaslighting. This book attempts to counter the gaslighting by providing fact-based information. Our goal is to motivate change. None of us can sit on the sidelines and allow a bitter minority to destroy our democracy. As Martin Luther King said. *In the end, we will remember not the words of our enemies, " "but the silence of our friends* Who are these friends with silent voices? They are the people we work and party with who appear to share our values and dreams, but when tested by a need to defend our values, they duck their heads or look the other way.

Caveat emptor! Simply translated, it means, "Buyer beware." Because we are encouraging the reader to become actively involved in programs designed to address these issues, we feel an obligation to warn you of the false friends and scammers who see social programs as a means to make a buck. These organizations have supposedly created their programs for the impoverished, but they provide little to no change, while taking money from the government to fund themselves. Others are those politicians that walk into neighborhoods speaking on change and what they can do, while pushing an agenda to win an election. Once elected, they ignore the disenfranchised voters who supported them. So, caveat emptor.

As Allan was writing/editing this book and seeking feedback from friends, he had an epiphany. No matter how hard he tried, he had a limited perspective on these issues. He is an old (79 years), Northern, white man, and as such, he sees the world through an old, Northern, white man's eyes. He needed another point of view. A mutual friend introduced him to Mikaya Gent Mills, a young, Southern, black woman. In the following paragraphs Mikaya provides a brief self-introduction.

> *From an Afrocentric perspective, I started to see my community that I knowingly love within the depths of my soul be targeted and gentrified. I saw those same people I used to grow up with in my southern neighborhood be on drugs, out on the streets, going without food, and no one to call on to help. This movement was embedded in me to do. My roots scream "black power, justice for all, and liberation!" I have spent 24 years of life discovering who I am, figuring out who my family was; wanting to know what*

about them made me who I was. I am a reflection of not only the ancestors of those who have created this path for me, but too, a reflection of those who I see on the streets. They are my brothers and sisters, and they are treated as such.

So as Allan Jones and I collaborate and write this book, this book will reveal the essence of a young black woman who has a story to tell from first-hand point of view. Be open to both perspectives. Be open to the understanding that we are both on a path of finding solutions to eradicate poverty and everything that comes with it. I am an aboriginal to this land we call the United States of America. I will not let my people fall nor will I let them suffer any longer. Ase'

I am honored and excited to collaborate with Mikaya. My collaboration with Mikaya produced an unanticipated benefit. I subconsciously expected her to have some vastly different views on the issues. It turns out that our views are much more alike than they are different when it comes to the solutions to the issues. I interpret that to indicate I have managed to keep my biases under control.

I have spent my life in service to this country in and out of the military, educating our children, and fighting the ills of poverty. I hope this book reveals to you what I have come to know; that poverty is the insidious corrosive agent that undermines the greatness of this country that I love. I hope this book is a rallying cry for you to no longer neglect poverty or the poor.

In 1985, about forty of the world's leading pop musicians gathered to raise their collective voices in an attempt to grow support for fighting poverty and starvation in Africa. They wrote, performed, produced, and distributed an inspirational song called, We Are The World[5] that remains popular to this time, several decades later. The chorus goes:

We are the world

We are the children

We are the ones who make a brighter day, so let's start giving

There's a choice we're making

We're saving our own lives

It's true we'll make a better day, just you and me

The two lines

"There's a choice we're making

We're saving our own lives."

Really spoke to me.

5. https://www.youtube.com/watch?v=9AjkUyX0rVw

The footnote link to the YouTube video is my gift to you. Watch the video and absorb the lyrics to lift your spirits. You may also enjoy trying to recognize the incredible singers. I should warn you that if you listen to the song, it gets stuck in your head for a couple of days.

Throughout this book, we encourage the reader to get involved – make a difference. None of us can fix all of the issues discussed. Realistically, none of us can fix any of the issues by ourselves. But big changes are usually an accumulation of little changes. As an example, consider this small effort I made years ago.

In the mid-1980s, I was working in the Corporate Research division of Digital Equipment Corporation in the department responsible for bringing new ideas into the company from universities around the world. In that role, I served as a volunteer on the Board of Directors for the Junior Engineering Technical Society (JETS). JETS provided a couple of cash scholarship prizes to be awarded at the annual National Science and Engineering Fair. I was asked to lead the JETS judging team for that year's competition, being held at Carnegie Mellon University (CMU) in Pittsburg, to select who would receive the JETS prizes. I agreed to do it if they would help me ensure we had minorities and women on our judging team. In the 1980s, this was an important issue.

At the competition, the judging team split up and went to view the presenters. Following the initial viewings, we reconvened to share our observations and pick 8 - 10 contestants to be semi-finalists. Then we all went back out to view the chosen ones we had not seen and selected four finalists, from which we selected the winners. During the initial viewing, I observed a young lady from central Florida who had done an amazing analysis of paper. What it is made from, how it is produced. What the resulting properties were (water absorption, tensile strength, thermal, electrical, and sound transmission and insulation properties, crushing strength, smell, translucence, etc.) Her display and explanation including her clear enthusiasm for her work were remarkable. You can tell, I was impressed. I asked her where she was going to college, and she said she was going to secretarial school because it was all her family could afford.

My immediate reaction was to track down my female judge and ask her to please observe this girl's presentation, and to be sure to ask her where she was going to college. The judge was a professor at CMU. She observed the presentation and was as impressed as I had been. When she heard about her secretarial plans, she asked the girl if she would be interested in coming to CMU. Leaving out the process details, the girl won the JETS scholarship, and the judge arranged a full ride scholarship for the girl to attend CMU with the promise from the professor to serve as her mentor.

I did very little physically to get this rewarding result. I was just doing what I always do - looking for a way to make the world a better place. With that mindset, I was receptive to the opportunities as they presented themselves. When I was asked to lead the team of judges, I heard it as an opportunity to provide some bright young students a chance to see female and minority adult scientists and engineers at no incremental cost. When I heard the bright female student was heading for secretarial school (No offense to secretaries intended.) I had already laid the groundwork to respond with my female judge.

The moral to the story is to always look for opportunities to move forward in pursuit of your goals. Small and simple steps can result in major leaps.

We hope this book reveals to you what we have come to know, that poverty is the great corrosive agent that undermines the greatness of this country that we love. We hope this book is a rallying cry for you to no longer neglect poverty or the poor.

Introduction

This book provides a listing of the major issues threatening our democracy that we must overcome, with suggestions for overcoming them. While researching the different relevant topics, it became clear that the average American is much like the authors in their level of understanding of the way our government works (or does not work). Allan has the luxury of being curious and retired, so he has both the inclination and time to improve his understanding. Mikaya has both the youthful enthusiasm and passion for a cause that drives her efforts. We hope that by telling others what we have learned, people who share our curiosity but lack the time will find this book informative and the message compelling. To assist you in validating our statements and provide additional information where you may want it, we have thoroughly footnoted the sources we used. How thoroughly? There are over 200 footnotes in this 200+page book. Material quoted from outside sources is shown in italics.

We must work together to fix this mess! One person cannot do this alone. Fortunately, we all have the opportunity to stand together!

Due to post-colonization, slavery, and the attack on black lives, many black people had to re-learn and re-discover values, self-esteem, love, and worth of self. Not only were they being dismantled in their environment, but also the toxicity of their homes created disorder to want to achieve success. In the community, being the first at something is better than not accomplishing anything at all. Whether that's being a first-generation high school or college graduate; first doctor in the community; first mayor. I look forward to the time when the "first black" stories move from "1 of 1" to a plethora of accolades being achieved throughout the nation and nobody notices because it won't be unusual or taboo, but the livelihood that exists.

Because of course they did. Why wouldn't they execute and perform to a higher standard than the notion that's given to them? We need to stop being surprised by the accomplishments being made and allow black people to flourish. But this should go for any "minority" that has barriers that stops them from performing, exploring, and reaching their fullest ability.

America has a lot to be proud of, but we must acknowledge that we also have some things to be ashamed of. America's greatest source of shame is poverty and everything that has transpired from it. It is obscene that we live in the wealthiest country the world has ever known, and yet children are going to bed hungry every night because their parents cannot earn a living. It is outrageous that the wealthiest country would gentrify ghettos to install a plethora of malls, car washes, and other buildings instead of re-establishing, restoring, and reinvigorating the minority neighborhoods. The War on Drugs caused and continues to cause the de-popularization of two parent households based on fraudulent criminal charges, an increase in prison cell occupancy, and ultimately an amplified demand for more foster care, and services to support homelessness, domestic violence, recidivism, and other societal issues. Americans should be ashamed of the alarming details in our history that intentionally distort the perception of middle- and lower-class citizens. To advance partisan ideology, government agencies are banning books and not allowing the teaching of some shameful events in American history.

Thomas Jefferson wrote that a well-informed electorate is a prerequisite to democracy[6].

The current republican efforts to constrain and distort public education is frightening.

---

6. https://tcf.org/content/commentary/a-well-informed-electorate-is-a-prerequisite-for-democracy

"Approximately 70 years ago, Republicans hit upon a winning formula: if the data disagree with your worldview, kill the data. Then, with no problematic data, claim that there is no definitive proof of reality and, in the words of Karl Rove, create your own reality.

• In the 1940s, faced with a highly effective group of economists at the young National Labor Relations Board, Republicans passed a bill banning the agency from hiring economists.

• In the 1990s, faced with high-quality research on gun violence, Republican Congressman Jay Dickey pushed through an amendment that effectively stopped federal funding for gun research.

• In February of this year, House Majority Leader Eric Cantor called for an end to federal funding of social science research.

• Now, Republicans are trying to kill high quality data on poverty, unemployment, violent crime, access to education and health care, and a variety of other key economic indicators."

Our research on the many issues threatening our democratic principles found that there was no single book that aggregated and integrated all the issues related to poverty and its impact on democracy under a common theme. There are books about racism, military defense, the economy, civil unrest, abortion, partisan politics, gun control, and countless other issues, but none of them provided the depth and breadth needed for the reader to understand how all of the issues are part of a larger system, and the only way to address them is systemically. The biggest issue, and the one at the root of many other problems, is poverty and the corrupt political, economic, and electoral systems that cause and perpetuate it. Using poverty as the unifying theme, the issues come together to show how all the solutions are interdependent.

When you step back and consider all the issues, poverty stands out in a couple of ways. In addition to poverty being a component of every other issue, poverty has one positive property. Poverty is not a divisive issue in the sense that nearly everyone agrees that we need to eliminate poverty. Most of the other issues have strongly opposing sides fighting for different solutions. There is no side opposed to eliminating poverty. Our challenge is to unite them to fight poverty.

This book provides accurate portrayals of the major issues with references to reliable sources for further learning. It illustrates how poverty, wealth, and income inequality are intricately woven throughout the entire fabric of our problems. After reading this book, you may not have changed your position on the issues, but you will have a more comprehensive understanding of them. If everyone is working from the same facts, agreement is more possible.

The conditions identified in this book did not get that way overnight. It has literally taken decades. Fixing the conditions will not occur overnight either. But that does not mean we can't fix them. We must begin immediately and persist.

This book is about solutions, but not blame, ownership, but not showmanship. Our goal is to unite everyone in addressing the conditions we discuss, not exacerbate the current divisiveness that prevents our productively teaming up to fix the problems.

The authors are independent voters with liberal, conservative, and progressive beliefs. We try not to fit into anybody's partisan mold.

In writing this book, we intend to be equally tough on Republicans and Democrats. Both parties share the blame for the conditions that existed way before the 21st century era. Each president, citizen, congress member, legislator, judge, and other governmental official shares the responsibility for America's failing.

Do you recognize these words? *trustworthy, loyal, helpful, friendly, " courteous, kind, obedient, cheerful, thrifty, brave, clean, and reverent"*? They are from the Boy Scout Motto. Let's add honor, shame, truthfulness, empathy, compassion, respect, admiration, pride, honesty, faithfulness, and consideration? These were the values we were taught for ourselves and our country. In 1980, Ronald Reagan referred to the US as *"... a shining city upon a hill whose beacon light guides freedom-loving people everywhere."* We maintained and lived by those values that the rest of the world admired and emulated for a couple of more decades. We still live by those values, and we suspect you do too. Let's consider what changed. The poverty in the US indicates that many of us need to recommit to those values. Not only recommit to those values, but create and establish some for yourselves that you can follow and believe in.

Hopefully, this book will illuminate the greed that has led us to the current underlying poverty issue and launch a movement to unite the 99% to restore some economic equilibrium and eliminate poverty.

We are aware of the problem of authors making statements that are of dubious veracity – without providing any source for their statement. We have tried to be diligent about providing you the source for the information presented. For the reader who wants to know more, we have provided footnotes to the sources we used for the information. All the sources are web-based, so they are readily available. In researching and writing this book, we read many excellent books and articles. We also spent time eliminating some that were misleading or inaccurate. To save you from wasting your time, we have provided many links to valuable and informative sources within the text so you can learn more while the issue is on your mind.

How can America have so much wealth and still have so much poverty? In the following chapters, we will discuss the major issues the US is facing and demonstrate the direct connection between the issues and poverty. The following is a list of issues that our elected leaders should have avoided or fixed.

- It has been nearly 10 years since Flint Michigan citizens have had clean, safe tap water. They unwittingly introduced lead-poisoned water into homes, due to cutting costs to a struggling city[7]. If this problem had occurred in the nearby affluent Detroit suburb of Grosse Pointe, it would have been fixed immediately. Realistically, it never would have been allowed to happen in an affluent community like Grosse Pointe. Both political parties blame the other side, but the bottom line is that this is not a partisan issue, it's a poverty issue. If you have no money, you have no power to get things done. You have people in positions of power who don't care about the well-being of men, women, and children.

- As of 12/20/2022, there had been 300 documented school shootings[8] in that year. Despite public support, our elected officials didn't even bring a bill to a vote on any meaningful gun control issues.

---

7. https://www.history.com/this-day-in-history/the-flint-water-crisis-begins

8. http://time.com/5167216/americans-gun-control-support-poll-2018

• Six months after the hurricane, eleven percent of Puerto Rico (PR) was still without electrical power – with a death toll of nearly three thousand.

• We fought in Afghanistan for over 16 years with little to show for the thousands of lives lost – on both sides.

• While the United States represents about 4.4 percent of the world's population, it houses around 22 percent of the world's prisoners. Innocent poor people (primarily minorities) sometimes spend months or more in jail waiting for trial because they cannot pay bail.

• We pay contractors and military equipment manufacturers huge sums of money while allowing our traumatized veterans to wait unconscionable lengths of time for treatment and to live in homeless tent cities or under overpasses. Disabled homeless veterans who have served in major wars can be found lying out in the streets. The agencies that should serve them are overcrowded, understaffed, and are not able to adequately serve them.

• K-12 public education in America is falling way behind other countries around the world. There is a growing disparity in the quality of education between affluent and poor communities. During the Covid-19 pandemic, children were conditioned to be at home and be educated by a teacher through online studies. Many kids did not have sufficient internet connections and/or computers to do their work. Children missed almost 3 years of traditional education.

• On any given night, there are over 500,000 people homeless in America.

• "Fake News" and the attacks on America's free press degrade a fundamental tool of democracy. America's Press is controlled commentary to disguise real information. Every news channel has biased misleading information that can be interpreted differently. It's gaslighting and propaganda. It is not all done to the same degree from network to network, but no network is innocent.

• The Economic Policy Institute report titled, "Income Inequality in the United States", dubbed the U.S. the "Unequal States of America" due to the size of the wealth gap.

• Today, virtually every single American is one really bad medical day from financial ruin. Did you know that medical bills are the number one reason for bankruptcy in the United States? Did you know that most people that go bankrupt due to medical bills actually have health insurance?

• The U.S. has the highest rate of maternal death related to childbirth and pregnancy of any developed country in the world.

• The economy is not working for the average American. Many people are working two or three jobs and still cannot pay their bills.

• The process for electing officials does not provide people who can fix big complex problems.

● Officials, in the name of the US government, are separating young immigrant children from their parents and imprisoning them, and they have lost track of over 1,500 of them.

● Forced labor (Slavery) and Sex trafficking are growing industries in the US.

These are not new issues. They have been around for years with sadly but truly little progress towards solving them. Their continuing existence and the lack of significant progress towards solving them have become the new normal. Our elected officials take extreme partisan positions, and each side blames the other for its intransigence in addressing them. What do all the issues have in common? People at the top of the food chain are making huge profits, while those beneath them are suffering. It does not have to be that way. People at the top of the food chain can still make a lot of money and nobody has to live in poverty. Politicians on both sides must show the courage to make it happen.

Part of the problem is that Americans are great pretenders. We are living in our dreams of the way we want America to be. Our children go to school in the imaginary safe schools of our dreams, and then they are not. We live thinking that if we get sick, we will get the healthcare we need and it will be affordable, and then it is not. We believe that everyone who wants to succeed and is willing to work hard can thrive in America, and then we learn about the tent cities of homeless people – including veterans. Our neighbors, who have lived next door for over a decade, will be our friends forever, and then our government deports the father for having come here illegally. In the words of the classic Arlo Guthrie's song, "*Good morning America. How are ya?*" The true answer is, "Not doing as well as we want to believe we are."

To fix the situation, we first must understand it. We use a wide assortment of current issues to illustrate the breadth and depth of the problems facing the US. In this relatively unique book, we have tried to provide a comprehensive look at the major issues of the day, with a little historical perspective on how we got to where we are. While the breadth is comprehensive, the depth is moderate.

This book begins with an explanation and examples of poverty in America – pointing out the pervasive nature of the issue. To illustrate that pervasiveness, we cover poverty's connection to politics, healthcare, the military, personal safety and security, incarceration and criminal justice, immigration, racism, public education, the economy, and the national debt. In many cases, it is a chicken and egg scenario. It is frequently a reciprocal relationship where it is difficult to determine which is the cause and which is the effect. The conclusion always comes out that without fixing poverty, we can't fix any of the other issues or if we don't fix the other issues, we can't fix poverty. It doesn't matter. We must fix poverty, one way or the other, or both.

To assist readers in ensuring they are not living in a bubble, the graphic below shows the bias of commonly used media sources. In writing this book, we have deliberately pulled information from sites across the political spectrum – while steering clear of the extremes (the "Utter Garbage" columns in the graphic that follows). Make a list of your primary sources of information and then locate them on the graphic. If they are all located in the same quadrant and not near the top center, you need to expand your perspective.

We had many graphics illustrating media bias from which to choose. We selected this one for its clever, multi-faceted, visual presentation of the potential bias. It is worth taking a few minutes to thoroughly explore the information presented. For example, sources lower on the graphic are rated lower on overall quality. Left and right are obvious. If you go to the link provided on the graphic, (www.mediabiaschart.com[9]) the link redirects you to h[10]ttp://www.allgeneralizationsarefalse.com/[11] (read the link name closely) We enjoyed that bit of humor. The author's explanation of the graphic provides an excellent lesson in media analysis and rating. The chart is now available as an interactive teaching tool at https://adfontesmedia.com/ including more current versions of the chart. Due to licensing protections the current version is not included. We can't copy it into the book, but you can go to their website and explore it.

The United States government is a complex system, composed of many intricately linked sub-systems. It is impossible to look at any single sub-system without exploring it in the context of the other subsystems with which it interacts. For example, social safety net programs, taxes, infrastructure, voting, and education are all directly or indirectly related – meaning that we cannot consider them in isolation. Because of the interrelated systemic nature of the problems, we have not attempted to propose solutions to the many individual issues. Doing so would be unrealistic. A proposal to fix one issue may well exacerbate a different issue. Having conceded that, it is still possible to examine and understand each of the issue subsystems individually. We have tried to balance those factors in presenting the information that follows. By using poverty as a focus point, we have tried to propose solutions to each issue in the context of reducing poverty – with the hypothesis that reducing poverty will have a positive effect on the rest of the issues.

---

9. http://www.mediabiaschart.com

10. http://www.allgeneralizationsarefalse.com/

11. http://www.allgeneralizationsarefalse.com/

This version of the chart is the latest available for copying into the book. Go to https://adfontesmedia.com/ for an interactive current version.

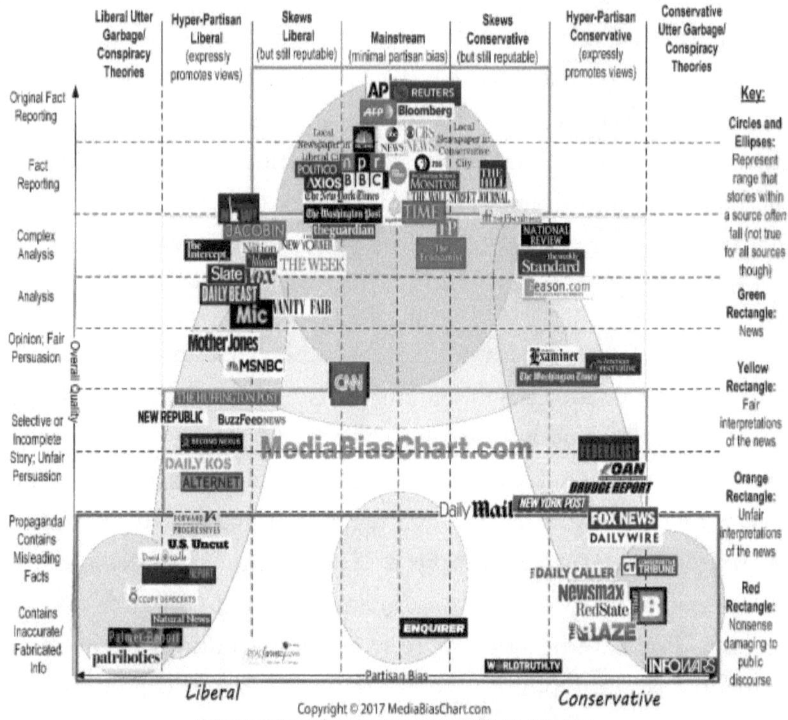

America needs to rekindle a healthy sense of shame, and then use that shame to motivate us to passionately fix our problems – starting with poverty.

Have you ever seen the 1975 production of *The Wiz*? You know, the black version of "*The Wizard of Oz.*" The Wiz provides a different narrative that can be recognized as the gateway of understanding self, before going back into a society to fix it. In the movie, you can compare the characters "Evileen" and "The Wiz" to the leaders of the government. People who have access to policies and legislation, use puppets to initiate action. They would prefer to call the shots while watching from a distance and seeing others suffer. For instance, the government likes to find solutions while creating more problems. This is in reference to the state of California and its government system, paying Californian citizens a stipend to be homeless, provide crackpipes and syringes to combat their drug problem. A California homeless man stated that "If you're going to be homeless– it's pretty fucking easy here. I mean, if we're going to be realistic, they pay you to be homeless here[12]." A health program is handing out free, sterile supplies, such as needles and crackpipes, to people with drug addiction issues. And soon, they'll be available in vending machines[13].

This "solution" is actually a "problem"? The state is enabling and initiating suicides among a vulnerable population. Remaining homeless when you are provided assistance to aid your addictions, is entirely by choice. But having a government system that pushes you to make a bad choice and live in this nature is shameful. Why aren't the service provider organizations saying anything about this? Because they're receiving grants and funds from the state and cannot afford to lose them. Why does no one talk about these issues? It's

---

12. https://www.foxnews.com/media/san-francisco-pays-homeless-california-residents-crime

13. https://www.whsv.com/2023/04/21/health-program-provides-free-needles-pipes-california/?outputType=apps#_853ae90f0351324bd73ea615e6487517__4c761f170e01683 6ff84498202b99827__853ae90f0351324bd73ea615e6487517_text_43ec3e5dee6e706af77 66fffea512721__84c40473414caf2ed4a7b1283e48bbf4_KESQ_9371d7a2e3ae86a00aab47 71e39d233d__0bcef9c45bd8a48eda1b26eb0c61c869_2520_0bcef9c45bd8a48eda1b26eb0 c61c869_252D_0bcef9c45bd8a48eda1b26eb0c61c869_2520A_0bcef9c45bd8a48eda1b26 eb0c61c869_2520health_0bcef9c45bd8a48eda1b26eb0c61c869_2520program_c0cb5f0fcf 239ab3d9c1fcd31fff1efc_users_0bcef9c45bd8a48eda1b26eb0c61c869_2520is_0bcef9c45b d8a48eda1b26eb0c61c869_2520helpful_0bcef9c45bd8a48eda1b26eb0c61c869_2520or_0 bcef9c45bd8a48eda1b26eb0c61c869_2520enabling

discussed, but because of propaganda distributed by the programs, the media will only show you so much, so it won't look as bad as it is.

When dealing with any aspect of poverty, you can't just look at it from a worldly point of view. If you look inside your local community, the environment, and the people associated with it, you will find the inner understanding of why it is hard to rise above societal standards that were unintentionally built for you to fail or be trapped. For example, the *Scarecrow* hangs from the rail while four crows negatively impacted his thinking, well-being, and belief about himself. A society will teach and emphasize that "You can't win. You can't break even, and you can't get out of the game[14]." What does that mean? No matter how close you come to succeeding or getting out of the environment you were raised in, something will prevent you from moving to the next step. This pushes you back to level 0. That is the narrative that becomes their reality.

This narrative happens entirely too frequently within the minority community. For example, not taking an opportunity such as an academic scholarship to a new state because your friends and family tell you that it's "too far", "you won't last" or "why would you leave us behind, we don't mean anything to you?" Another scenario is being at the wrong place at the wrong time because you decided you wanted to act out before you leave for the last time. If you're strong enough, you will remain confident and coordinated to strive forward on your path. If you're easily motivated by the comments and thoughts, you are likely to not get out of the game.

As you read this book, I want you to imagine yourself as being Dorothy. Not really knowing too much about where you came from

---

14. https://www.google.com/

search?q=you+can't+win+the+wiz+lyrics&rlz=1CAJCUZ_enUS1032&oq=you+can't+wi

n&aqs=chrome.6.0i355i512j46i512l2j0i512j46i512l2j0i512l4.7241j0j7

or what's in your view. You have all these social problems that have caused poverty in your community, state, nation, and world. In order to find solutions, you have to be aware and discover what the root of each problem is. The why, how, when, what, and where these issues stem from. Just like Dorothy didn't understand who and what she was until she met different parts of herself that she needed to work on; propelling forward, once she acknowledged that it started with her, she was able to go home and fix the problems not only in her own life but also in her community. How will you know what needs to be fixed if you don't know in detail what's going on?

Poverty in America

The book's message is that poverty is a deadly threat to democracy. Poverty is pervasively interfering with the way we run the country and we must reduce poverty to restore democracy. Poverty is not just some statistical fact related to income or savings. Poverty is also a devastating psychological burden that crushes the human spirit. As a society, and particularly for political discussions, we try to put numerical labels on poverty, but quantitative data can miss the point: people are much more than mere numbers. If people cannot afford to feed, house, and clothe their children, provide them with healthcare, and keep them safe, then – regardless of their income – they feel impoverished. If poverty's impact stopped there, it would be bad, but the devastating effects of poverty permeate society in every way imaginable. Poverty doesn't just occur in black communities. It affects a wide range of citizens across all social, racial, cultural, and economic groups.

We should bear in mind the following words from Thomas Paine's Common Sense pamphlet. *"Society in every state is a blessing, but Government, even in its best state, is but a necessary evil; in its worst state an intolerable one: for when we suffer or are exposed to the same miseries by a Government, which we might expect in a country without Government, our calamity is heightened by reflecting that we furnish the means by which we suffer."*

Government is both the cause and solution to Poverty. It is up to us to determine which.

As years go by, we are reminded how the late-great Marvin Gaye's iconic song "Mercy, Mercy Me" predicted what is going on in the United States of America. He sings *"Mercy, Mercy Me, oh, things ain't what they used to be. What about this overcrowded land? How much more abuse from man can she stand?"* We as people abuse our own people and land. America has a way of being there for its people. Provides aid, security, alliance when needed, housing, assistance when asked; But for how long? To what degree? Almost half of the United States has struggled with financial stipulations such as feeding kids, clothing, food & shelter; inflation (increases with food, gas prices); and other necessities that provide sustainability to the common household. We drill hundreds of thousands of holes into our homeland to pick up fossil fuels to provide gasoline to our vehicles. Our air is polluted and contaminated because of industrial facilities, combustion, and chemicals that flood the skies. We are not only killing our animals, we're killing each other. *"Mercy, Mercy me, ah things ain't what they used to be. Radiation underground and in the sky, Animals and birds who live nearby are dying."*

America has severe problems. Known and unknown problems that are poorly recognized and censored by new apartments buildings and tourists being shown the great lifestyle but not the reality of what is really going on. But we all see it. Everywhere we go, it doesn't matter if you're in Texas, California, Wyoming, Oklahoma, or Florida. We see the rundown neighborhoods, the homeless veterans, and families with children outside begging for food. We see police brutality, the racial profiling, and discrimination amongst all groups. We ultimately make three decisions: (1) help by providing resources, (2) watch for a second, give them a smirk or smile, roll up the windows, and stare back at them, or (3) just ignore what's going on completely and pretend what you see does not affect you. But in truth, it affects everyone. It has an influence on every citizen in the United States. Within these noticeable problems, there are always solutions to combat any issue and problem that is at hand. If we look at the long-term impact that poverty has had on the American people, it is astonishing that our society is still one of the richest countries on the planet.

We often hear people talking about American exceptionalism and cite it as the reason we should lead the World. We need to be more aware of how others may perceive us. By focusing on our supposedly exceptional qualities, Americans blind ourselves to the ways that we are a lot like everyone else with our racist attitudes. In many cases, we treat white immigrants better than we treat native born Black and Brown people. Many Americans are proud patriots until it's time to help some of those racial minorities who were born, raised, and native to this land. The minorities already living in the US have a harder time getting the opportunity to succeed than those who come from overseas.

We turn a blind eye to the needs of these people while we entice others to come into the United States. For example, we open our borders to known countries seeking refuge. We provide them with scholarships, housing, jobs, and a stipend to survive. Meanwhile, we have citizens who stay in camps outside, receive little to no housing assistance (if not the shelter), have to claim disability, (which provides income, but removes the ability to work), and treat them with cruel discrimination because they have a stench from ragged clothes and a basket they push around that has their last valuables with them. We are no better than other countries.

Our faith in American exceptionalism makes it harder for Americans to understand why others are less enthusiastic about U.S. dominance, are often alarmed by U.S. policies, and are frequently irritated by what they see as U.S. hypocrisy. In many ways, America is exceptionally good, but there are also some less than glorious behaviors that are not. It does not matter whether the subject is possession of nuclear weapons, conformity with international law, or America's tendency to condemn the conduct of others while ignoring its own bad actions. Ironically, U.S. foreign policy would probably be more effective if Americans were less convinced of their own unique virtues and less eager to proclaim them.

For a thorough exploration of American exceptionalism, read the excellent article at Foreign Policy[15]. America has justly earned the reputation of a major international aggressor. It is time we stopped leading that category. Some people doubt we are the aggressor. Try this thought experiment.

Pretend you are a citizen of the world (or an alien from outer space) observing Earth and assessing its activities. How would you perceive America's position in the world? We talk a good game about democracy and human rights, but what kind of an example do we really set? We tell the world that democracy is the best form of government, but here at home there are major efforts underway to limit the voting rights of large numbers of our citizens, especially the poor who are pilloried as not being intelligent enough to vote. Our Supreme Court has said in Citizens vs. United that people with lots of money can essentially buy elections. It's not one man – one vote; it's x dollars – one vote.

On the human rights side, we are the world's most prolific jailers – by far. The American prison industrial complex is a cash generator – largely on the backs of young black male prisoners. Let us not forget the way we treated Native Americans, slaves, or the Japanese we put in internment camps during WWII, and using the atomic bomb – not once, but twice, a mob of misled political supporters attacking the US capital declaring the last presidential election stolen, and separating immigrant children from their parents and holding them in cages. According to The State of America's Children® 2020 report,

---

15. http://foreignpolicy.com/2011/10/11/the-myth-of-american-exceptionalism

children of color are disproportionately transferred to the adult criminal justice system, where they are tried and prosecuted as adults. In 2017, Black youth represented 54 percent of youth prosecuted in adult criminal court but only 15 percent of the total youth population[16]. Let us not forget the way we treated Indigenous Natives by genocide; the Tulsa, Oklahoma bombing of Black Wall Street in 1921; the enslavement of Africans and Natives destroying cultural traditions, or the Japanese being put in internment camps during WWII between 1942 and 1945. Imagine then being Secretary of State and sitting down with your counterpart from another country and trying to speak from the moral high ground. In the early 20th century, we were sitting pretty on that high ground, but it is eroding as we speak. Partisan leaders are promoting prohibiting teaching our children about our historical shameful behaviors. Instead of spending so much time and energy on military planning and operations, we need to pull back and get our own house in order.

Let's go back and spend a few minutes discussing Tulsa. For most Americans growing up White in the 1950s, Tulsa was just a city in Oklahoma. My history courses never mentioned the Massacre on Black Wall Street of 1921 that killed 300 black people, due to white looters, rioters, fires, and vigilantes. But it's worse than that. I graduated from the US Naval Academy in 1967, and still had not heard about it. Gradually, over the next 50 years, I saw it mentioned in racism reports. More importantly, as we write the next chapters of history, large elements of society are fighting to keep this shameful chapter from being included.

Since our primary issue is Poverty, yes, America is exceptional in that area too, exceptionally bad!

---

16. https://www.childrensdefense.org/policy/resources/soac-2020-youth-justice

"A recent study[17] by Timothy Smeeding, Lee Rainwater, and Gary Burtless showed striking differences in western countries' rates of relative poverty, which they defined as 50 percent of the median adjusted disposable personal income (ADIN) for persons (adjusted for family size). They also measured deep poverty, defined as 40 percent of the median ADIN. Using data from the Luxembourg Income Study, the researchers showed that the United States has the highest relative poverty (and deep poverty) rates among those countries observed (see figure)."

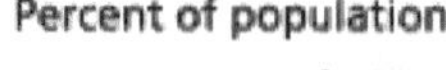

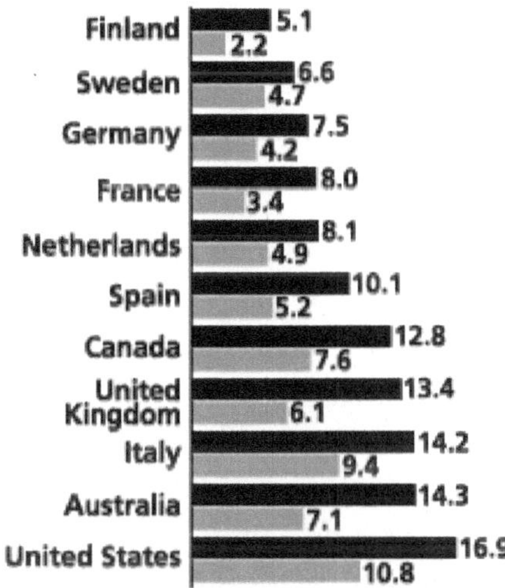

2002 data

17. https://www.prb.org/povertyintheunitedstatesandotherwesterncountries

Source: Luxembourg Income Study, "Key Figures: Relative Poverty Rates"

Virtually every problem that our society is dealing with has a reciprocal cause and effect relationship with poverty. For example:

- Homelessness –

o Poverty can cause homelessness. Between 2007-2020 there was a total of 580,466 accounted for who were experiencing homelessness[18]. This includes Individuals, people in families, chronically homeless individuals, veterans, and unaccompanied youth.

o Paying for housing/rent can cause poverty.

- Crime –

o Poverty can make people desperate enough to commit a crime. A 1% rise in poverty would amount to a 2.16% rise in crime and 2.57% rise in violent crimes[19].

o A criminal record can make it difficult to get a job and avoid poverty. (A report released by the Bureau of Justice Statistics[20] in 2020, finds that of more than 50,000 people released from federal prison in 2010, a staggering 33% found no employment at all over four years post-release,

---

18. https://endhomelessness.org/homelessness-in-america/homelessness-statistics/
    state-of-homelessness/

19. https://teacherscollegesj.org/how-does-poverty-affect-crime-rates/

20. https://www.prisonpolicy.org/blog/2022/02/08/employment/

and at any given time, no more than 40% of the cohort was employed. People who did find jobs struggled, too.)

● Healthcare –

o Poverty makes people delay going to the doctor's office until their condition is chronic instead of when they first see symptoms. (In 2021, around 30 million people in the United States had no health insurance[21].)

o Healthcare costs can be financially devastating – leading to poverty.

This list barely scratches the surface of the all-encompassing and insidious impact of poverty. It would take a multivolume encyclopedia to discuss them all. That is not our goal. We only hope to provide enough examples to make the reader aware that poverty is a real and growing danger to democracy, and we must unite to defeat it. Chapter 8 suggests some tactics that might be useful.

We have more than 1.5 million households living in extreme poverty. That is nearly twice as many as there were 20 years ago. The current rise in civil discord, crime, and hostility is directly connected to the growing poverty issue. For a deeper understanding of the issue of poverty in the US, read the recent UN report excerpted below. Consider this absurdity. *"While funding for the IRS to audit wealthy taxpayers has been reduced, efforts to identify welfare fraud are being greatly intensified. The United States now has probably the lowest degree of social mobility[22] among all the rich countries."* Our elected officials recognize the need to collect more taxes to pay for the government's many programs and services. They should support a

21. https://www.statista.com/statistics/200955/americans-without-health-insurance/

22. *https://www.npr.org/sections/goatsandsoda/2017/12/21/572043850/u-n-investigator-on-extreme-poverty-issues-a-grim-report-on-the-u-s*

bipartisan tax bill that results in more money for the poor and more taxes for the rich, not the current approach that more aggressively taxes the poor and middle class while giving tax breaks to the wealthy.

We ought to all work together to support people, programs, and ideas that benefit the many at the cost to a few, not the current situation where the efforts of the many are providing huge profits to the few – aka the top 1%. Be angry with the 1% who suck the wealth out of the economy instead of paying a living wage, while millions of children go to bed hungry every night because their parents, who both are working two jobs, can't pay their bills. That's real and it's happening every day. Meanwhile, we are spending trillions of dollars fighting terrorists who have only a small actual impact on our lives. Largely because of poverty, thousands of Americans are killed every year in this country, not by terrorists, but by their frustrated and angry fellow citizens. If we must fight a war, let's fight a war on poverty in America.

Let's start by dispelling the myth that poor people are responsible for our poverty issues. The most frightening and discouraging statement in doing the research for this book comes from an OXFAM report[23].

Issue #1 - Poverty is a choice made by the people in power.

Poor people do not choose to be poor. The poor do not get to make that choice.

---

23. https://www.oxfam.org/sites/www.oxfam.org/files/file_attachments/bp210-economy-one-percent-tax-havens-180116-en_0.pdf

"But at the end of the day, particularly in a rich country like the USA, the persistence of extreme poverty is a political choice made by those in power."

Stop and think about that OXFAM report[24] statement. Many of the millions of Americans living in poverty are not there because of anything they did or choices they made. They are poor because the people in power callously chose policies that fueled more poverty. Consider Congressional bills to reduce Social Security, Welfare, Healthcare, and other social safety net programs while at the same time giving tax breaks to the top 1%. Poverty is the visible and all-encompassing symptom of the problem; but politics motivated by greed is the cause – and our democratic system is the potential solution. The only conceivable silver lining to this cloud is that those in power can also decide to eliminate poverty, and as voters, the 99% have the means to decide who has that power.

There are countless books and studies of the destructive, crushing, physical, and emotional impact of poverty on its victims. This book acknowledges this phenomenon while taking the conversation to another level. Poverty hurts more than people. Poverty hurts our country. It fuels most of the great ills that have been getting worse. Eliminating poverty is more than a humanity issue. It's also a democracy issue. Poverty is the root cause of many of society's major issues like crime, racism, disease, anti-immigration, terrorism, abortion, unwanted pregnancy, poor education, and divorce. If everyone 's basic needs (e.g., physical and emotional safety and security) were met, most of these issues would be minor annoyances, not major problems. We can't fix any of them if we don't fix poverty first.

---

24. https://www.oxfam.org/sites/www.oxfam.org/files/file_attachments/bp210-economy-one-percent-tax-havens-180116-en_0.pdf

Over 2,000 years ago Aristotle wrote,

"POVERTY is the parent of crime."

It still is!

Poverty is a national and international disgrace. Nobody should be living in abject poverty. Nobody should be dying from poverty. If they are living in these harsh conditions, they are not fully aware of their circumstances or they find ways to escape the essence of poverty. If they do know, they realize they are not afforded the same opportunities as those who have money, cars, a stable residency, decent clothing, and a stocked refrigerator. Those are absolute statements, so you may feel the need to challenge them. If so, please tell me who should be allowed to live in abject poverty. If they are living in these harsh conditions, they are not fully aware of their circumstances or they would find ways to escape the essence of poverty. If they do know, they realize they are not afforded the same opportunities as those who have money, cars, a stable residency, decent clothing, and a stocked refrigerator. If some people are thinking, "Those lazy bastards living in poverty are not willing to work for a living.", then read on, because, for the most part, those people do not exist.

Look at these two different scenarios provided by the two different co-authors from two cultures describing their lives in different eras of the 20th and 21st century. Both of them came from low-income families and are living comfortably today. Allan is nearly 80 years old from the northeast and Mikaya is not quite 25 and grew up in Texas, but they have reached many of the same conclusions when it comes to the dangers of poverty.

[Perspective 1 - Allan]

1. He grew up in Maine in the 1950s and 60s, when each generation did a little better than the previous one, and as the winners of WWII America was riding high economically, militarily, culturally, industrially, and ethically – setting an example for democratic rule in countries around the world.

2. People flocked to America from other countries to share in and contribute to our freedoms and our prosperity – and we welcomed them. Capitalism was King! The economy was booming. People were working. It was a time when income and wealth were distributed fairly so everyone benefited. But, gradually, things changed.

3. The opening of China and independence in India opened up vast worker pools that drained our good paying manufacturing jobs and our ineffective response to that meant that there were no replacement jobs, initiating a downward spiral to poverty.

4. Unregulated capitalism allowed greed to skew the way corporate income was shared. More of the money began going to owners and executives, and less to the average worker. Gradually, this subtle shift tipped the balance and began to affect everything we do. People were working hard but falling behind economically.

5. Political unrest and public resentment grew as poverty grew. The most glaring result of that imbalance is the election of Donald Trump. People were angry and dissatisfied with the way their government had allowed this wealth inequality issue to put so many Americans into poverty. Trump was elected because he promised to fix it, but he's someone who benefits and perpetuates the very system that funnels economic gains into the rich class. In short, he conned his populist followers.

[Perspective 2- Mikaya]

1. She grew up in the late 1990's and early 2000's where she lived in two different households, while still living under the same conditions of society. One, my mother and my stepdad, who stayed in the projects of Oak Cliff, Texas. This was known as the hood. Everything was within walking distance, but as you walked down to Blockbuster you'd find yourself running into crackheads, rundown homes, and violence at the bus stop.

2. Being young she never realized how many times her siblings and she were left alone just so her mom and stepdad would be able to go to work. Her mom worked for nursing companies, while her stepdad fixed airplanes. They would sometimes argue over the late payments and funds not being added into accounts which resulted in domestic violence and drug use by her stepdad. There were no good schools in that area, so her siblings and she stayed at her grandparents' house in the suburbs of Dallas.

3. One would think that because they were obtaining a better education and lived with her grandparents for the time being, that, as a collective, they had money. They lived in a home built from the ground up in a very nice community. Today, her grandmother works as the lead accountant for the district of Dallas, and her grandfather is an entrepreneur. In reality, once both retired from their full-time jobs, they realized they were still living as barely middle-class citizens. Having to take on other jobs just to make "ends meet" because taxes took more from their Social Security than they could afford.

4. Both households' experiences led them to obtain more than minimum wage income, but because of how America's

democracy works, they still suffer at the hands of poverty while trying to dig out of a hole. This is not the American Dream.

It is unacceptable that a few people in power have tilted the economy to allow themselves to accumulate so much wealth, while so many are severely suffering from the lack of it. Politicians argue that they want to reduce taxes, but the deficit is too high, and the social safety-net programs are too expensive. The simple, unspoken truth is that there is more than enough money available to eliminate poverty if Congress had the political strength and personal courage to go get it from the super-wealthy and invest it in infrastructure and public service jobs.

How many times have we heard, "We can't afford to provide everybody with government healthcare. It will add too much to the deficit." We have heard the same thing about Social Security, infrastructure spending, public education, and other major federal programs. This statement might be true if government income/revenue were a fixed number, but who says it must be? Our elected representatives are going about the process from the wrong direction. They start with the amount of money available and then argue over what programs and services to include and what to exclude. Instead, they should be stepping back and having a conversation about what kind of country we want to be, what programs it will take to achieve that vision, and then figuring out how to pay for it; and it should not be a partisan issue.

Then we have the Debt Ceiling. Yes, we have an archaic, impractical, absurd, and harmful policy called the Debt Ceiling. After following the planning and budgeting policies and procedures to fund the federal programs and services, the respective agencies run their programs and spend their budgets. The budgets were intended to keep spending within certain limits – known as the debt ceiling. Congress ignores the debt ceiling until it rears its ugly head like a massive boulder on a railroad track. Congress must convene and agree to move the boulder so the train can proceed. It is an inconvenient obstacle. Congress already voted to spend the money there should be no need to vote again to spend the money they already voted to spend. During the 2023 negotiations over the debt ceiling, conservatives are demanding cuts to social programs, largely having a negative impact on the lower income elements of society. Liberals and progressives are leaning towards increasing the taxes on the wealthy to provide better living conditions for the poor. Cuts to social programs lead to a dystopian poverty society.

We are the wealthiest country on the planet, and yet we have between 5 and 15 percent of Americans living below the poverty line. Whichever point along the line we choose between those two estimates, that equates to 15 – 45 million citizens! If our leaders' vision for America includes millions of citizens living in poverty, it is time to change leaders.

We are not advocating a 'Robin Hood' solution of taking from the rich and giving to the poor. We are suggesting we need a progressive tax program to create infrastructure and public service jobs. Congressperson Alexandria Ocasio-Cortez (AOC) has called for a return to the higher tax rates of the Reagan years[25]. Republicans are calling her proposal crazy, but Peter Diamond, Nobel laureate in economics and arguably the world's leading expert on public finance says it makes sense. And if we are looking for an example when it worked, we did it in the US for 35 years after WWII – the most successful period of economic growth in our history."

---

25. https://www.nytimes.com/2019/01/05/opinion/alexandria-ocasio-cortez-tax-policy-dance.html

Isn't it interesting that when most of the MAGA crowd want to "make America great again", they're referring to either the period directly after WWII or the Reagan years – both of which represent significantly higher top tax rates? As it stands, more and more Americans find themselves working hard but falling further behind – many into poverty. They get angry and frustrated – and in some cases, crazy. That craziness is manifesting itself in social and political unrest that is threatening our democracy.

There is enough wealth in the US that nobody should be forced to live in poverty. The problem is not a matter of the quantity of wealth; it is a matter of its distribution. The wealth in the US is concentrated in the top 1%, while people are starving and dying from curable diseases because of poverty. The situation is intolerable and fixable! Throughout this book, we will repeatedly point out that we need to reclaim some of the money that the top 1% is hoarding. The reason is not that we have any animosity towards them or their success. It is like bank robber Willie Sutton said in 1933 when asked by the judge why he robbed banks, Sutton simply replied, *"Because that's where the money is."* Unlike the robbed banks that were left with nothing, the 1% will still be wealthy beyond most people's imagination.

Periodically, we hear about needing to raise the debt limit. Let's begin with the recognition that the whole concept is absurd. The federal government does its thing and spends money to run the country. They lack the discipline to keep their spending within their budget, so they pass bills that spend more than is available under the debt limit. Then they must raise the debt limit to keep the country from defaulting on the debt. Everybody agrees defaulting is unacceptable. So, what are the options? All we hear about are two. 1. Raise the limit. 2. Cut spending. This is where it gets outrageous. At this point, you can't cut spending. We have already spent it. One side threatens not to agree to raise the limit unless the other side agrees to cut spending. On the surface, this sounds like a reasonable negotiating tactic, but it's disingenuous. As a part of the legislative process, both sides decided to spend the money. You cannot change your mind at this point. That is called reneging on a debt. Congress should change its rules and not allow itself to approve a spending bill that will cause an overdraft without including a rider that simultaneously raises the debt limit.

We started writing this book five years ago to provide ourselves with the hope that America would stand up for itself. As we researched and analyzed the situation, we gradually realized that Trump is not the problem. He is just another symptom of the real problem. America's (and to a major extent, the world's) real problem is the outrageous wealth and income inequality policies that allow the top 1% to amass unimaginable fortunes while countless people barely survive or die from abject poverty, and the greed and amoral beliefs that lead the wealthiest 1% to do it. Military Defense, the 'War on Drugs', Incarceration, Healthcare, and Big Pharma are all major issues in America; but Poverty, largely driven by wealth and income inequality, is both the symptom and the cause of most of these issues.

Before we get all smug about those rich guys with all the power being to blame for poverty, stop and consider whether the rest of us are using our power (however limited) to fix the problem. Have we actively engaged in politics over some issues we care about? Was eliminating poverty something we fought for? As you read this book, begin making a list of steps you can take to improve things.

Years ago, I had the pleasure of listening to Colin Powell speak to an auditorium full of high school kids at The Westminster Schools in Atlanta, GA. Following his prepared remarks, he took questions from the audience. One student asked him, "What do you do when you give someone an order and they fail to carry it out?" The audience was expecting him to describe some form of punitive steps. Instead, they heard him talk about treating it as a learning opportunity as he tried to figure out what he, himself, had done wrong. Why did he think, wrongly, that the person would be able to accomplish the task? In considering what is happening in America we need to ask ourselves, "What are we doing wrong?", and "What can we do to fix the problem?" We hear a lot about the top 1%. Do not forget that the rest of us represent 99%. That is a powerful voting block if we organize and use the power.

Trump said he wants to Make America Great Again. We do too. However, that raises the questions, "When was America great, and what made it so?" There were two aspects to America's greatness. The first was our following a democratic path that pursued a vision that encouraged and enabled everyone to be prosperous. The second was inclusiveness and diversity that everyone really meant everyone. Within both paths of greatness, we have to believe that it took time to successfully get there. Through industrialization, slavery, genocide, Jim Crow Laws, Ku Klux Klan, and bombings of black churches our history has made bloody decisions that we must also recognize. This raises more eyebrows to the question "When was America great, and what made it so?"

How bad is the Poverty problem?

According to the US Census Bureau[26], the official poverty rate in 2020 was 11.4 percent – up one percentage point from 2019. This equates to about 37.2 million people.

- 12.8 million children live in poverty.

- 4.7 million senior citizens live in poverty.

---

26. https://www.census.gov/library/publications/2021/demo/p60-273.html

- 3.8 million working-age adults with a disability live in poverty.

- 2.4 million work full-time all year and live in poverty.

- 5.7 million work less than full-time and live in poverty.

If you want to know more about poverty in the US, The Brookings Institution produced a comprehensive report on poverty called "Behind the numbers: Millions seeking a path out of poverty[27]."

America is a thriving country. Nobody should be hungry, homeless, or living below the poverty level. We should all be able to agree upon that. Some politicians maintain that 'we can't afford it'. At the same time, we have billionaires with vast fortunes. Most Americans would support some form of taking money from the ultra-wealthy to fund infrastructure programs and public service jobs and skill training that enable people to get away from needing the social safety nets.

As voters, we share the responsibility for the millions of our fellow citizens living in poverty because we continue to elect representatives who have not fixed this problem. When we re-elect representatives who failed to try to fix the problem, we are rewarding the wrong behaviors. America bases its economy and its culture on the simple concept of rewarding good behaviors and punishing bad ones. In psychology, they call it 'behavior modification' or 'operant conditioning'. Remember Pavlov's dogs salivating when he rang the bell? We do it with our children – rewarding good behaviors and punishing bad ones. In business we say, "You get what you pay for." We have to find a way to stop rewarding politicians for behaviors that perpetuate poverty.

---

27. https://www.brookings.edu/blog/up-front/2018/09/12/behind-the-numbers-millions-seeking-a-path-out-of-poverty/

In order for our elected leaders to fix problems, they have to see that the community wants conditions to change. Officials have to know that their citizens are aware of the problems and have the determination to do something about it. To better comprehend the breadth and severity of the issues, leaders seek input from organizations that are working with mental health, homeless, incarcerated, and violent clients. Instead of building collaborative partnerships that can bridge the gap, they feed money into these organizations. Sadly, in many communities, their organizations exist in silos, blind to the potentially collaborative relationships. Some organizations have never heard of other facilities in their surrounding community. Representatives have a chain of command but if no one is protesting about poverty and the need for a cure, then they won't resolve the issues. The ultimate goal with organizations is to provide the:

1. **Opportunity**: having resources and key essentials that make their organization valuable.
2. **Partnership**: collaborating with organizations to establish partnerships.
3. **Community connectivity**: referring and connecting organizations to clients and clients to organizations.
4. **Success**: meeting the needs of clients and customers to supply benefits and produce ultimate success.

Poverty in America has sadly earned the use of the adjective *Systemic*, meaning it has an insidious impact on nearly every facet of life in this country. At an individual level, there is usually some precipitating event like a medical emergency, PTSD, or loss of a job that causes the problem. However, poverty is also a systemic problem at the national level. It is not due to any single condition or event. It is both the cause and effect of many national problems. To fully understand both the causes and effects of systemic poverty in America, we must examine each major subsystem like healthcare and criminal justice and understand how they are related and cumulatively produce an untenable situation.

Being poor can make you poor. In his book DL Hughley, a comedian and social activist, illustrates the insidious nature of poverty. He points out that poor people pay more for groceries because they are less likely to have access to big-box discount stores and cannot afford to buy in bulk. *"Because of this, low-income households pay 6 percent extra per sheet. Only in America can you be too poor to wipe your ass! You stink, I'm broke!"* Poor people also pay more for car insurance – regardless of their driving record – over $500 per year more. Bank overdraft fees, minimum balance requirements and predatory lending practices can push the poor deeper into poverty. Those who are living in low-income areas tend to buy more clothes, jewelry, and fancier cars outside of paying for their other bills. With a delusional mentality, people trick themselves into believing that they "have it" when in fact they don't. This creates poor judgment of their reality, which now instead of getting out of the poor man's mindset, you have driven yourself further down the path of struggling. It costs more to be poor.

America is losing its luster as the land of opportunity. It is not. In his book Kurt Andersen reminds us,

> *"These days, if you grow up poor in America, you have less than a one-in-four shot of becoming even solidly middle class—one in three if you're white, one in ten if you're black. If you grow up right in the economic middle, the chances are you won't move up at all. On the other hand, if you come from an upper-middle-class or rich household, the odds are strong you'll remain upper middle class or rich as an adult."*

The MSN presentation titled "How Many Children Live in Poverty in Your State[28]?" provides a state-by-state description of poverty in America. The report is talking about children. It's sad and scary. No matter where we live, there is an unacceptable level of poverty. Children who live impoverished and those who grew up impoverished have something similar in common, trauma. They have this traumatic experience of not having any and having to "grind" and "hustle" to get it. They become accustomed to living in survival mode, always feeling like they have to live on the edge, that "tomorrow I can be back in the same place I was in, struggling." Many times, those who have successfully "got out the hood" have a troubling time adjusting to their new financial gain. Poverty leaves bruises and wounds on children.

Divisive extremists have convinced us that the social safety-net issue is just a black problem. Social safety net programs are a collection of societal programs supporting low-income blacks, browns, and whites (essentially everybody in America) in remarkably similar proportions. Because there are more whites than blacks in America, more whites require public assistance than blacks do[29]. Most people do not choose to take advantage of social safety net programs; circumstances force them to. While we may not agree on the means to fix them, we can all agree to work together to fix the circumstances. Fixing the circumstances is a one-time major cost followed by a less expensive maintenance cost, while social safety-net program costs go on forever with continuously rising economic costs and emotional suffering.

Under current conditions, people are living in poverty and the government must decide how to provide for their survival. There are two things wrong with that simple short statement. The government

---

28. https://www.bing.com/search?q=how+many+children+live+in+poverty&FORM=AWRE

29. http://content.time.com/time/magazine/article/0,9171,156084,00.html

should not have to provide direct assistance in the form of giving people money, and people should have more than just enough to survive. Programs that provide direct assistance to the needy are required for immediate relief of dangerous conditions, but they perpetuate the problem. It is a classic example of treating the symptom while ignoring the cause. Instead of giving away money, the government should spend money on building infrastructure and providing services that the country needs. That creates jobs. Those jobs must pay a living wage.

How can we be the wealthiest country on the planet and still have these outrageous economic conditions? The simple and obvious answer is that the wealth is concentrated in a ridiculously small percentage of the population and the politicians appear to be feebly unwilling to take any of it from them. Most Americans are not upset that a few citizens have done extremely well financially. The uber-wealthy have achieved the American dream beyond most reasonable expectations. We cheer for them and hope someday to become one of them. The thing that causes people's anger and unrest is realizing how many Americans are living in poverty – at truly little fault of their own. A combination of societal, cultural, economic, demographic, geographic, racial, and political factors have converged to create an environment that greatly limits their opportunity for success. By any measure, America has enough wealth to allow some people to be extremely wealthy while also ensuring that nobody has to exist in extreme poverty. Unfortunately, because of greed and an under-regulated capitalist economy, we fall far short of that ideal. Read, "Why the U.S., One of the World's Richest Countries, Struggles with Diseases of Poverty[30]" for a depressing reality check.

---

30. https://www.huffingtonpost.com/entry/america-diseases-of-poverty_us_5a69f610e4b0dc592a0fe66a

Following the Great Depression, the US created several Social Safety Net programs like Welfare, Food Stamps, housing, and education assistance, Social Security for the elderly, monthly stipends for single mothers and the disabled, public healthcare, and a minimum wage. These programs fueled the post WWII economic growth. Putting money into the hands of the consumer created real jobs and everyone benefited. In the early 1970s, these programs came under political pressure and began being reduced. For example, changes in welfare eligibility reduced the number of families on Welfare from 4.6 million in 1996 to 1.1 million in 2017. It was not done because 3.5 million of them no longer needed assistance. It was done because the Congress was afraid to raise the money to pay for the program. The people in power decided it was okay for people to live in poverty. The decline in enrollment does not represent a commensurate decline in poverty. To the contrary, it resulted in an increase in poverty.

The problem is not that a relatively small number of Americans have done well. That's the American Dream and we all hope to live it. The problem is how they did it. Most of the wealth gains of the few at the top have come at the expense of a vast number of working-class citizens. In recent election cycles, people wanting to reverse the current conditions that provide huge economic advantages to the wealthy and powerful have supported efforts to tax the wealthy more heavily as a part of a plan to reduce poverty. The wealthy people targeted for the proposed tax increases struck back by inaccurately describing these efforts using the dreaded "Socialism" tag and label the efforts as "Income Redistribution" or "Wealth Redistribution" programs. Ironically, the very wealthy got wealthy by a long-term, gradual, but unspoken and unsustainable income and wealth redistribution program that moved much of the wealth into the fortunes of the top 1%. If things do not change drastically, the amount of poverty in America will continue to grow. As that inequity and inequality become more apparent, they cause anger and resentment that manifests itself as social, cultural, political, civil, criminal, and racial unrest. These conditions threaten our democracy.

The evidence is clear. Middle-wage workers' hourly wages are up 6% since 1979, low-wage workers' wages are down 5%, while those with very high wages saw a 41% increase. While the rich are getting richer, everyone else is losing ground[31]. Senator Bernie Sanders states[32] his concern on the issue.

> "The rich-poor gap in America is obscene. So, let's fix it – here's how
>
> *The United States cannot prosper and remain a vigorous democracy when so few have so much and so many have so little. While many of my congressional colleagues choose to ignore it, the issue of income and wealth inequality is one of the great moral, economic and political crises that we face – and it must be dealt with.*
>
> *The unfortunate reality is that we are moving rapidly toward an oligarchic form of society, where a handful of billionaires have enormous wealth and power while working families have been struggling in a way we have not seen since the Great Depression. This situation has been exacerbated by the pandemic."*

The impact of this inequity is even greater than it appears above because the numbers do not emphasize the continuing growth in the degree of difference between the rich and poor, and the unavoidable

31. https://www.epi.org/publication/charting-wage-stagnation/

32. https://www.sanders.senate.gov/op-eds/the-rich-poor-gap-in-america-is-obscene-so-lets-fix-it-heres-how/

collapse of the middle class if conditions do not change. If the percentage difference were stable at today's levels, the results would be devastating. Unfortunately, the percentages are following trends that will make the problem even worse. The resulting concentration of wealth hurts the economy by diminishing the consumer spending power that drives the rest of the economy.

Next time you go to Walmart, look around at the employees. They work for us. Really! We are paying part of their salary – and not just by purchasing things in their store. Because Walmart pays them so poorly, our tax dollars are providing the social safety net money that they are eligible for. At the same time, several members of the Walton family who own the company are on the list of the 25 wealthiest people in the world! If we raised the minimum wage to a living wage, then people who work in retail and other low paying jobs would not have to supplement their earnings with Welfare. All companies should be required to pay a reasonable living wage to their employees, and the Walton family members will still be obscenely wealthy.

At some point in the past 40 years, the people at the top realized that they had the power to determine how much everyone in the company was paid – or maybe they always knew but previously chose not to abuse that privilege. During the recent past, outsourcing and automation became options. Many American jobs were going overseas for cheaper labor costs or being performed by robots. As a result, the business owners/company CEOs/Presidents could force their employees to accept lower wages or cut their jobs completely. At the same time, they could increase productivity and profits; and pay themselves more money. This pattern became a cycle of more money for the boss, with no pay increase for the workers who kept their jobs, and no money at all for those whose jobs went away.

Stockholder benefits are another example of paying the wealthy at the expense of the workers. People with money invest their money (buy stock) in companies to provide capital for the general growth and operations of the company. If the company is profitable, the investors get a dividend. (Some stocks do not pay dividends. Some investors count on increased share value.) Under the present system, the people at the top of the company pay themselves very well. Next, they reward the investors by keeping growing the company; and the worker-bees with no power and few options, keep on working for a smaller and smaller piece of the corporate pie. We do not have a problem with the hierarchy. What concerns us are the percentages. The present-day revenue sharing model creates unsustainable income and wealth inequality.

There was an article in the Washington Post on July 17, 2014, titled, "Capitalism that works[33]". The footnote below is a link to the article. It is not recent, but it's still relevant. We highly recommend you read it.

Post WWII, when a company was profitable, everybody (management, investors, and labor) benefited in a proportion that raised everybody economically. Management thought long-term strategically and investors expected to hold their stocks and watch their value grow over time. Gradually, the focus shifted to more tactical, short-term maneuvering. They eliminated their apprenticeship programs (too long term) and then complained that they could not find qualified and adequately trained workers. They have reduced wages and eliminated benefits by obtaining their workers through temp agencies. They have slashed investment in research and development and long-term product development while devoting more funds to buying back their own stock, which causes the value of outstanding shares to rise. These practices are

---

33. https://www.tampabay.com/opinion/columns/column-capitalism-that-works/2188936/

great for rewarding major investors and corporate chief executives. Unfortunately, they drive down living standards and erode the United States' economic power and exacerbate America's pervasive poverty problem. Our political leaders need to regulate our economy more actively. Poverty in America is not a hidden problem. It is an in-your-face problem demonstrating the prevalence of poverty and an example that our current political leaders are failing to properly serve their constituents. When elected officials fail, our democratic foundation is threatened.

Issue #2 - Homelessness should not be an issue in a country with so much wealth.

One of the most visible and devastating manifestations of America's poverty problem is homelessness. Our democracy cannot morally tolerate having millions of homeless people. It creates resentment and divides us, adding to the tolerance and long-suffering of socially dangerous conditions. Actually, poverty itself does not divide us. People in power use the devastating economic and emotional impact of poverty to divide us. The longer a problem like homelessness persists, the more it becomes a part of the fabric of society and the less people notice it as a problem. We become so accustomed to living with it that we lose track of its insidious nature and the resulting other issues that are caused and exacerbated by it. We know things are bad, but we have forgotten how things were better before poverty hit us.

When we see a homeless person on the side of the street, we typically see a single person. However, studies show that half of the homeless people are families – they are the hidden homeless; living in tents, scattered around in shelters, or at a family member's house. Those who are chronically homeless have been experiencing homelessness for a numerous years while also dealing with mental illness, substance abuse, or physical disability. Just imagine creating and raising a family while living in the streets to survive.

Poverty manifests differently in different areas. The following two perspectives illustrate some of the differences.

[**Perspective 1 - Allan**] In my volunteer work with homelessness agencies in Northern Virginia, I had the opportunity to tour a homeless shelter. It was a beautiful facility, managed by a remarkable woman. As we walked around, we saw several preschool aged kids closely following their mothers around. They were clean, healthy, well fed, well clothed, and by all appearances, happy. I could not help but think how lucky and unlucky they were at the same time. Lucky to have this facility with a fully equipped playground, toys, a library, and other kids to play with. Unlucky to be so poor that this had to be their home. Some of the residents at the shelter are there to escape some form of abuse, but the primary reason for most of them is poverty.

[**Perspective 2 - Mikaya**] I have had the privilege of working with the homeless first-hand. Going into facilities as a case manager, as outreach, or just a liaison, I have seen the conditions endured by those who are experiencing homelessness and what a shelter really looks like in Dallas, Texas. In 2022, I went to different organizations and facilities outreaching to those who are impoverished between the ages of 16-24. The company I worked for offered young adults resources such as jobs, certifications, some form of housing, and more. I went into one facility that housed men and women who had families. As soon as I walked in there was a lingering smell, kids with unkempt hair walking around, serving jail food, and no actual clothes to provide. The majority of the families were black. The shelter was full to capacity.

When we spoke with those who fit our target market, they demanded a job, transportation, and daycare. They wanted some type of income to provide for their families. They didn't want to obtain certifications, barely wanted housing; their need was to make money. Those who began the process of receiving these resources soon stopped responding to messages and calls; Not because they didn't have time, they felt like the services were not really going to benefit them. They felt that they were going to be taken advantage of.

These two perspectives illustrate how in different parts of the United States the culture and treatment of people who are dealing with homelessness and the facilities that are run are completely different. You have some organizations who have the right idea to sponsor and help those in need but fail to make it feel like a home for them to grow and leave. To gain self-sufficiency, you need to have facilities like homeless shelters, transitional housing, and placement homes.

Unfortunately, some greedy unscrupulous operators take a devious self-serving approach and operate under the concept that "if I make it look a certain way, they will not feel at home, they will not want to stay for a long period of time, and I can make the profit off the government to run this idea." Fortunately, most operators actually make it a safe place for these men, women, and children to gain confidence in themselves, find healthy resources that benefit them, and provide a way to give them a plan. The problem is, both work but the turnaround rate of poverty is still very high. One illustrates greed and selfishness, the other humanity and charity.

The problem began about 25 years ago when America shifted towards a post-industrialized economy. That shift had a profound impact on the lower-wage-level earners. The economy shifted from well-paying manufacturing jobs to minimum wage service jobs, temporary, and part-time jobs. This transition meant that people could not earn enough, even working multiple jobs, to support a family. The move to part-time jobs allowed employers to dodge providing benefits like healthcare insurance and paid vacations. If you worked 40 hours per week (full time), the employer was required to provide vacations, healthcare, and other benefits. Their solution was to make most positions part-time and therefore not eligible for benefits. The employees not only lost their benefits, but they also earned less income. The deleterious conditions fell disproportionately on African-Americans, Latinos, and other minorities; and became another manifestation of America's subsurface racism. Data from the Kaiser Family Foundation discovered that Hispanic people had the highest uninsured rates at 21.2% and 19.0% as of 2021. Black people had uninsured rates of 10.8% and 10.9% respectively.

Four identifiable structural factors that led to the growing homelessness problem are:

1. Factory automation,
2. Rising housing costs,
3. A diminishing government "safety net",
4. Gaslighting by those in power changing people's perceptions of the homeless population (stigmatizing poor people as lazy).

While the cost of housing has been rising, the real earning power of low-income citizens has been diminished. Where subsidized or affordable housing is available, the providers o[f the subsidies force the applicants for the properties to pay ever-increasing portions of their income towards housing – creating a condition described as 'shelter poor'. Between December 2017 and September 2022, the median rent for newly leased units rose nearly 32 percent, with nearly all of that increase occurring in 2021 and 2022.[1] One study from the US Government Accountability Office found that average rent increases of $100 a month were associated with a 9% increase in homelessness in several areas.

> *"Since the mid-1970s, affordable housing has become increasingly scarce and beyond the reach of many people living in poverty because they are forced to contribute increasingly larger proportions of their income towards housing. Moreover, once they are homeless, they find it increasingly difficult to get themselves back into affordable housing. There are several causative explanations for this new phenomenon.*

> *● The loss of affordable housing units (changed to full-priced housing) and the failure of government and private contractors to build new low-cost homes.*

> *● Community opposition to low-income housing (NIMBY syndrome).*

> *● The federal government's withdrawal from housing production.*

> *● The inability of lower-class incomes to keep pace with rising rents.*

● *The functioning of the mortgage finance system[34]."*

[We shortened these bulleted items from the source version. Go to the link in the footnote for more details.]

Who are these homeless people and where do they come from? If you were asked to describe a homeless person, the visual image that usually comes to mind is of an underfed, unshaven, unkempt male of undetermined age. That is the person we typically see standing at a traffic intersection holding a handwritten sign asking for money. In reality, the homeless community is remarkably diverse in many ways. The following information about various homeless sub-populations is summarized from several selected web-based resources. In analyzing the information, the numbers varied considerably from source to source. However, even if the numbers are inconsistent from study to study, the issues are very real. We have listed the populations to illustrate the breadth and interconnectedness of the problem and the subsequent challenges created in solving the issues causing homelessness. Many of the homeless population fit into multiple categories (e.g., elderly, veteran, substance abuser). In most cases, the connection between homelessness and poverty is obvious. As you read the descriptions, prepare to be saddened and amazed. The categories include:

● **Families** represent about 34% of America's homeless population.

o More families experience homelessness in the United States than in any other industrialized nation.

o A typical homeless family consists of a single mother with her two young children.

---

34. *https://web.stanford.edu/class/e297c/poverty_prejudice/soc_sec/hcauses.htm*

o One in 30 American children experience homelessness annually[35]. (This number is hard to believe so I provided the source.) Fifty-one percent are under age five.

o More than 2.5 million children are homeless each year in America.

▪ You will typically see a family of three. A mother with 2 children, a boy, and a girl. Sometimes the father is included in the family. They are staying either in a beat-up car for transportation, or the mother and children are sheltered in a Women and Children homeless shelter because without a marriage license or proof of marriage, the father is displaced.

● **Veterans** (This is truly shameful.)

o Between 130,000 and 200,000 veterans are homeless on any given night—representing between one fourth and one-fifth of all homeless people.

o Three times that many veterans are struggling with excessive rent burdens and thus at increased risk of homelessness.

---

35. https://www.air.org/centers/national-center-family-homelessness#_853ae90f0351324bd73ea615e6487517__4c761f170e016836ff84498202b9 9827__853ae90f0351324bd73ea615e6487517_text_43ec3e5dee6e706af7766fffea512721_ A_0bcef9c45bd8a48eda1b26eb0c61c869_2520staggering_0bcef9c45bd8a48eda1b26eb0c6 1c869_25202.5_0bcef9c45bd8a48eda1b26eb0c61c869_2520million_0bcef9c45bd8a48eda 1b26eb0c61c869_2520children_c0cb5f0fcf239ab3d9c1fcd31fff1efc_children_0bcef9c45bd 8a48eda1b26eb0c61c869_2520in_0bcef9c45bd8a48eda1b26eb0c61c869_2520the_0bcef9 c45bd8a48eda1b26eb0c61c869_2520United_0bcef9c45bd8a48eda1b26eb0c61c869_2520 States

o Conservatively, one out of every three homeless men who are sleeping in a doorway, alley, or box in our cities and rural communities has put on a uniform and served this country.

▪ Veterans who have served this country for many years and have received medals are pawning their prize possessions just to not be on the street for the night. There are many disabled veterans who sit on the side of the road with unacceptable conditions waiting for someone to provide them services.

● **Youth** – Some with their families and some on their own.

o Some are fleeing physical or sexual abuse.

o Some are members of homeless families.

o A disproportionate number are LGBTQ.

o Some are substance abusers.

▪ There is a cohort of accompanied minors and young adults between the ages of 16-24 who have been kicked out, have run away from home, or have dealt with some sort of sexual abuse that pushed them away from their families. Those who are pregnant youth are with older men who may groom and sexualize them into believing that where they are is where they are supposed to be.

● **People with disabilities**

o 42.8% of sheltered, homeless adults experienced disability.

o Reliance on relatively small Supplemental Security Income (SSI) payments – which average 44 percent below the federal poverty level – makes it difficult for people to retain permanent housing.

o Families and disabled people have been disproportionately hit by increasing homelessness.

▪ Typically, you will see those who are disabled in a wheelchair, with a walker, or a cane. You will discover that they are between the ages of 35-75 years old. Usually, you will see them on the street because although they obtain some Social Security checks, they do not have a distinct location to house those who are disabled. You will see them either on the streets, close to a hospital, or a shelter.

● **Ex-offenders** – people who have served their prison time.

o Incarceration and homelessness are mutual risk factors for each other.

▪ Researchers generally estimate that 25-50% of the homeless population has a history of incarceration.

▪ Compared to adults in the general population, a greater percentage of inmates have been previously homeless, illustrating that homelessness often precipitates incarceration.

o Some government-subsidized housing has rules prohibiting ex-offenders from using them.

▪ Those individuals who are re-entering society after serving a sentence have a very hard time receiving services. They are still treated like criminals and can hardly find any work. If they do, it is an underpaid job with high maintenance. You will see them trying to turn over a new leaf while conflicted by the temptations of drugs, violence, and fast money.

● **Elderly** – People over 60 years old. (These are our grandparents. ☹)

o People 60 and older make up more than 30 percent of the nation's homeless population.

o The U.S. is facing a graying of the homeless. By 2050, there are expected to be 95,000 elders living without stable housing - which is more than double the current population for this age group. We can't let that happen.

o Increased homelessness among elderly persons is largely the result of poverty and the declining availability of affordable housing among certain segments of the aging.

o Throughout the nation, there are at least 9 seniors waiting for every occupied unit of affordable elderly housing.

▪ The elderly are usually the most underserved because they ostensibly have affordable housing for them, but the cost is deceptively and rigidly high. They have been homeless or displaced for more than 2 years. They are self-sufficient through Social Security however, it pays for their minimal needs such as medication, food, hospital appointments, and transportation. This causes dismay for those who would rather stay in shelters than transition to elderly housing.

● **Mental Illness** – People in need of psychiatric help.

o According to the Substance Abuse and Mental Health Services Administration, 20% to 25% of the homeless population in the United States suffers from some form of severe mental illness.

o People with poor mental health are more susceptible to the three main factors that can lead to homelessness: poverty, disaffiliation, and personal vulnerability.

o Because they often lack the capacity to sustain employment, they have little income.

o Delusional thinking may lead them to withdraw from friends, family, and other people. This loss of support leaves them fewer coping resources in times of trouble.

o Mental illness can also impair a person's ability to be resilient and resourceful; it can cloud thinking and impair judgment. For all these reasons, people with mental illness are at greater risk of experiencing homelessness.

▪ Typically, those who are dealing with a mental illness are those who have been isolated, abused, grew up in dysfunctional households, who stop taking medication because the cost is too high to pay for, substance abusers and/or those who have been neglected by their friends and family. Those who are dealing with a mental illness have seen things of violence and terror that add delusion to the conversation they may have with someone. Underneath discombobulated words they provide a story of the pain they've been through. Those who are dealing with a mental illness are interestingly misunderstood the most.

● **Substance abusers** – alcohol and drugs

o The Substance Abuse and Mental Health Services Administration (2003) estimates 38% of homeless people were dependent on alcohol and 26% abused other drugs.

o Substance abuse is often a cause of homelessness.

o More than 1 million people are homeless, with approximately 30 percent of these people suffering from mental illness and 50 percent chronically addicted to drugs, alcohol, or both.

o Approximately 70 percent of homeless veterans are estimated to be substance abusers.

▪ Within every category that makes up the homeless population, lie many people who are drinking and smoking to deal with the pain of living in poverty. Because most are in the streets or living in shelters, liquor stores are walking distance and the "plug" is a phone call away. This creates an illusion that people would rather give their paychecks to help their substance use than receiving help. You also have those who will always be deemed as substance abusers based on their mental capacity.

The categories vary but their needs are remarkably similar in scope and different in the degree to which each client needs each service. The purpose in listing and describing these various homeless populations is to bring them together in the consciousness of the reader and create a realization of the interconnectedness of the issues, while at the same time recognizing the disparities and overlaps of the resources needed.

That sums up the population. Now we need to consider the service costs. Most homelessness cost analyses include things like shelter, transportation, food, clothing, counseling, etc. While acknowledging that other costs exist. Most cost analyses do not include public healthcare, education, and criminal justice costs.

- **Healthcare** - Homelessness and health care are intimately interwoven. Poor health is both a cause and a result of homelessness.

  o Inadequate health insurance is itself a cause of homelessness. Many people without health insurance have low incomes and do not have the resources to pay for health services on their own. A serious injury or illness in the family could result in insurmountable expenses for hospitalizations, tests, and treatment. For many, this forces a choice between hospital bills or rent.

  o Health care is even more of a problem for people who are already homeless. Homeless people are three to six times more likely to become ill than housed people (National Health Care for the Homeless Council, 2008).

  o Homelessness precludes good nutrition, good personal hygiene, and basic first aid, adding to the complex health needs of homeless people.

- **Public Education** – If a child has no home, how does he or she register for or attend school? When parents enroll their children into school, they can let the school system know of their situation. This allows the student to receive free breakfast, lunch, and after-school meals. The issue is not the meals, but their learning abilities. Depending on how many years the family has been impoverished, the child might be illiterate, may have a learning disability, or need extra help in the classroom. Children who are smart and brilliant in their grade level, still face the battle of not receiving Wi-Fi and internet to complete assignments.

o Education is critical to earning a living. Lack of an education and the community support that comes with it result in social and cultural disadvantages – potentially leading to increased healthcare and criminal justice costs.

o Impoverished children are frequently provided meals – sometimes the only meal they receive all day. Sadly, adolescent children can be cruel and engage in food-shaming – picking on the less fortunate, discouraging them to miss vital nutrition.

o Without a job, the child will struggle to get out of being another generation homeless.

- **Criminal Justice** – Any port in a storm. Recidivism is at an all-time high because employers are reluctant to hire ex-offenders. Some ex-offenders realize that they have greater opportunity in prison than in society, always receiving the short end of the stick. They are abetted by going back into the same environments that got them involved in violence, crime, and substance abuse.

o Survival is an extraordinarily strong instinct. If a person can't make a living, they'll resort to crime.

▪ From the perspective of the homeless, being arrested may be a good thing. They get:

● Three meals a day.

● A warm, soft, clean, and safe place to sleep.

● Personal hygiene facilities.

o The cost to arrest, process, house, and release a person is greater than the cost to provide homeless services outside the criminal justice system.

When we think about the impact of homelessness, we typically consider its impact on the homeless individual(s). We also need to consider the impact on the community. This impact includes both tax dollars spent and the strain it puts on social agencies, individuals, and families. Short-term situational homelessness is a problem, but it's the long-term chronic homeless population that drains the budgets of hospitals, emergency rooms, police departments, jails, schools, mental health, poverty, and homeless programs. The article, "The Effects of Homelessness on Society[36]", provides a helpful human understanding of the issue.

---

36. https://classroom.synonym.com/the-effects-of-homelessness-on-society-12084361.html

"The Homeless Census provides us with numbers, statistics, and demographics. But the people behind the numbers are often our neighbors, loved ones, friends, and coworkers.

● He served his country and did three tours in Iraq. He experienced death, war, and battle. He came home with an honorable discharge, post-traumatic stress disorder, and few employment opportunities. One piece of bad luck followed another until he found himself sleeping in the alleyway of a shopping center. He just wants a job and the chance to get his life together again.

● She is a woman of a certain age, a homemaker married for 30 years before her partner left her. The last thing she would ever do is to become a burden to her grown children who live in different states. They think Mom is doing OK, but Mom is not OK. You see, she lost the house eight months ago and has been sleeping in the car every night since and visiting libraries in the daytime trying her best to blend in."

Virtually every community has some homeless residents, so the community must respond to the problem. That typically means operating homeless shelters and associated support services – including housing, police, health, food, and medical services. Local, state, and federal tax dollars, sometimes supplemented by charitable and religious organizations, support these costly services. Even with these funding sources, the programs are frequently underfunded to meet the needs of everyone in distress. If you are homeless, you are in survival mode – meaning that you will do whatever you have to do to survive. That may mean panhandling (begging), recycling (dumpster diving), and if that fails, stealing.

As the problem grows, citizens begin complaining about the sanitary, visible, and olfactory presence of these homeless people. In response, the local government passes stricter laws governing (sometimes prohibiting) squatting, panhandling, and recycling. Remember, these people are in survival mode. Arresting a person for being a public nuisance is a minor inconvenience to the homeless person, but a growing expense to the community to locate, arrest, process, try, feed, house, and release these people. If the first offense is a ticket and a fine, it is sure to lead to a subsequent arrest because the person has no money to pay the fine.

Most communities provide some shelter for the homeless – but not enough for everyone who needs it. The result is tent cities where people use scrounged materials to create makeshift shelters under overpasses, in alleyways, and in clearings in the woods. They sleep on public benches, in business doorways, hallways, or any place where they can feel some degree of comfort and safety. The county must address the best way to meet their sanitation needs (toilets). Providing public toilets is a cost but having homeless people urinating and defecating in public places is humiliating, embarrassing, unsanitary, unpleasant, and unsightly.

The next physical need is food. Once again, they are in survival mode. If they get caught stealing food, it is a minor inconvenience to them, but a significant cost to the community. As a bonus for committing a crime, the county feeds them in jail. If they successfully steal food from the grocery store, paying customers pay for it. We all do. The stores include losses from theft in calculating how much to mark up the products in the store to still be profitable.

Considering all the evidence and looking at several programs across the country that have tried it, the best solution for all concerned, the homeless and the not-homeless, is to provide adequate housing and homeless services combined with an active job creation and placement program to re-establish these homeless people as productive members of society.

Up to this point the news has all been depressing. Homelessness appears to be an intractable problem without the funds required to solve it. However, appearances can be deceiving. The appearance of the problem is real. The appearance of a lack of funding is not. Recent studies that looked at the total costs of services for a homeless person living on the street show that these total costs are about three times as much as the cost to provide a comprehensive program that includes housing and support services. In other words, communities are already spending more than enough money than what is needed to fix the problem for larger numbers of people. They are just not spending it wisely.

Several cities have proven it is less expensive (and much more humane) to provide housing and services for the homeless within a system than to support them living on the street. Some counties are mandating that restaurants and other food sellers donate leftover food to shelters instead of throwing it away. Operating the shelter, providing maintenance and janitorial services, collecting, and preparing food, and serving and cleaning up after a meals program are potential jobs for the people living in the shelter.

*The most recent report along these lines was a May Central Florida Commission on Homelessness study indicating that the region **spends $31,000 a year per homeless person**[37] on "the salaries of law-enforcement officers to arrest and transport homeless individuals — largely for nonviolent offenses such as trespassing, public intoxication or sleeping in parks — as well as the cost of jail stays, emergency-room visits and hospitalization for medical and psychiatric issues."*

By contrast, getting each homeless person a house and a caseworker to supervise their needs would cost about $10,000 per person."

The reason this obvious solution has not been more widely implemented is that the existing system is composed of a collection of independent service providers, funding sources, and administrative agencies. These agencies cooperate and collaborate, but they are not centrally managed as a single integrated system. The solution appears to be finding some organization, program, or individual to take the lead and deliver a better program for less money.

The list of types of homeless people included veterans. Homelessness in general is a shameful fact in America, but homeless veterans take that shame level down to deplorable. These vets believed in and fought for 'The American Dream' while the rest of us benefited from their

---

37. *https://shnny.org/uploads/Florida-Homelessness-Report-2014.pdf*

service and sacrifice. It seems unconscionable that we cannot put in place the programs needed to assist these heroes to become productive and prosperous members of society. Here are a few basic facts to quantify the problem[38].

"Most homeless veterans (96%) are single males from poor, disadvantaged communities. Homeless veterans have served in World War II, Korean War, Cold War, Vietnam War, Grenada, Panama, Lebanon, Operation Enduring Freedom (Afghanistan), Operation Iraqi Freedom, and the military's anti-drug cultivation efforts in South America.

• The number of homeless female veterans is on the rise: in 2006, there were 150 homeless female veterans of the Iraq and Afghanistan wars; in 2011, there were 1,700. That same year, 18% of homeless veterans assisted by the VA were women. Comparison studies conducted by HUD show that female veterans are two to three times more likely to be homeless than any other group in the US adult population.

• Veterans between the ages of 18 and 30 are twice as likely as adults in the general population to be homeless, and the risk of homelessness increases significantly among young veterans who are poor.

• Roughly 56% of all homeless veterans are African-American or Hispanic, despite only accounting for 12.8% and 15.4% of the U.S. population, respectively.

---

38. https://nchv.org/veteran-homelessness/

• About 53% of individual homeless veterans have disabilities, compared with 41%of homeless non-veteran individuals.

• Half suffer from mental illness; two-thirds suffer from substance abuse problems; and many from dual diagnosis (defined as a person struggling with both mental illness and a substance abuse problem).

• Homeless veterans tend to experience homelessness longer than their non-veteran peers do: Veterans spend an average of nearly six years homeless, compared to four years reported among non-veterans."

While only 8% of Americans can claim veteran status, veterans make up 17% of our homeless population. In 2022, **19,565** Veterans experienced sheltered homelessness, and **13,564** Veterans experienced unsheltered homelessness. Even if the number is only half of the lowest estimate, it is grossly unacceptable. Homelessness is a costly problem that can be fixed without greatly increasing the amount already being spent. We need non-profit organizations to sponsor and support our homeless vets until they are self-sufficient. They supported us. It's time to return the service.

Yes, we need to reduce or eliminate homelessness, and the programs and services described in the preceding paragraphs have proven to be effective. On the other hand, if we fix or eliminate poverty, then homelessness will be greatly reduced for most of the population, the economy will flourish, and democracy will thrive.

Issue #3 - America's children are literally starving and suffering lifelong damage from poor nutrition.

Most people have no idea how serious and extensive the child nutrition problem is. Nor are they aware of the costs of allowing hunger and poor nutrition to exist in America. Today's situation reminds me of a Fram oil filter TV commercial from many years ago with the catch phrase, *"You can pay me now, or pay me later."* It was a variation on the proverbial sayings, "An ounce of prevention is worth a pound of cure.", and "A stitch in time saves nine." Their point was quite simple and straightforward. It is usually cheaper and more effective to spend a little now to prevent a problem than to wait and end up spending a lot more later to repair it. This concept is perfectly applicable to nutrition. By providing good nutrition to children during their growth and development stages, society can avoid the larger physical and mental health costs down the road. In this case, there is a potential for a double return on the investment. In addition to avoiding the aforementioned health costs, adults who grew up with good nutrition are more likely to be wage earners and taxpayers instead of unemployed or unemployable citizens relying on a range of costly social safety net programs.

WebMD sums up the nutritional health issues as follows.

> *"Healthy Eating in Children: Problems Caused by Poor Nutrition[39] - Topic Overview, Children who eat poorly are more likely to develop certain long-term health problems and complications, including:*

---

39. *https://www.webmd.com/parenting/tc/healthy-eating-in-children-problems-caused-by-poor-nutrition-references*

• *Osteoporosis[40] in later life.*

• *Cardiovascular diseases. Growing up eating foods high in fat, sugar, and salt can increase the risk for high cholesterol[41], high blood pressure[42], and atherosclerosis[43] as an adult.*

• *Type 2 diabetes[44], which in children is linked to being overweight[45], being physically inactive, and having a family history of type 2 diabetes[46].*

• *Certain breathing problems[47], such as asthma[48] in children who are overweight[49]."*

Each of the conditions listed is physically, emotionally, and economically debilitating, leading to long-term financial costs, emotional, psychosocial, and physical discomfort. Malnutrition or undernutrition during early childhood weakens the child's resistance to disease and slows intellectual and physical development – conditions that cannot be corrected later in life. There are children who are suffering right now, waiting for their next meal. Both the parent and the child lack the proper nourishment. Without frequent intake of fruits, vegetables, and balanced meals their bodies are slowly losing calcium. As children grow, their adolescent bodies

---

40. https://www.webmd.com/hw-popup/osteoporosis-menopause

41. https://www.webmd.com/hw-popup/cholesterol

42. https://www.webmd.com/hw-popup/high-blood-pressure-hypertension

43. https://www.webmd.com/hw-popup/atherosclerosis-8374

44. https://www.webmd.com/hw-popup/type-2-diabetes

45. https://www.webmd.com/diet/obesity/features/am-i-obese

46. https://diabetes.webmd.com/guide/diabetes_symptoms_types

47. https://www.webmd.com/lung/breathing-problems-causes-tests-treatments

48. https://www.webmd.com/hw-popup/asthma

49. https://www.webmd.com/diet/obesity/video/obesity-risks

require calcium to develop strong bones. Bones begin to greatly reduce their calcium intake by the time they reach early adulthood, making it critical to get enough calcium as a teen. Teens who do not meet calcium requirements have higher risks for brittle bones, bone breakage, stunted bone growth and osteoporosis later in life.

In addition to the health and nutrition costs, there are psychological and social costs. Many children go to school to nourish their stomachs as much as their minds. For them, the food they receive at school is their primary source of nutrition. 35 million people in the U.S. are hungry or don't know where their next meal is coming from, and 13 million of them are children. If another country were doing this to our children, we would be at war.

Young children are extremely sensitive to the way their peers view them. For some, it is an internal perception issue. The child subconsciously thinks, "They have food, and I don't, therefore, they matter, and I don't." Whether it's an internal or an external perception, the stigma of not being able to afford to purchase a meal creates a psychological scar and a social barrier to the child's emotional and intellectual development. Young black and brown children become traumatized in their early adolescent years which promotes more issues in teenage and adulthood. This lack of development frequently leads to poorer academic performance, social awkwardness, inability to get or hold a job, and a lifelong dependency on social safety net programs. 'Pay me now or pay me later' clearly applies! Cutting back on child nutrition programs is an ill-advised solution. It becomes another link in the poverty chain that hangs around their necks and weighs them down.

In other countries around the world, hunger and famine are the result of a lack of food. Not so in the US. Every year, Americans throw out forty percent of the available food[50], or about $165 million worth. This uneaten food could feed 25 million Americans. The problem is in getting the available food to the people who need it in a sanitary, low-risk, cost-effective manner. The lack of access to nutritious food is a poverty, liability litigation, and logistical issue, not a supply issue.

> *"Waste Land: Does the Large Amount of Food Discarded in the U.S. Take a Toll on the Environment?*
>
> *According to the Agriculture Department, each year Americans toss more than 25 percent, of all domestically produced food. A 2009 study[51] showed that a quarter of U.S. water and 4 percent of U.S. oil consumption annually go into producing and distributing food that ultimately ends up in landfills."*

Producing, delivering, consuming, and disposing of food involves many steps, and in aggregate, is awfully expensive. Throwing away forty percent of food each year, as millions of families, youth, veterans, and individuals go without food is extremely foolish, harmful and wasteful. These meals could be given to hungry populations.

---

50. https://www.npr.org/2012/09/21/161551772/the-ugly-truth-about-food-waste-in-america#_853ae90f0351324bd73ea615e6487517__4c761f170e016836ff84498202b99827__853ae90f0351324bd73ea615e6487517_text_43ec3e5dee6e706af7766fffea512721_Forty_0bcef9c45bd8a48eda1b26eb0c61c869_2520percent_0bcef9c45bd8a48eda1b26eb0c61c869_2520of_0bcef9c45bd8a48eda1b26eb0c61c869_2520the_0bcef9c45bd8a48eda1b26eb0c61c869_2520food_c0cb5f0fcf239ab3d9c1fcd31fff1efc_worth_0bcef9c45bd8a48eda1b26eb0c61c869_2520of_0bcef9c45bd8a48eda1b26eb0c61c869_2520food_0bcef9c45bd8a48eda1b26eb0c61c869_2520each_0bcef9c45bd8a48eda1b26eb0c61c869_2520year

51. *https://www.scientificamerican.com/article/earth-talk-waste-land/*

There is a reasonably narrow range of estimates for the total costs for food in America. For the purpose of discussion, we have chosen one in the center of the range. We could use numbers half their size and the problem would still be compelling.

Considering just US fruits and vegetables (no meats), the broad range estimate of the annual cost to produce them is $412 million dollars. There is even better agreement on the percentage of the food that is wasted. The number is about 40% or $165M. We have nearly fifty million hungry citizens in a country that is throwing away $165M worth of food every year. We must do better. Think about the situation across the economy. Companies in the food industry manage to be profitable while the system throws away forty percent of their product. We need to find a way to increase profitability by reducing waste and at the same time finding a way to feed our hungry citizens. We must also consider the ecological/environmental costs that come with dumping food in landfills.

California recently passed a law encouraging food donation by protecting the donors from liability. One of the reasons that stores and restaurants throw away food is the fear of liability if the food they give away spoils and a recipient gets sick. (44 percent of manufacturers, 41 percent of restaurants and 25 percent of retailers identified fear of liability as their primary barrier to food donation[52].) In California, food represents the largest portion of waste sent to landfills. If you want a bit more information about the food waste situation in America, we recommend the following articles.

- "What Do Restaurants Do With Leftover Food?[53]"

---

52. http://www.wastetodaymagazine.com/article/california-passes-food-donation-law/

53. https://www.huffingtonpost.com/the-daily-meal/what-do-restaurants-do-wi_b_5469841.html

● "Wasted: How America Is Losing Up to 40 Percent of Its Food from Farm to Fork to Landfill[54]"

Poverty is a choice made by those in power. So are hunger and poor nutrition. Just six days after Sonny Perdue became Department of Agriculture Secretary, Purdue rolled back the Healthy, Hunger-Free Kids Act introduced in 2010 by President Barack Obama and former first lady Michelle Obama[55]. This was part of a larger program to undo everything the Obama administration had accomplished - even if it hurt the citizens. The rollback would reduce whole-grain requirements, allow higher levels of sodium entrees, and restore higher-fat and sweetened milk to school meal programs. Perdue's rule revision stipulated that pizza was a vegetable! This issue is not black or white. The concentrated tomato sauce on pizza has real nutritional value, but it is not a vegetable. PolitiFact provides an analysis of the issue[56]. The goal of our representatives should be to make things better, not to score petty partisan political points. We all need to get politically involved and work to elect statesmen, not politicians. If we can get them to focus on solving problems like poverty, we can reduce hunger and poor nutrition at the same time.

---

54. https://www.nrdc.org/sites/default/files/wasted-food-IP.pdf

55. https://www.csmonitor.com/EqualEd/2017/0502/USDA-secretary-announces-halt-on-school-nutrition-standards

56. https://www.politifact.com/factchecks/2011/nov/22/democratic-national-committee/republicans-pizza-vegetable-school-lunch/

Politics

Do you remember being taught the Preamble to The Constitution in grade school?

> *We the People of the United States, in order to form a more "perfect union, establish justice, ensure domestic tranquility, provide for the common defense, promote the general welfare, and to secure the blessings of liberty to ourselves and posterity, do ordain and establish this Constitution of the United States of America."*

In the constitution, who does 'We The people' apply to? The preamble was written in 1787, and then enacted in 1789. During that time, 'The people' did not include everyone. The preamble only applied to those who were white European male citizens. It excluded children, people of color, women, or ethnic backgrounds. America, during that time period, was deeply divided by race, region, industrialism, and politics. As time pushed forward, we have seen different amendments equating the roles of all citizens, yet still allowing or emphasizing separation by race and gender through laws and policies. Where is the union if our government is divided? How do we seek justice if we have policies, laws, and regulations that say otherwise? How do we ensure domestic tranquility when there's domestic terrorism and killing of our own? How do we promote general welfare if the government does not listen to the concerns of its own people?

According to a January 2022 Gallup report, Congress approval rating[57] was around 18%.

---

57. https://news.gallup.com/poll/389096/congressional-approval-sinks-democrats-sour-further.aspx

America is exceptional in many ways. One of the most important ways is our ability to respond to threats. Historically, those threats were in the form of sudden attacks like Pearl Harbor and 9/11, the economic crash in 2008, and the 2020 COVID pandemic. But heads up America, we have a new problem! The current political and economic threats crept up on us more gradually and are less dramatic in their appearance, but potentially even more devastating in their impact than anything we have faced in a long time. The historic threats associated with poverty like healthcare, the military, and the economy, now also need to include climate change, incarceration, racism, campaign finance, infrastructure, voter suppression, and the list goes on.

We are somewhat familiar with most of these issues because we hear our elected officials proclaiming their partisan positions all the time. What we do not hear or see are many sincere efforts to work together democratically across party lines to solve the problems. In fact, we see the opposite. The Senate passed a bill to provide healthcare to military veterans in response to injuries they received when they were exposed to toxic materials that they inhaled from burn pits in Afghanistan. While the bill was being finalized in the house, preliminary agreement was reached separately on a wide range infrastructure and economics bill that the Republicans opposed. Both bills were good for their constituents, but some Republicans behaved like infants whose candy had been taken and voted against the veterans' bill when the revised version came back up for final approval. It was the same bill they had voted for the previous week with one minor unobjectionable parliamentary procedural modification. Comedian and activist John Stewart spoke up and publicly shamed them into acting responsibly. Instead of passing a bill that permanently fixed the problems, the Republicans passed a short-term solution that would need to be periodically renewed - giving them repeated opportunities to extract some political gain each time. The next day, they passed the bill. There are similar examples where the party roles are reversed. Politicians should not be playing political power games at the expense of their constituents.

This explains Congress' 18% approval rating.

I was speaking with a sincere, intelligent conservative friend of mine and the conversation got around to politics - specifically politicians. I made the comment that a leading Republican was lying. Without hesitation, she replied, "All politicians lie." As I began to rebut her, I realized that she was right. The issue is not if they lie, but how much. Some lie far more than others, but they all lie. That is a sad state of affairs.

The US Congress, both House and Senate, should be places where responsible debate on critical issues takes place. Instead of focusing on addressing important issues that improve conditions for their constituents, every issue becomes a partisan football. Their goal is not to pass bills that make things better for all of their constituents, but to keep the ball until they have the opportunity to score a highly partisan goal that has much more limited benefits. Everything is perceived through a partisan lens and reacted to for partisan gain, not the greater good for all citizens.

A recent example of the need for elected officials to collaborate across party lines is the train derailment in East Palestine, OH, in February of 2023. What were the news stories about for the first few days? They talked about the short and long-term damage and both sides blamed the problem on the other party. Republicans made a big deal over the fact that Transportation Secretary Buttigieg had not made an immediate visit to the disaster site. Think about that. If he had immediately visited the site, valuable rescue resources would have been diverted to support his visit. Instead of immediately visiting the site, he formed a task force to manage all aspects of the derailment.

We needed leaders of both political parties to come together to clean up this mess and then to take appropriate legislative and regulatory steps to prevent further wrecks. One little-known fact that emerged while studying the East Palestine derailment is that the US averages over 1,000 derailments per year. That's about three per day. We should have known this and already begun developing a plan to fix the problem. Oh, wait! We have a plan, but partisan squabbling is blocking its passage. Our rail system is a major part of the country's infrastructure. Updating our infrastructure is not some future issue, it is an immediate need that requires bipartisan commitment and support, not blaming and finger pointing.

Fixing poverty should not be a partisan issue. Poverty affects every citizen, Republicans and Democrats, liberals, and conservatives alike. There may be some contentious conversations about how to fix poverty, but we should all agree that we need to fix it. As a citizenry, we have become partisan and almost tribal, buying into starkly different views of our country. As you read this book, try to think as a citizen, but not a partisan. A citizen is led according to principles that provide the lens through which we look at conditions and determine our positions. As conditions change, our principles remain steadfast. We look at situations, apply our principles, and determine our positions. Set aside whatever current position you may believe in and allow your humanity and logic to be open to exploring new ways of looking at the issues.

At this point, we need to clarify a few terms. The word democracy is based upon two ancient Greek words, demos – meaning the citizens, and kratos – meaning power. In our current times, there are two common meanings or uses of the word "Democracy". In one case, it refers to a <u>style</u> of government by the people. In the other case, it refers to a particular <u>form</u> of government where the majority rules directly. The US is a democratic style of government, but not a democratic form. The US form of government is a republic. The majority still rules but through elected representatives, and there are significant constitutional protections in place for the minority.

Trump's Big Lie that led to and encouraged the January 6th insurrection should be seen as a flashing warning light that these intended constitutional protections regarding free speech are being misused, misinterpreted, and are under attack. If you say something I disagree with, the Constitution gives you the right to say it. Ironically, as a citizen, I have an obligation to fight for you to have the right to say it. I also have the right to tell the world that I disagree with what you said. That is freedom of speech. For public safety reasons, society has put some constraints on freedom. For example, you cannot yell, "FIRE!", in a crowded theater. There is another important distinction that applies. If a person says something that is not true, but they believe it is, they are not lying, they are just wrong. In order for the statement to be a lie, it must be intended to deceive. We used to value the truth and despise lies. Lately, lying no longer has a political cost. There is another frequently cited misconception regarding free speech. It is true that you are mostly free to say whatever you want. However, publishers and the media are not required to broadcast it. Society has devised a new tactic for fighting something another person says that they disagree with, called, "Cancel Culture" where if you comment or say something that is not in agreement with what others believe or think, you will be canceled. It is a new phrase for an old practice that goes back centuries by other names like shunned, boycotted, and ostracized. It is constitutional, but harmful because it intimidates thoughtful people and discourages them from sharing the truth as they see it. Because of this trend, those that have their own belief systems and voices are now conforming and limiting their speech to protect themselves from being canceled.

Both houses of Congress used to be democratically deliberative bodies where civil discourse was the norm. For democracy to work, truthful conversations are essential. It is time for our elected officials to stop behaving like partisan politicians and start behaving like humanitarian statesmen. They must stop worrying about getting re-elected and start doing what is best for their constituents and the country. They might be surprised to find that by doing the latter, they may achieve the former. So, why don't they fix it? The 1% are making huge profits with things as they are, and they spend large sums to influence political decisions to maintain their advantages. The lobbyists lead the voters on wild-goose chases concerning red-herring issues that divide the voters and make progress impossible.

That is where we come in as voters. We must stop voting for candidates for red-herring issue reasons and start rewarding candidates who act in the best long-term interests of the country. Red herring issues distract from addressing poverty and in fact feed the deepening of poverty in America. Our motivation to not chase these hot button divides is that poverty weakens our country and way of life more than any other issue. For example, regardless of which side of the abortion/pro-life or gun-control/gun-rights issues we are on, that single issue should not be the reason we support a particular candidate. It makes no sense for a low-income voter to support a candidate because that individual shares their view on gun control or abortion but who opposes social safety net programs, denies climate change, gives tax-breaks to the wealthy, opposes raising the minimum wage, is against equal pay for equal work, and opposes universal healthcare. All those latter issues are important to every middle and low-income family's security and prosperity. But 1% use red-herring issues to distract these voters – convincing citizens to vote unconsciously against their own self-interest on all the other issues. Every voter needs to look at the big picture. We need to provide school civics courses that debunk red-herring issues and illustrate how they can harm the country. Instead, there are active efforts to ban books in school districts across the country. Look at the books on the list. Many of them are on the list because they provide truthful and needed information for voters.

The current crop of politicians reminds me of Alice talking to the Cheshire cat. "Would you tell me, please, which way I ought to go from here?" "That depends a good deal on where you want to get to," said the Cat. "I don't much care where—" said Alice. "Then it doesn't matter which way you go," said the Cat. We cannot afford to have our politicians lost and unsure where they want to go – other than to get reelected. If they fail to serve the people, we need to tell them where to go – that unpleasant place down below! We need to elect humanitarians and statesmen to lead the country, people to whom 'power' is only desirable as a means to making the country better.

America's democracy has had a couple of exceptionally good centuries, but recent events give us reasons to question our global status. Are we potentially looking forward to a major fall? Perhaps we should start by looking back a couple thousand years or more to where there are several historical examples of empires or civilizations failing. George Santayana reminds us, *"Those who cannot remember the past are condemned to repeat it."* So, let us look at the most famous study of why a major civilization failed, "*The History of the Decline and Fall of the Roman Empire*" by Edward Gibbons. According to Gibbons' work, the following is a list of the issues that brought down the mighty Roman Empire.

1. Decline in Morals and Values

2. Public Health
3. Political Corruption
4. Unemployment
5. Inflation
6. Urban decay
7. Inferior Technology
8. Military Spending

Now consider the issues disrupting American society today. The parallels are overlapping and frightening. Each of the eight issues leads to poverty, and poverty destroys democracy.

1. Decline in Morals and Values – Living in chronic poverty makes people do things that go against their fundamental values and beliefs in order to survive. The public has been conditioned to passively accept lies from their politicians.
2. Public Health – Catastrophic medical bills are the single largest cause of family poverty. COVID exacerbated the issue. These same conditions cause the maternal death rate in the US to place us among third-world countries.
3. Political Corruption – New York voters elected a confessed liar, George Santos, to the House of Representatives. Since the election, countless additional lies have been revealed and confirmed. Because the Republicans need his vote, they are not censuring or removing him. So, many critical economic bills are stuck in congress, unable to pass and reduce poverty.
4. Unemployment – COVID had a direct impact on unemployment when businesses were forced to close to control the spread of the pandemic. In an evil side-effect, COVID caused major supply-chain issues – delaying and denying access to essential supplies and materials. Partisan squabbling prevented agreement on infrastructure funding

and public service programs that would have alleviated poverty.

5. Inflation – Interruptions in oil and electric supplies led to price increases on everything. The resulting increase in inflation, accompanied by job losses, put people on the road to poverty.

6. Urban decay – Most major urban centers in the US are struggling culturally, economically, and socially. Politicians use these conditions to divide us and weaken our ability to survive, let alone thrive.

1. Inferior Technology – In a misguided quest to maximize short-term profits, the US ceded its leadership in high tech innovation and manufacturing. Our North American manufacturing and assembly industries must have the latest technology chips to build communications devices, military weapons, appliances, automobiles, and countless other products. It does us no good to have the best missiles if we can't get the chips needed to use them.

1. Military Spending – The US is spending so much on military defense, we have less money for infrastructure and public service projects that provide jobs and reduce poverty.

This is not a history lesson. It's a warning. If you evaluate the eight items on Gibbon's list, you can see where poverty is an element of each one. For more details about each of these issues, read the website article, "Why Do World Powers Decline and Fall?[58]" You need not take the time to consider individually the Soviet Union, the Egyptian civilization, the Persian Empire, the Mongol Empire, and others. The point is that being great is no guarantee of remaining

---

58. http://www.freemaninstitute.com/RTGdecline.htm

great. Remaining great requires avoiding the pitfalls that brought down the great civilizations from the past. Our democracy is at great risk today.

Following WWII, America established itself as a dominant world leader militarily, economically, politically, culturally, industrially, and ethically. We enjoyed a prolonged period of growth and prosperity that all Americans shared. Workers united, and unions worked with management to ensure fair labor pay and practices. We made progress on social issues like integration and women's rights. We were heading in the right direction. Each generation did a little better than the one before it – until now.

We are now experiencing a quiet erosion of the actualization of the American dream. It happened slowly, over many years, and as a result, it did not alarm anybody – sort of like the boiled frog. According to the parable, if you suddenly put a frog into boiling water, it will jump out, but if you put the frog into warm water and then slowly bring it to a boil, it will not perceive the danger and will be cooked to death. Americans are becoming that boiled frog. In many ways I totally disapprove of what is happening to America. However, in a strange way I am grateful that it may awaken the American spirit in time for us to jump out of the pot before the American way of life we all love is totally cooked – and dead.

Our revered Founding fathers told us:

> *"Prudence, indeed, will dictate that Governments long established should not be changed for light and transient causes; and accordingly, all experience hath shewn, that mankind are more disposed to suffer, while evils are sufferable, than to right themselves by abolishing the forms to which they are accustomed. But when a long train of abuses and usurpations, pursuing invariably the same*

> *Object evinces a design to reduce them under absolute Despotism, it is their right, it is their duty, to throw off such Government, and to provide new Guards for their future security. —Such has been the patient sufferance of these Colonies; and such is now the necessity which constrains them to alter their former Systems of Government."*

These words are from our Declaration of Independence. The Founding Fathers were highly intelligent, wise, innovative, and thoughtful men. Thomas Jefferson anticipated our current need to adapt to the times when he said,

> *I am certainly not an advocate for frequent changes in laws" .and constitutions But laws and institutions must go hand in hand with the progress of the human mind. As that becomes more developed, more enlightened, as new discoveries are made, new truths discovered and manners and opinions change, with the change of circumstances, institutions must advance also to keep pace with the times. We might as well require a man to wear still the coat which fitted him when a boy as civilized society to remain ever under the regimen of their barbarous ancestors."* Thomas Jefferson[59] - July 12, 1816

America has reached a point where we need to re-examine ourselves and make some changes in our fundamental practices to modify our political behaviors to better reflect our values and the cultures of the people. Adapting to change is not unconstitutional. Jefferson voiced the need for it. America has gradually lost its luster and may be overdue for a close examination of its political processes. Bear that in mind as you read this book. There is an often-used proverb that

---

59. http://www.let.rug.nl/usa/presidents/thomas-jefferson/letters-of-thomas-jefferson/ jefl246.php

may be appropriate for this time: "When life gives you lemons, make lemonade." I consider the current political and social conditions an overflowing basket of lemons. However, if we can use it to motivate people to stop being complacent and step up to change things, perhaps we can make some lemonade.

Those who cannot remember the past are condemned to repeat it".

~ George Santayana

Those who are indigenous and aboriginal to this land (native Americans and slaves) have come too far to be told not to remember their past, only what others have taught them. Some states are banning the teaching of Critical Race Theory and reparations in their schools. It's history, not pornography or anarchy. As we go forward, it is a reminder to "know thyself" and be aware of the government that created the laws that pushed you into this historical blindness, broke down our minds to fear and conform into laws and regulations, history, and a systemic education that continuously fails us. Question, understand, and become knowledgeable on the laws and constitutions to be able to protest what is seen harmful and dangerous to who you are.

A democracy is strongest and most successful when the citizens rule by consensus, not coercion. The partisan animosity currently sweeping the country uses ethnic and cultural differences to divide us – making consensus more difficult to achieve. Remember, our strength is in being united.

Our lack of cultural memory in some cases was deliberately imposed on us by the settlers who stole the land and limited access to learning its history. Their collective memories and cultural histories must be much more than only what others have taught. If you are a member of a marginalized cultural subgroup, 'know thyself' and beware that the government that created the laws has also pushed you into this cultural blindness. Question, understand, and become knowledgeable on the laws and constitutions to be able to protest what is potentially harmful and dangerous to who you are. As you gain a better understanding of who you are, you will also develop an appreciation for your role in making America great for everybody. At the same time, others will learn to appreciate and value you.

America's democratic system and processes are essential to solving the issues facing us. Recent events have pushed ensuring our electoral system is reliable and fair to the head of the list. As voters, we must believe in our electoral process as the first step in having faith in the people we elect. Our democracy is predicated upon fair and free elections. Before he was elected the first time he ran, Trump planted the seeds to convince people that if he lost, it was because the election was stolen ((The Big Lie!). He denigrated members of the press that challenged his lies and worked at the local and state levels to put his supporters into offices with the power to sway the election results his way. The January 6th, 2021, attack on the nation's Capital was instigated by Trump based upon his continuing claim that the election was stolen. In early 2023, despite overwhelming evidence to the contrary, many Republicans still believed the 2020 election was stolen. We have to restore Americans' faith in this fundamental democratic process. Congress now has the 1/6 Select Committee's report. Members of Congress must set aside partisan issues and serve as statesmen to act in the best interest of the country.

Issue #4 - America is not the greatest country in the world anymore.

If you have not seen the <u>Newsroom</u> series, we highly recommend it. It is available on YouTube, Amazon Prime, and HBO streaming.

Take a few minutes to watch Jeff Daniels[60] as Will McAvoy, the news anchor responds to the question, "What makes America the greatest country in the world?" He articulately sets the stage for the rest of this book.

Jeff Daniels' character concludes his comments with a reminder that the first step in solving a problem is recognizing that you have one. His closing line is a recognition that, "America is not the greatest country in the world anymore!" The thing that haunts me about the clip is the expression on the face of the young blonde student who naively asks the question about American Exceptionalism – fully expecting warm and fuzzy platitudes in response. Her expression perfectly represents the Americans who believe, or want to believe, that America is still the greatest country in the world. In many hearts and minds, America is still the greatest country, providing a shining example to the rest of the world in many areas. Sadly, we no longer are. In case he went too fast, he said:

> *"We're seventh in literacy, 27th in math, 22nd in science, 49th in life expectancy, 178th in infant mortality, third in median household income, number 4 in labor force, and number 4 in exports. We lead the world in only three categories: number of incarcerated citizens per capita, number of adults who believe angels are real, and defense spending, where we spend more than the next 26 countries combined, twenty-five of whom are allies ... We sure used to be the greatest nation. We used to stand up for what was right. We fought for moral reasons. We passed laws, struck down laws for moral reasons.* **We waged wars on poverty, not poor people.** *We sacrificed. We cared about*

---

60. https://www.youtube.com/watch?v=bIpKfw17-yY

our neighbors. We put our money where our mouths were. And we never beat our chest. We built great big things, made ungodly technological advances, explored the universe, cured diseases, and we cultivated the world's greatest artists and the world's greatest economy. We reached for the stars, acted like men. We aspired to intelligence, we didn't belittle it, it didn't make us feel inferior. We didn't identify ourselves by who we voted for in our last election. And we didn't ... we didn't scare so easy. We were able to be all these things, and to do all these things, because we were informed. By great men, men who were revered. First step in solving any problem is recognizing there is one."

(Credit to Aaron Sorkin who wrote those words. I love this clip. I have it bookmarked and go back and watch it occasionally. Aaron Sorkin should be required to produce stuff like this all the time. The current Trump spectacle would make a great model.)

We might be tempted to dismiss the previous quote as TV fiction, so let's consider a non-fiction source, The Wall Street Journal[61].

"Data: Wall Street Journal/NORC poll. Chart: Axios Visuals

Rarely does one poll stare so deeply into the soul of a nation and tell its story. But a new Wall Street Journal-NORC poll exposes generational and political divides[62] that echo loudly and transformatively across our culture, politics and governance.

---

61. https://www.axios.com/2023/03/28/america-core-values-economy-poll

62. *https://www.axios.com/2022/09/12/two-americas-index-democracy*

Why it matters: Bill McInturff[63], the pollster on earlier editions of this survey, told The Journal that the combined toll of political division, COVID and the lowest economic confidence in decades appear to be having "a startling effect on our core values."

"Patriotism, religious faith, having children and other priorities that helped define the national character for generations are receding in importance to Americans," The Wall Street Journal's Aaron Zitner writes[64].

"Tolerance for others, deemed very important by 80% of Americans as recently as four years ago, has fallen to 58%."

The findings: NORC[65] at the University of Chicago polled 1,019 adults this month by web and phone *(margin of error: ±4%)*.

Asked to describe the state of the nation's economy, 1% (not a typo) chose "excellent." 56% said a four-year college degree is "not worth the cost because people often graduate without specific job skills and with a large amount of debt." 33% said they have very little or no confidence in public schools.

Look at the tectonic shifts from a Journal/NBC poll 25 years ago, in 1998:

- *Patriotism is very important: Dropped from 70% to 38%.*

- *Religion is very important: Dropped from 62% to 39%.*

63. https://twitter.com/pollsterguy?lang=en

64. https://www.wsj.com/articles/americans-pull-back-from-values-that-once-defined-u-s-wsj-norc-poll-finds-df8534cd

65. https://www.norc.org/Pages/default.aspx

- *Having children is very important: Dropped from 59% to 30%.*

- *Community involvement is very important: Dropped from 47% to 27%.*

- *Money is very important: Rose from 31% to 43%.*

The bottom line: The poll quantifies a generational and political divide that shows a rot at the very soul of our nation."

A casual look at the five things on the list doesn't mention poverty. However, if you ask yourself what is the cause of each change, poverty shows up immediately. Consider the drop in the perceived importance of 'Patriotism'. If your sense of economic security has dropped and poverty is threatening your safety because the government is not doing its job, then it is easy to understand why people would be less patriotic towards that failing democracy. We could explore each of the topics and find poverty as one of the major factors.

While poverty plays a role, misleading media sources exacerbate the problem. Former Fox News talking head Tucker Carlson and his collaborators in the far-right media bubble have established a whole new lexicon of racist words and phrases like 'Legacy Americans', 'Critical Race Theory (CRT)', 'White Replacement Theory ', and other innocuous and non-threatening sounding terms to politely espouse their racist white supremacist beliefs. If it stopped there, it would be sad but not outrageous. But it does not stop with the new language. They use the language to advocate for unacceptable discrimination and inequities based on race. This additional step has many negative impacts, the most egregious of which is to divide

Americans into subgroups that fight among themselves instead of uniting to defend themselves and each other.

How did we allow ourselves to get into this predicament? The recent series of events have illustrated how inadequately and inaccurately the current system for electing our leaders is functioning. Disgust and disappointment with the current partisan political conditions compelled us to spend the time to better understand why the system produced results that do not represent the will of our citizens. After researching the problem, we have a reasonably firm grasp of its breadth and depth. We also have developed a preliminary vision of a process for defining and implementing a solution to the problem.

Democracy and capitalism are still the best bases on which to build, but we need to learn from our history and refine some of the rules (those much-maligned regulations) to ensure the system produces the outcomes we want. Innovation and responding to crises are both American strengths. It's time to apply those strengths to our current political, social, and economic conditions. Poverty and the rest of the issues require a functioning Congress to engage in intelligent, civil, rational debate and resolve them.

In presenting each of the issues, we looked at numerous online sources and when metrics were cited, we provided the most commonly used estimates. We could debate the accuracy of the numbers associated with any of the following issues, but that is not the point. The point is that even if the numbers are only one-half as bad as those presented, they are outrageous and unacceptable; and they are all indicators that an immensely powerful minority of our citizens is severely stressing the fabric of our society, and in some cases tearing it apart.

According to Business Insider, the United States is the 13th wealthiest country in the world (based on per-capita – total wealth divided by total population). Despite this situation, many unacceptable issues and conditions exist. Some are symptoms, some are causes, and some are effects, but they all combine to paint a dire picture of the pressures on average Americans.

Most of the problems and issues in the following pages would be greatly reduced, if not eliminated, if everybody had a home to live in, food to eat, a job that paid a living wage, access to affordable healthcare, safety from physical attack, and a quality education. There is enough wealth in America to provide every citizen with all these things without causing even minor pain to the very wealthy who would be required to pay a more equitable share of the cost.

Unfortunately, with wealth comes power, for good or evil, and the wealthy have the power to fight any efforts to change the current conditions. However, they represent only 1% of the population and the rest of us outnumber them 99 to 1. It is important to also realize that we have some wealthy individuals who are not avaricious. Some of them are generous humanitarians. Sounds like a simple solution, and it is. Too simple, because the greedy members of the 1% use their wealth to buy gaslighting media messages that divide the 99% into small competing fractious groups that end up canceling out each other's votes. While we fight amongst ourselves, we will not have the time, energy, or resources to fight them. Our challenge is to energize, educate, and activate the 99% so that we work as a united front to change things.

Remember the "American Dream"? It was not a narrow tunnel-vision dream. It was a broad dream that included wonderful opportunities and happiness for everybody. The Dream included more than simply financial status. It included a sense of self-worth, a loving family, a feeling of safety and security and many other tangible and intangible things. The dream included a vision that every generation would be more prosperous and successful than the one that preceded it. For decades, it was more than just a dream. Following WWII, it was a reality for many of us. It's not clear when it happened, but the level of prosperity for each generation peaked and has turned downhill. There are many factors that drive the changes in America's prosperity. The socialization process occurred when an individual's standards, motives, behaviors, and moral ethics changed to conform to those regarded as desirable and appropriate for his or her present and future role in any particular society[66]. Fixing poverty will cure many of them. It will allow them to re-discover and/or form their own standards, shifting their attitudes to go after their own "American Dream". The fortunate part of the global economic situation is that America's overall economy continues to lead the world, or so we are told, and choose to believe.

As we looked around and read what was happening in the world, we were both disappointed and angry that the Dream is not only no longer within reach of many people; but also, completely beyond the realm of their ability to dream it. We must work together to restore the Dream.

Remember when:

---

66. https://www.sciencedirect.com/topics/social-sciences/
   socialization#_853ae90f0351324bd73ea615e6487517__4c761f170e016836ff84498202b99
   827__853ae90f0351324bd73ea615e6487517_text_43ec3e5dee6e706af7766fffea512721_S
   ocialization_0bcef9c45bd8a48eda1b26eb0c61c869_2520is_0bcef9c45bd8a48eda1b26eb0c
   61c869_2520the_0bcef9c45bd8a48eda1b26eb0c61c869_2520process_0bcef9c45bd8a48ed
   a1b26eb0c61c869_2520whereby_c0cb5f0fcf239ab3d9c1fcd31ff1efc_role_0bcef9c45bd8a4
   8eda1b26eb0c61c869_2520in_0bcef9c45bd8a48eda1b26eb0c61c869_2520any_0bcef9c45
   bd8a48eda1b26eb0c61c869_2520particular_0bcef9c45bd8a48eda1b26eb0c61c869_2520s
   ociety

- Kids grew up in a neighborhood where people did not lock their doors.

- The next generation made more money than their parents.

- When you went out to play, your mom told you to come home when the streetlights came on?

- Every mom in the neighborhood acted as if she was your mom and everyone knew each other like a family.

In many areas across the country, times have changed.

- People not only lock their doors, but they also have alarm systems, live in gated communities, carry guns, and have cameras that display every moment of what is happening in the vicinity..

- The past couple of generations' financial situation has been the same or worse than their parents'.

- Playing kids are under constant surveillance and supervision, many sadly confined to home life on their gadgets instead of experiencing their childhood.

- In other neighborhoods, moms are working, and the kids are on their own, leaving the child to develop faster and quicker. Raising children has become an industry – from nannies to day-care centers.

This is merely the essence of our changing times. In some locations, neighbors, the environment, and other children cannot be trusted. Neglecting moral values and implementing laws in a society has impacted the traditional generations that we knew once before. Surely, the American people did not elect representatives and expect them to create this situation.

America is a republic, governed by the people. People vote to elect the representatives who make the decisions that create, keep, or change the conditions in the country. Typically, that would mean that the people have chosen the current situation. Why would we do that? Clearly, some people have chosen it, but it does not make any sense that most Americans would choose to create rules that would result in the current unacceptable conditions. It is not enough to intellectually choose a better way. We must fight and vote to make things better. Every election where the winner does not fight in the best interests of his/her constituents, democracy loses strength.

Issue #5 - We need an informed and empowered electorate.

In order for a democracy to thrive, the people with the responsibility for electing the leaders, our citizens, must be well informed. Today's citizens are undereducated and misinformed (deliberately). We hear about banning books, prohibiting the teaching of subjects like the history of slavery, Fox News must pay $787.5M for knowingly and deliberately lying to its viewers in covering the 2020 election, and the list goes on. This book is designed to provide the reader an overview of the major issues, hoping to provoke interest in some. From provoking interest, we hope the footnote links to additional information will facilitate your deeper understanding

The US is becoming an Oligarchy. Following the principle of Occam's Razor, the most logical explanation for our current political situation is that a powerful minority has managed to take control of America's election and economic systems and is currently ruling America. That is not how a democracy should work. The situation is not the result of some cabal or conspiracy among a sinister group of greedy immoral people – the Deep State. Instead, it is a confluence of interests. Independently, individuals and groups having common interests in amassing obscene collections of wealth have evolved a situation that allows them to enrich the few at the expense of the many – regardless of the societal impact. Unregulated capitalism has allowed greedy individuals to game the system and create an unsustainable level of poverty brought on by wealth and income inequality. A broken election system has enabled and allowed them to do it.

We must also include the realization that America is competing in a global marketplace. Based upon our beliefs in human rights and ethical values, our economy is controlled by regulations, (minimum wage, EEOC, etc.) some of which add to the cost to make, sell, and deliver products. Our global competitors do not mandate these behaviors, allowing them to make and sell similar products for less. Economists are trying to find a model that ensures everybody's rights are protected. Because America is one of the world's largest and most desirable consumer markets (and many Eastern European countries share our values) we have some leverage to demand that foreign suppliers wanting to do business here must either enforce similar human requirements or pay a human tariff that can be used to compensate American workers, making the lower cost no longer a competitive advantage. This is another economic issue that our elected leaders must resolve. Partisan political bickering is divisive and counterproductive. Instead we must collaborate and cooperate – using the leverage that being the biggest and most desirable economy in the global marketplace affords us – to establish and enforce international financial rules and regulations that ensure all the workers are treated fairly and humanely and the participating countries and companies are profitable.

Most people who run for public office do so from a sincere desire to serve the public. After we elect them, they run into an unfortunate reality, referred to as:

The Politicians' Infinite Loop to Despair

1. **I** want to serve my community.
2. To serve, the voters have to (re)elect me.
3. To get the people's votes, I need to raise money.
4. Wealthy people provide most of the money to support me.
5. I got elected.
6. I must please the people with money.
7. I do what the money people want.
8. I try to serve the people who elected me.
   a. Step eight loses to step seven.
9. Go back to step 3.

You may have noticed, there is nothing in this infinite loop designed to drive quality of life higher for most people. As the middle-class loses out, the motivator becomes finding someone to blame to redirect that anger and get reelected. In doing that we chase misadventures (wars for instance) that make poverty worse.

America leads the world in military spending, incarceration rates, and deaths due to gun violence! Of the three, only military spending may be a good thing – and we discuss military spending in more detail elsewhere. We do have the world's largest and most costly military and we deploy it across the world, ostensibly in defense of freedom and human rights. Unfortunately, there are not any parallel grand benefits to the incarceration rate or gun violence.

Incidentally, we tried a few different search phrases, trying to find a list of areas where America leads the world in good things. We got countless lists of bad things, but truly little on the good side. Slate.com provided the best list of good things[67] we could find.

Why Did Dylan Roof Shoot Nine Black People in a Church? Just asking the question in that way triggers four clichéd responses. He shot them, so it is a gun control issue. There were nine people killed so it was an act of domestic terrorism. They were Black, so it is a racial issue. They were in church, so it is a religious issue. After exhausting the red herring issues, then we turn to the nuanced issues. He was a reclusive person who fantasized about apartheid, so it is a mental health issue. He was bullied. He does not have a job. He is poor. He does not have any friends. .... And the list goes on.

What is the reason nobody is talking about? All the reasons listed above are merely symptoms of the underlying festering sore in America. POVERTY! The previous list included his being poor, but that is just a symptom of the systemic problem of poverty. If they are poor, or things are not going well for them, the first response by many people is to find someone to blame for the problem; and typically, that someone is not themselves. They look at their surroundings, the conditions, and the people, and convince themselves that 'they' (somebody else) is to blame. They talk to others who share some of their problems and collectively agree that some other group is causing their problems. Ironically, many of those other groups have similar problems to their own, based on the same underlying causes. This rancor stews and boils until the lid blows off and some poor soul breaks. Sadly, they frequently ignore the people who are actually to blame for their unfortunate circumstances – the

---

67. http://www.slate.com/articles/news_and_politics/politics/2012/07/

the_greatest_country_in_the_world_the_usa_is_tops_in_cheese_production_and_these_2

3_other_categories_.html

1% who created and continue to exacerbate the economic conditions with no regard for their devastating and demoralizing impact on the rest of the citizens. The 1% spend money on media sources to convince their victims that those other people are to blame.

Do we genuinely want to stop the senseless killings? Of course we do! But forget about taking away their guns. They are the symptom, not the cause. If the citizens did not have guns, they would find another way to express their rage. There are countless diverse happy communities, so it is not a racial issue. We truly can all get along. Most of the churches teach most of the same values, so it is not a religious issue. Forget about all the other proposed issues. If we want to stop the killings, then we have to fix the economy, so everyone has a legitimate opportunity to live a comfortable, prosperous, happy life. Happy people do not kill other people unless they are sociopaths, and there is no simple solution to that problem. If everyone were able to earn a decent living, it would change everything. I guess we must treat the symptoms for now, but we also must put more effort into treating the cause.

The French are sending a ship to take back the Statue of Liberty. We are not living up to the words on her tablet:

> *"Give me your tired, your poor, Your huddled masses yearning to breathe free, The wretched refuse of your teeming shore. Send these, the homeless, tempest-tost to me, I lift my lamp beside the golden door!"*

For centuries, the rest of the world viewed America as a shining example of democratic rule. The US has always been a country composed of a diverse pool of immigrants from countries all over the world. People admiringly described the US as a "melting pot" where its strengths and values were the result of incorporating the best elements from many cultures. Notice the past tense. America's core values are being lost or trampled. Racism and economic pressures on individuals, fed by a divisive narrative that encourages people to blame the other person for their troubles, weaken the majority's ability to unite and act in their own best interest. The Founding Fathers built this country upon ideals like life, liberty, the pursuit of happiness, common good, justice, equality, diversity, truth, patriotism, separation of powers, representative government, checks and balances, individual rights, and freedom of religion. Many of these fundamental values are currently under serious attack.

This issue breaks down into poverty, jobs, and security. Unless you are an indigenous Native American, somewhere along the line your ancestors were immigrants. Immigrants and Native Americans built America's greatness. They discovered the great inventions and innovations that created companies that fueled the economic growth of the country. People flock here from countries all over the world because we provide opportunities for personal growth and success. In a growing, thriving economy, with jobs for everyone, immigrants are a valuable resource. When the economy is stressed, the challenge is not to get rid of the immigrant resource. It's to fix the economy. As with the other shameful issues, if everyone felt financially secure, immigration would not be an issue.

A ridiculously small number of immigrants come here to do us harm. Most of the people who do Americans harm are Americans. That is a security issue, not an immigration issue. Those who can gain from pushing us towards the fringe describe these infrequent attacks as an immigration issue. We cannot allow the fringe to drive the discussion. Once again, most Americans are or have friends, family members, and neighbors who are to some degree immigrants – some of whom are illegal. We do not want to get rid of them or punish them. We want to normalize them. We all pretty much agree that we need a better system for managing our borders, humanely and rationally correcting the problems with people who are here illegally, and controlling illegal immigration. We need a centrist, rational solution, not an extreme emotional reaction.

For decades, children came here innocently and became our friends and neighbors. How can we even consider punishing them for that? Most Americans do not want to. But a few politicians, citing a bogus Replacement Theory[68], for partisan reasons are trying to deport them. President Barack Obama introduced Deferred Action for Childhood Arrivals (DACA) in 2012 to shield people from deportation who came to the United States as children. A person's DACA status is renewable, lasting two years at a time, but it does not provide a pathway to citizenship. People in the program are eligible for a range of benefits, including permission to remain in the country and get work permits, through which many obtain health insurance from their employers. Working under DACA has also allowed them to pay for school, pursue higher education and, in some states, drive legally and qualify for state-subsidized health care. Over 90% of DACA recipients work and pay income and Social Security taxes[69].

DACA recipients are frequently confused with Dreamers. They are not the same thing. Separate legislation called the Dream Act, would have given its beneficiaries a path to citizenship. Dreamers now fall between the ages of 16 and 35. Most Dreamers come from Mexico, Central America, South America, and Asia. The US issued Dreamer status to about 800,000 people. Dreamers must be enrolled in high school or already have a diploma or G.E.D. to qualify.

---

68. https://immigrationforum.org/wp-content/uploads/2021/12/Replacement-Theory-Explainer-1122.pdf

69. https://www.stilt.com/blog/2020/02/do-dreamers-pay-taxes/

The economic impact of the Dreamers is hard to measure, but one study has determined that those covered by DACA contribute nearly $42 billion annually to the U.S. economy and pay $3.4 billion more in taxes[70] each year than they consume in benefits. You may have believed the gaslighting that convinced people that the immigrants were a drain on our economy. Not so!

People who have been listening to the gaslighting about the replacement theory may be surprised by these facts. The anti-immigration racists and the lying 1% are gradually eroding the democratic principles that once made America great. Pervasive poverty is the deadliest weapon in their arsenal.

Issue #6 - Kids in cages.

Within the past decade, Central American immigrant children were being isolated from their parents and imprisoned separately by US government officials (Kids in Cages!). The inhumanity of it is unfathomable. This situation is about both politics and racism. America has some historic shameful early national examples of greed – slavery and the way we treated Native Americans come to mind as not-so-glowing examples of American exceptionalism. They were not only examples of greed; they were also egregious violations of human rights. Lest we think we have put those days far behind us,

---

70. https://americansforprosperity.org/how-dreamers-are-contributing-to-america/#_853ae90f0351324bd73ea615e6487517__4c761f170e016836ff84498202b99827__853ae90f0351324bd73ea615e6487517_text_43ec3e5dee6e706af7766fffea512721_The_0bcef9c45bd8a48eda1b26eb0c61c869_2520economic_0bcef9c45bd8a48eda1b26eb0c61c869_2520impact_0bcef9c45bd8a48eda1b26eb0c61c869_2520of_0bcef9c45bd8a48eda1b26eb0c61c869_2520the_c0cb5f0fcf239ab3d9c1fcd31fff1efc_than_0bcef9c45bd8a48eda1b26eb0c61c869_2520they_0bcef9c45bd8a48eda1b26eb0c61c869_2520consume_0bcef9c45bd8a48eda1b26eb0c61c869_2520in_0bcef9c45bd8a48eda1b26eb0c61c869_2520benefits

consider present-day examples like the way we treat immigrants and the proportion and racial mix of our prison populations.

If those immigrant families had come here from northern Europe and were white skinned, blue-eyed boys and girls, the situation would be quite different. We would be seeing support programs being organized to adopt and care for the families. Instead, we heartlessly disregarded their human rights and needs. We must do better.

> *"Trump's Child Detention Camps Cost $775 Per Person Every Day - The daily cost[71] for a child in a detention camp is more than a stay in a deluxe room at the Trump International Hotel in Washington, D.C."*

These $775 per-day luxury facilities that the kids live in at the border detention centers are tents and chain-link fences. It is reasonable to assume that the suppliers' cost per child is significantly less than $775 per-day, leaving obscene profits for the providers. The companies and organizations profiting from housing these children have long and close ties to politicians and political parties. The American people are paying obscene amounts for a service that is morally repugnant. While our ability to handle arriving migrant children humanely and responsibly at our southern border has improved, we still have a long way to go[72].

Assuming the government could possibly justify the separations, we would have to demand that the responsible agency would be meticulous in ensuring the safety and well-being of the children. But they were not! Steven Wagner, Acting Assistant Secretary for the Administration for Children and Families at the U.S. Department

---

71. *https://www.gq.com/story/trump-detention-camps-cost*

72. https://www.nytimes.com/2021/08/06/us/politics/migrant-children-shelters.html

of Health and Human Services testified before the Permanent Subcommittee on Investigations of the Committee on Homeland Security and Governmental Affairs of the United States Senate on April 26, 2018. He reported,

> *"From October to December 2017, ORR (Office of Refugee Resettlement) attempted to reach 7,635 UAC and their sponsors. Of this number, ORR reached and received agreement to participate in the safety and well-being call from approximately 86 percent of sponsors. From these calls, ORR learned that 6,075 UAC remained with their sponsors. Twenty-eight UAC had run away, five had been removed from the United States, and 52 had relocated to live with a non-sponsor. ORR was unable to determine with certainty the whereabouts of 1,475 UAC. Based on the calls, ORR referred 792 cases, which were in need of further assistance, to the National Call Center for additional information and services[73]."*

We LOST 1475 children! General John Kelly, said that the refugee children we are separating from their parents will *"be taken care of — put into foster care or whatever"*? Is this what he meant by "or whatever." The problem gets worse. When the parents are released or deported, it is exceedingly difficult for the parents to locate and reunite with their children.

> *"As President Donald Trump's administration ramps up the prosecutions of parents crossing the border illegally and separates their children, Pastor's case offers a glimpse into how challenging it is to reunite them. Homeland Security Secretary Kirstjen Nielsen has defended the practice, saying*

---

73. *https://www.acf.hhs.gov/orr/grant-funding/unaccompanied-children-released-sponsors-state*

children are taken from any criminals imprisoned for breaking the law.

But once immigrant families, many asylum seekers from Central America, are separated at the border, they struggle to find each other among the three behemoth federal agencies in charge of their care. Advocates say few procedures are in place to ensure they reunify.

"In many cases they may never," said Michelle Brané, executive director of the migrant rights program at the Women's Refugee Commission, a national advocacy group. "We have seen children as young as 18 months deported without their parents and more commonly, parents deported without their children. Parents arrive in Central America with no idea how to get their children back[74]."

We are doing this. You and I. The US government is doing this. The US government is us! We have been stigmatized and divided to the point where we are losing track of our basic human values. The following poem, by German Lutheran pastor Martin Niemöller, chastised the German intellectuals for allowing the Nazis to attack groups in their society. The parallels with what is happening today are terrifying.

"First they came for the Socialists, and I did not speak out—

Because I was not a Socialist.

Then they came for the Trade Unionists, and I did not speak out —

---

74. *https://www.houstonchronicle.com/news/houston-texas/houston/article/Immigrant-families-separated-at-border-struggle 12938759.php*

Because I was not a Trade Unionist.

Then they came for the Jews, and I did not speak out—

Because I was not a Jew.

Then they came for me—and there was no one left to speak for me."

This must stop! Enough of this racism crap! We are much more alike than we are different.

Let's play a brief mind-game. Start at the beginning – really – at birth! We begin by imagining a purely hypothetical setting in a hospital nursery in a totally integrated middle-class area. The parents are all non-racist – and some of the marriages are bi-racial. All the families have comfortable incomes. All the parents have the same high expectations for their children. All the parents have similar high expectations for the rest of the children in their community. The families represent all the major religions and cultures of the world. Although this community is hypothetical, it is not a far-fetched scenario. If you think about it, you may know of a community like this one.

The lucky children born into this community will play together and become close friends, totally ignoring the ethnic, cultural, racial, or religious differences. At some point during their growth, they will become curious and want to learn about the differences. This knowledge will not divide them; it will grow their bonds of friendship.

Some of the children will be smarter than others are. Some will be more athletic than others are. Some will build things. Some will be artists. There will be countless differences; but they will not hate each other for their differences. In fact, their differences will strengthen and enrich the community. Go to the local major mall and watch the young children in the play area. They will play and interact with total disregard for their differences. There has to be a lesson for all of us in their behavior.

If our communities are not like this one, what can we do to make them so? Start the change. Talk with one friend and get them on board. Then enlist another. Keep growing the program until it becomes a movement that creates reality.

Is there anything in the scenario that defies logic? If not, then what happened that we have all the intolerance and hatred in society? How did those innocent children become racist? Rogers and Hammerstein said it very well in their controversial song from South Pacific, "You Have to be Carefully Taught"

"You've got to be taught to hate and fear,

You've got to be taught from year to year,

It's got to be drummed in your dear little ear,

You've got to be carefully taught.

You've got to be taught to be afraid,

Of people whose eyes are oddly made,

And people whose skin is a diff'rent shade,

You've got to be carefully taught.

You've got to be taught before it's too late,

Before you are six or seven or eight,

To hate all the people your relatives hate,

You've got to be carefully taught!"

There is another meaning that we have been missing in these powerful lyrics. Consider the issue of families of poor people living on government assistance for generations. What would happen if the ideas in this book were implemented, and everyone had the opportunity for a job paying a living wage. How do we handle people who do not want to work? Why do they not want to work? After a brief discussion of the usual excuses, we realized that they were not born that way. They had to be carefully taught. Any solution we implement must include time to change the people's self-image and expectations.

Why do intolerant racists behave that way? It usually occurs at the intersection of poverty and greed. If people work hard but are stuck in poverty, they can be convinced by people seeking to take advantage of them that 'those people' or 'others' are responsible. From there it is a short step to envy or hate them and become angry, misguided racists. Who is convincing them? They are the greedy ones who are profiting from their poverty.

If poverty is the evil condition that causes so many problems, why do we have a war on crime, but not a war on poverty? The frightening but indisputable answer is the usual one – money. If you watch a crime drama TV show, at some point the detectives always fall back on the fundamental principle – Follow the money! There are profits to be made by the few at the top in the war on crime, but a war on poverty benefits the masses who have no power to fight the battles.

History has many examples of the masses being fed up with the elite getting all the wealth. Our democratic process may take longer than previous examples like the French Revolution, but the 1/6 insurrection may be symbolic of the first royal head's falling into the basket of the guillotine.

Bryan Stevenson created two emotionally evocative memorials[75] to remind us of our national problem with racism (see the links below). One of the memorials places the visitor face to face with lynching, the other connects our past to our current issues with mass-incarceration of blacks in America. They are both enormously powerful. Take a few minutes to read the article and watch the video. Then let's return to our recurring theme. If they all were living a prosperous and happy life, would these atrocities have happened? Probably not! They would not have been in fear for their own economic survival, and resentful that those other people were a threat to them. In fact, they would have feared jeopardizing their happy lives with such unlawful and abhorrent behavior.

This country grew to its well-deserved greatness through two centuries of good neighborliness and a sense that everyone should have an opportunity to thrive and be secure and happy. We should all be dismayed at several recent developments. What would some of the industrial leaders from our past think if they could see what has happened to their great companies? The individuals who founded and led these companies made a lot of money – and they deserved it. At the same time, they paid the people who worked for their companies a decent wage and the result was a strong American middle class – with the ability to be good customers for these companies.

Visionary corporate leaders who made lots of money built this model without crushing their workers. Henry Ford recognized that for there to be a large public market for automobiles, the working class needed to earn enough to be able to buy cars. During the incredible growth days of Digital Equipment Corporation (DEC),

---

75. https://www.cnn.com/travel/article/lynching-memorial-montgomery-alabama/

    index.html?sr=fbCNN042618lynching-memorial-montgomery-

    alabama0942AMVODtopVideo

CEO Ken Olsen made the conscious decision to spend the additional money it took to locate facilities in many small towns in New England rather than concentrate them near the corporate headquarters in Maynard, Mass. It was more a social conscience than a corporate financial decision. His stated reasoning was that if at some future point Digital was to fail, he did not want to cause a town or a region to fail.

You do not have to look beyond your local community to find an example of corporate greed and disdain for the public. Several years ago, Amazon Inc. purchased land in Prince William County (PWC) VA for building multiple data centers. That began the problem. In selecting the property, instead of locating in the Industrial Park, Amazon selected a piece of property near the center of the Town of Haymarket and adjacent to the Rural Crescent Area with little of the infrastructure needed for data centers (literally across the street from the Walmart Superstore). A data center voraciously consumes electrical power and fresh water. The Industrial Park already provides these utilities. The property Amazon selected does not. To correct this deficiency, Amazon went to Dominion Power (DP) and asked DP to provide it. (DP had previously worked with PWC economic development to court Amazon – expecting they would locate in the Park.) To deliver on their request, DP would need to run lines from its nearest major substation through, over, under, or around established communities. What ensued was a battle that the people of PWC won (temporarily) – forcing an acceptable routing of the power lines.

The community is fortunate to have a remarkable, charismatic, strong woman, (Elena Schlossberg), who leads the "The Coalition to Protect PWC[76]". (Check out the website for the up-to-date status of the current battles.) She and her core team of volunteers waged an

---

76. http://www.protectpwc.org/

almost four-year long battle against the potentially harmful impact of the project. They have gathered bi-partisan support from local and state politicians in support of their efforts. In addition, they have united the entire community in opposition to the project. DP tried a tactic of divide and conquer by proposing several possible routes that would threaten various communities, expecting the communities to each look out for themselves – thus weakening the overall community resolve. The Coalition did an outstanding job of uniting the threatened communities and battling these DP efforts.

Early proposed routes for the high voltage transmission lines included lines that went:

- Through the Rural Crescent – land with tough and clear zoning restrictions designed to preserve the natural wildlife flora and fauna as well as the agricultural, historical, and equestrian environment.

- Through residential subdivisions – including across golf courses.

- Through a historically black community with roots dating back to before the civil war.

- Through parts of downtown Haymarket.

Amazon could have avoided all this drama and strife if it had located the data centers in the Industrial Park. They chose this fight. To add insult to injury, Amazon and DP want the DP customers to pay for the dedicated line (okay, it's not technically a dedicated line, but what was proven in the evidentiary hearing before the State Corporation Commission Judge was that Amazon was the sole driver for the project.) If any citizen decided to build a new home on the top of a hill several miles from the nearest power line, the citizen would have to pay to have the power line run to the property. For some demented reason, Amazon and DP are insisting that the DP customers should pay for Amazon's personal extension cord. There is a reasonable and less objectionable solution that the Coalition will support that includes a hybrid solution that follows pre-existing rights-of-way and the interstate highway, burying the lines where they would be objectionable as power towers. Amazon is immensely profitable. Asking the DP subscribers to pay for the installation of their power line is just plain greedy. A small, united group of citizens collaborated to beat a corporate giant like Amazon. Democracy can work if dedicated citizens unite to make a difference.

Considering this issue, I wondered about the implications of applying Moore's Law to the situation. Basically, Moore's Law says that computers will continue to get smaller and faster. If you apply that to data centers, (They are essentially large computer installations.) then eventually a data center will fit in a volume the size of a refrigerator. Meanwhile, we will have these enormous unneeded dystopian buildings taking up space.

Leaders like DEC's Ken Olsen would have started with the primary criteria that the building of a new facility should benefit the community and worked with them to achieve it. Today's corporate leaders, with the gargantuan power of an Amazon, start with the assumption that they can run roughshod over the common citizens to maximize their corporate profits and personal wealth. PWC local elected officials have supported the coalition up to this point, but DP has enormous political influence across the state, and our local politicians' peers from other parts of the state who receive financial support from DP could have outvoted them. They stood with the people so far. Kudos to Elena and her dedicated Coalition team for fighting a fight nobody thought they had a chance to win.

Today's examples of greed are just as self-serving as these earlier examples, but on a financial scale that is almost beyond imagination. Executive salaries have skyrocketed from a 40:1 ratio compared to employees to over 400:1. It is difficult to conceptualize how much money some of the Wall Street crowd is making. The Oscar-winning movie <u>Inside Job</u> paints a vivid picture of how selfish, greedy people caused an economic crash that brought the whole world economy to its knees. Millions of people around the world have lost their homes, jobs, and/or their life savings as a result. At the same time, these greedy financial executives paid themselves bonuses for their efforts. Some of the most highly compensated people did not create anything of value to anyone but themselves. Yet they walked away with hundreds of millions of dollars that came from average working people.

It boggles the mind to hear statements from these Wall St. leaders like, "We have to pay executives a 'competitive' salary in order to attract the best people." There are three rational but incredulous reactions to this statement. Ask the Board members of these companies:

1. If you are presently paying $40M in salary and bonuses, are you saying that you cannot find another outstanding person who is willing to work for only $20M?
2. Since you have paid them so much money, we should be able to assume that they are the best and the brightest. If so, why is it that these geniuses allowed the entire financial house of cards to tumble?
3. Why doesn't the attitude of paying more for quality people apply to average workers?

Over time, the corporate leaders have gamed the system and created rules that demand and reward their behavior – at the expense of the employees. Employees used to participate in the success of the company through profit sharing. If the company was profitable, then the company shared those profits with the employees. However, the rules have changed. The executives figured out that they could manipulate the P&L calculations to minimize the profits. If the company revenues are up, then the leadership pays shareholders, board members, and executive's big bonuses. Aw shucks, after they paid all those bonuses, the company is barely profitable – so extraordinarily little is available to share with employees.

When the economy takes a downturn and there is less demand for the products and services, the executives still reap their big rewards, but they lay off the workers. When the market begins to recover, management delays hiring back the workers to keep profit margins high. Meanwhile, the company asks the people still employed to work harder to make up for the shortage of help. Because they do not want to lose their jobs, the employees work harder, but the company does not pay them more. The sad irony is that the greedy executives take credit and get bonuses for the improved productivity of the employees resulting from the employees busting their backs just to keep their jobs.

Whatever happened to the days when corporate leaders who were asked what their company's greatest asset was would respond, "It's our employees." They treasured them, trained them, and rewarded them. In return, employees felt loyalty to the company. Many people in my parent's generation worked for the same company their whole careers, rising through the ranks along the way. Unfortunately, in today's corporate environment, employees are just a commodity in the process of delivering products and services.

Under Ken Olsen's[77] leadership, Digital had a "No layoffs" policy. Actually, Ken called it a tradition, not a policy. In a high-tech company like DEC, the technology and products were continuously changing and evolving. If his company discontinued a product, DEC gave the affected employees priority in hiring into any other part of the company. This included training them for the new position. For example, because Digital had facilities scattered around the New England states, Digital operated its own helicopter air service. Ken saw an opportunity to do something special, so he staffed his air service with former Vietnam helicopter pilots and mechanics. Joe Green, the WBZ Boston Traffic Copter pilot had radio links to the DEC helicopter pilots and was able to provide people all over New England with immediate reports of any major traffic issues, even though those issues were geographically far beyond the usual WBZ traffic copters' flight patterns. A reporter once asked Joe Green what he thought of the DEC pilots. He said that they were the most professional group of pilots he had ever had the pleasure of working with.

When the company decided it could no longer afford to operate its air fleet, rather than lay off the people, Ken Olsen provided counseling and training to transition them to other jobs in the company. Years later, when the corporate fortunes waned, he established the "Engineers to Education" program that encouraged employees with technical skills to transition into K-12 teaching positions – and paid for their education and training. Eventually, DEC was broken up and the pieces sold off. However, the reasons for the company's failure as a business had nothing to do with the fact that Ken treated his employees well. In today's environment, it appears that all the emphasis is on rewarding shareholders and corporate executives, with extraordinarily little regard for the worker-bees. That emphasis has led to our current untenable situation of financial hardship (poverty) and social resentment.

---

77. http://www.nytimes.com/2011/02/08/technology/business-computing/08olsen.html

Now, let's look at what these ultra-rich people do with all their money. Some truly appear to have a social conscience and through foundations, they do good work. The Bill and Melinda Gates Foundation, supported generously by Warren Buffet, is an example of this group. While their good work is laudable, their powerful potential for mitigating the greed in the system by advocating more sanity in determining executive compensation and better treatment for employees is largely untapped.

People with remarkable talent, brilliance, sacrifice, and hard work justifiably earn rich rewards. However, the system of income versus value and effort is broken, so there appears to be a need for some form of control and leveling. It is unconscionable for some people to be making billions of dollars while others in this country are losing their homes and malnourished. The recent debates over the tax breaks for the top 1% of the population make it apparent that the top 1% could give up 10% more of their earnings and still live way beyond comfortable. Meanwhile, children are starving in America. That is just wrong!

There is still another unresolvable piece to this Greed puzzle. There are people who have become extremely wealthy in America who also profess strong religious convictions. They wear their religion on their sleeves like some badge of honor. They spend millions of their dollars campaigning for social issues and promoting their beliefs. Yet these same people continue to acquire all the gaudy trappings of wealth and display them ostentatiously. Can't they see their own hypocrisy? One of the Christian teachings is about the rich man trying to get into Heaven. From Wikipedia[78]:

> *"The saying was a response to a young rich man who had*
> *asked Jesus what he needed to do in order to inherit eternal*

---

78. http://en.wikipedia.org/wiki/Eye_of_a_needle

life. Jesus replied that he should keep the commandments, to which the man stated he had done. Jesus responded, "If you want to be perfect, go, sell your possessions and give to the poor, and you will have treasure in heaven. Then come, follow me." The young man became sad and was unwilling to do this. Jesus then spoke this response, leaving his disciples astonished. ...I tell you the truth, it is hard for a rich man to enter the kingdom of heaven. Again I tell you, it is easier for a camel[79] to go through the eye of a needle than for a rich man to enter the kingdom of God[80]".

Apparently, this parable does not get much play in executive offices and boardrooms in America.

Capitalism is a fundamental element in the greatness of our country. However, unfettered capitalism has demonstrated the potential to foster temptations to greedy behavior. People talk about "the Golden Rule". It is a universal principle across most religions that says, *"Do unto others as you would have them do unto you."* In today's corporate world, they follow a different Golden Rule, *"He who has the gold makes the rules."* The concentration of wealth among a small powerful portion of society is resulting in changes to the rules that favor the wealthy over the rest of society. We must elect representatives with the courage and wisdom to fight for more rational income and wealth equality.

For those who believe that the Golden Rule is a Christian teaching, they're right, but only partly. It is a value that is found in most of the world's religions.

---

79. *http://en.wikipedia.org/wiki/Camel*

80. *http://en.wikipedia.org/wiki/Kingdom_of_God*

Here are Norman Rockwell's notes on the way that the Golden Rule is expressed

in different religions...

THE GOLDEN RULE
IS COMMON TO ALL RELIGIONS

BUDDHISM.   Hurt not others with that which pains yourself. *Udanavarga.*

CHRISTIANITY.   All things whatsoever ye would that men should do to you, do ye even so to them: for this is the law and the prophets. *Bible, St. Matthew.*

CONFUCIANISM.   Is there any one maxim which ought to be acted upon throughout one's whole life? Surely the maxim of lovingkindness is such – Do not unto others what you would not they should do unto you. *Analects.*

HEBRAISM.   What is hurtful to yourself do not to your fellow man. That is the whole of the Torah and the remainder is but commentary. Go learn it. *Talmud.*

HINDUISM.   This is the sum of duty: do naught to others which if done to thee, would cause thee pain. *Mahabharata.*

ISLAM.   No one of you is a believer until he loves for his brother what he loves for himself. *Traditions.*

JAINISM.   In happiness and suffering, in joy and grief, we should regard all creatures as we regard our own self, and should therefore refrain from inflicting upon others such injury as would appear undesirable to us if inflicted upon ourselves. *Yogashastra.*

SIKHISM.   As thou deemest thyself so deem others. Then shalt thou become a partner in heaven. *Kabir.*

TAOISM.   Regard your neighbor's gain as your own gain: and regard your neighbor's loss as your own loss. *T'ai Shang Kan Ying P'ien.*

ZOROASTRIANISM.   That nature only is good when it shall not do unto another whatever is not good for its own self. *Dadistan-i-dinik.*

"We have committed the Golden Rule to memory,
let us now commit it to life."
EDWIN MARKHAM

Excerpts from the research of the artist, Norman Rockwell, including extracts from "The Norman Rockwell" Album published by Doubleday & Co., Garden City, New York, 1961.

The cover, this page, and succeeding pages are reprinted with permission of the Curtis Publishing Company.

The primary and obvious victims of Kids in Cages are the kids themselves. It is safe to say that all of them come from poverty conditions. There are no rich white kids in cages. The kids pose no existential threat to anyone. However, there is another victim, democratic accountability. The kids are valuable pawns in the immigration/incarceration industry profits game, while also dividing the average citizens and voters and distracting them from forcing the elected representatives to focus on ceasing this inhumane program and fixing poverty. In a similar vein, we must also think about those who are sex-trafficked and sold. They too are victims, prisoners, and pawns to those who are inhumane, pedophiles, and offenders. But, while our government creates programs that rescue those who are being trafficked, it also creates concentration camps for children who are not from this land. This inconsistency has its roots in poverty.

Jobs and the Economy

Do you know how hard it is to obtain a job in this modern society? You may have dreamed of going to college in grade school, had your dream career job planned out to a tee, knew what you wanted to study and knew the programs you wanted to be a part of. Then you went off to a prestigious school you hoped for and worked your ass off. You maintained a high-level grade point average (GPA) and made sure you participated in all the school activities. You graduate with your bachelor's degree and obtain all the knowledge you could about your career field. You then apply for jobs in your field. What does the employer say is an expected requirement? **EXPERIENCE!** You need experience to do the work. How did you forget about the experience portion? We've spent so much time trying to learn how to do the job and what to do when we get there, that we never had any work experience to be hired for the position. So unfortunately, you have to settle for another job that you don't want just so you can make ends meet. You were expecting to make $94,000-$150,000 annually in a corporate office, but now you've lowered your standards to $32,000-$48,000 annually in a part-time fast-food job, or a job that's close to your line of work. I am pretty sure we've all been through this, and if not, these are college students' scary new realities.

Nowadays, it is safe to say that Generation Z does not want anything to do with Corporate America jobs. They have no intention for life after high school once they receive their diploma. Their new quality of life is obtaining a quick buck by streaming on social media platforms. For some it works successfully, for others they crave attention so badly, they lose themselves in the process. Social media has taken over the workforce. How were they able to do that? This generation does not want to be involved in the minimum wage level of thriving. As of now, minimum wage is under $18 in every state. That is horrible. States should be ashamed. How can we still use the same wages from the beginning of our economic development and steadily grow? Government services do not alleviate all the dire needs of those who believe it is still enough to supply someone with the new standard of living? Poverty is severe, wanting assistance. Most states will assume that those who ask for assistance are in a better situation than they put on their paperwork and application, but how can you judge someone without actually knowing what's in their pockets? No matter how it seems or looks, you can never know what a person is really dealing with until you've been living in their shoes.

Collecting taxes for government spending to boost the economy does not imply creating more government employees. Most of the money will be paid to private companies who get contracts to do the work. Congress, through a process of debate and discussion, decides what infrastructure and public service work needs to be done and allocates money to pay for the work. RFPs (requests for proposals) are issued, and private companies compete for the contracts. The bids/proposals are evaluated, and the winner gets the contract.

Some people tout Capitalism almost as a religion. It is not. It's an economic and political system. At its most fundamental level, capitalism means private ownership. It also has no heart or conscience. According to the International Monetary fund[81]:

> *"Capitalism is often thought of as an economic system in which private actors own and control property in accord with their interests, and demand and supply freely set prices in markets in a way that can serve the best interests of society."*

---

81. http://www.imf.org/external/pubs/ft/fandd/2015/06/basics.htm

However, some CEOs have convinced themselves that it is their job to charge as much as possible for their products – regardless of the consequences to the consumer. Nirmal Mulye, the chief executive of a small drug company called Nostrum Laboratories, defended his decision[82] to the Financial Times to quadruple the price of a 65-year-old antibiotic. What he's saying:

> *I think it is a moral requirement to make money when"*
> *you can ... to sell the product for the highest price... I agree*
> *with Martin Shkreli that when he raised the price of his*
> *drug he was within his rights because he had to reward his*
> *shareholders... This is a capitalist economy and if you can't*
> *make money you can't stay in business."*

Notice that he charges high prices to reward his shareholders, not his employees. CEOs are typically major shareholders, so this attitude for rewarding shareholders is self-serving. Gradually, greed took over as those with power exercised that power to enhance their own situation at the expense of the lesser empowered employees. Those in power have implemented a long-term strategy that has resulted in their getting most of the income – and now they are fighting to protect that advantage by throwing around terms like socialism and communism. Capitalism can still work, but the present conditions clearly show that without better controls, some people will abuse it.

Poorly regulated banking, investment, and insurance companies caused a major financial crisis in the US in 2008 and more recently in Europe and the US. In Q1 of 2023, Silicon Valley bank failed, followed by a number of others. It should never have happened again. Following the 2008 failures, the US and international banking industries worked with their respective governments to pass

82. https://www.axios.com/nirmal-mulye-nostrum-laboratories-drug-prices-31c32cc2-5c22-4e1a-a560-4ed4792664eb.html

regulations to prevent another failure. The regulations worked, so in typical political misjudgment, the governments gradually rolled back the regulations and PLOP! Banks began failing again.

It is not just banking industry companies that need to be better regulated. Under-regulated industries in the US have created the greatest income disparity, and consequent poverty increases, in decades. In our past the government recognized a problem when some corporations grew to the point that they held a virtual monopoly in their market – allowing them to set prices that were not good for the national economy. Standard Oil and AT&T were examples of the government stepping in when unfettered capitalism was harming the marketplace. The time has come to look at income and wealth distribution in that same light!

America has a serious income disparity problem. Let me provide a personal illustration. A friend of mine has been working in a mailroom for several years without a pay raise. He is locked in. He needs the job, so he cannot threaten to quit. If he did, the employer would simply say, "Go ahead. We can get someone else to do the job for that price." The company would be CORRECT, but it would not be RIGHT, because the executives and shareholders in the company have received pay raises, dividends, and bonuses every year. The company could get someone else to do the executive's job, probably for less, but they don't. They continue to pay the execs generous to outrageous salaries while paying the employees as little as they can get away with. Until we regulate how the system works, there is no incentive for the executives to do anything differently. We need to find a way to require companies to pay a living wage to all their employees.

A Living Wage means more than a living for just the wage earner. All of the small and large businesses that depend on wage earners to be their customers struggle when the average citizen has no discretionary money to spend. The economy enters a death spiral heading for financial collapse.

How do you get the economy back on track? We need to find a means for getting some of the hoarded wealth back in the game and distributing it fairly and efficiently. This is not a new challenge. We have faced it before and fixed it before. We start by using a progressive tax system that continues to encourage people to strive to earn great wealth, while also contributing to the overall growth of the economy. This has two elements.

1. Design and implement a major progressive tax reform that collects the money needed to fund national, state, and local public service jobs and infrastructure projects.
2. Determine, implement, and adjust as needed a Living Wage – not just a surviving wage. A surviving wage does not provide the discretionary money that drives the rest of the economy. A living wage allows families to enjoy life.

The wealthy will still have enough money to have their yachts, palaces, and airplanes, with more money than they could ever spend. Meanwhile, poverty, crime, suffering, financial stress, and deprivation will be reduced and comfort, and joy will be increased for everyone. Everybody wins. Nobody loses – unless the avaricious wealthy consider it a loss if some of their hoarded wealth is used to make the economy work for everyone. Get over it!

Issue #7 - We need to stop measuring the economy by how well rich people are doing.

How many times do we hear the talking heads on the evening news talk about 'The Market' – meaning the stock market? Now, how many times do they mention the Poverty Index and some current score? The answers are typically "Frequently' and 'Never". Poverty has to become as important an issue as the stock market. We need to track it and be more aware of it.

Eliminating poverty is not just about fairness, it's also about sustainability! According to the Pew Research report, "Racial, gender wage gaps persist in the US despite some progress. ", white men out-earn black and Hispanic men and all groups of women. In the United States, income inequality, or the salary gap between the rich and everyone else, has been growing markedly by every major statistical measure for some 30 years. (Take a couple of minutes to watch the video linked below to get a better appreciation of the magnitude and urgency of the problem.) Income disparity is so vast that America's top 10 percent now average more than nine times as much income as the bottom 90 percent. Americans in the top 1 percent are paid stunningly higher. They average over 40 times more income than the bottom 90 percent. However, that gap pales in comparison to the divide between the nation's top 0.1 percent and everyone else. Americans at this lofty level are taking in over 198 times the income of the bottom 90 percent combined. The disparity in numbers is simply impossible to imagine. Watch the video[83].

Poverty is the result of an unfair and unsustainable level of income inequality. According to a Forbes Magazine article in May of 2018:

> *"CEO Pay Skyrockets To 361 Times That of The Average Worker.*

---

83. https://www.youtube.com/watch?v=Gk5OJBry2ss

If you have any doubt about our country's disappearing middle class, check out the current CEO-to-employee pay gap. In the 1950s, a typical CEO made 20 times the salary of his or her average worker. Last year, CEO pay at an S&P 500 Index firm soared to an average of 361 times more than the average rank-and-file worker[84], or pay of $13,940,000 a year."

That is NOT comparing the CEO at the top to the LOWEST paid worker. The comparison is the CEO at the top to the AVERAGE employees' wages. If companies paid their employees a living wage, there would be less poverty and stronger families. Why? Because parents would not have to work multiple jobs to pay their bills, allowing them more time for family and parenting activities.

Issue #8 - Unsustainable income and wealth inequality

Is income inequality a problem? The uber-wealthy earned it, right? To a certain degree that is true. However, they did not earn it all by themselves. If they are ultra-wealthy, that condition is usually the result of the efforts of many people who worked for them producing the products and services they sold to get rich. In the current largely unfettered or under-regulated US capitalistic economic system, the people at the top can determine how much of the revenue goes to the workers and how much goes to the executives and shareholders. If they decide to skew the balance so that most of the revenue goes to the executives and shareholders, they can. However, when that occurs, it affects everybody, not just that company's employees. For example, "Walmart's low-wage workers cost U.S. taxpayers an

84. https://www.forbes.com/sites/dianahembree/2018/05/22/ceo-pay-skyrockets-to-361-times-that-of-the-average-worker/#a5c02393e59c943d6a75a9241140faca340616293776d

estimated $6.2 billion in public assistance including food stamps, Medicaid, and subsidized housing, according to a report[85] published to coincide with Tax Day, April 15". Just a reminder; we (the taxpayers) paid $6.2B to supplement Walmart employees' pay[86] while "Walmart Inc. paid its median worker $19,177 last year, and Chief Executive Doug McMillon earned $22.8 million, ...At Walmart, the CEO Makes 1,188 Times as Much as the Median Worker" That is just one company. It is a national problem.

We cannot fix poverty without addressing income and wealth inequality. If someone tries to call it wealth redistribution or socialism, call it "Bullshit"!

Since 1978, the cost of:

- College tuition increased by 1,120%.

- Medical care increased by 601%.

- Housing Costs increased by 380%.

Meanwhile, the pay of:

- Typical workers rose by just 10%.

- Minimum wage workers fell by 5.5%.

- Average CEOs increased by 37%.

America is in danger of becoming an oligarchy. (Definition: An oligarchy is an organization controlled by just a few businesses or

85. https://www.forbes.com/sites/clareoconnor/2014/04/15/report-walmart-workers-cost-taxpayers-6-2-billion-in-public-assistance/#a5c02393e59c943d6a75a9241140faca31a361263720b

86. https://www.wsj.com/articles/at-walmart-the-ceo-makes-1-188-times-as-much-as-the-median-worker-1524261608

individuals. They have enough power to turn the organization to benefit them to the exclusion of other members. They maintain their power through their relationships with each other.) During the past few election cycles, Conservatives have accused the Liberals of wanting to engage in income redistribution – as though it is a bad thing; and perhaps it is. Over the past couple of decades, the very wealthy have used their money and power to redistribute income from the middle class to the very wealthy. In 1970, the average CEO earned $25 for every dollar the average worker in the company made. By 2000, that ratio was $90 to $1[87]. In 2017, it is $271 to $1. Looking at the issue from the other end, the bottom 80% of the population owns only 7% of the financial wealth. In 2005, the combined wealth of the 400 wealthiest people was greater than the combined wealth of the other 155,000,000 US Citizens.

In politico-speak, the Republicans consistently refer to these wealthy people as job creators. It is just not true. The wealthy invest their money in financial instruments to make more wealth, not create more jobs. Nick Hanauer in his TED Talk titled "Rich people don't create jobs[88]" does an excellent job of making this point. In Hanauer's explanation, consumers create jobs by buying products and services. Instead of trickle down, it is trickle up. If the middle-class workers earn a reasonable wage, they spend their money buying stuff. The more stuff they buy, the greater the demand for the stuff. Greater demand leads to companies needing to produce more stuff. To produce more stuff, the company needs to hire more people. Voila! Jobs created! The people with jobs pay taxes, enabling the government to fund more projects and the cycle continues to grow the economy. If the employer only pays a meager wage, the workers can only afford the essentials necessary for survival. Paying a living

---

87. http://fortune.com/2017/07/20/ceo-pay-ratio-2016/

88. http://www.youtube.com/watch?v=CKCvf8E7V1g

wage provides some money for discretionary spending – buying stuff.

Trickle-down economics is a cruel myth. During the 2017 federal budget discussions, Republicans were pushing for major corporate tax breaks saying that CEOs will use the money to reinvest in the company and create more jobs. However, at the Wall Street Journal's CEO Council meeting, Gary Kohn, Trump's top economic advisor, was surprised when the moderator asked the room full of CEOs how many of them would reinvest that proposed tax break, only a few of them raised their hands. Most said they would return it to their shareholders or use it to buy back stock. This sentiment is consistent with responses that economic reporters have been getting for months.

> *"A new Congressional Research Service report finds that the 2017 Tax Cuts and Jobs Act had little measurable effect on the overall US economy in 2018. And, no, the tax cuts didn't come remotely close to paying for themselves by turbocharging the economy as President Trump repeatedly promised. This was a surprise to few, since most independent analysts predicted more than a year ago that the law would have little economic impact[89]."*

It is time to consider a different model of income redistribution. We need to make the wealthiest citizens the job creators they pretend to be. In this model, the wealthiest citizens would pay a much heavier tax (call it the "Infrastructure and Public Service Tax"). It would be a progressive tax (The more you make, the more you pay.) and individuals making less than $400,000 (or some other reasonable number) a year would be exempt. The government would spend

---

89. *https://www.taxpolicycenter.org/taxvox/new-congressional-study-finds-little-economic-benefit-2017-tax-cuts*

the revenue generated from these taxes on rebuilding America's crumbling and outdated infrastructure and paying for public services. We would not be giving money away to people just because they need it. We would be building things (power and water distribution grids, highways and bridges, and maintenance projects, water and sewer systems, renewable energy facilities, schools, etc.) and providing essential services (teachers, firemen, policemen, healthcare, national research labs, etc.). We need these things to maintain and improve our way of life. All of them create real productive essential jobs, reducing the unemployment rate and lessening the strain on social safety-net programs. The vast majority of the jobs would not be government jobs. Private contractors would rebuild the infrastructure, paid for by tax dollars, and pay a living wage.

The Multiplier Effect

There is an added benefit to these spending programs. Applying what economists describe as the multiplier effect, every job directly created by a government contract results in the creation of 2 – 5 additional local jobs. The benefits of this approach include:

- More people have the personal satisfaction of earning a living.

- Fewer people are relying on social safety net programs – reducing the tax burden associated with funding them.

- Because these people are now earning a living, they will be paying taxes – helping fund additional needed infrastructure projects and creating additional jobs.

- More people working means more people consuming goods and services, so all companies benefit.

- This model keeps the country's financial wealth working to the benefit of all its citizens, not just the wealthiest.

Please do not try to convince us that the wealthiest people 'earned' that money. Certainly, they deservedly earned a lot of money; but then they got greedy. They were not satisfied with a lot. They wanted more. In the words of ESPN's Chris Berman and the rest of the Monday Night Football crew, "C'mon, man!" The disparity they have created between executive and worker compensation is irrational, inexcusable, – and unsustainable. For a brief, thoughtful discussion of the cause and effect of income inequality, read, "OF THE 1%, BY THE 1%, FOR THE 1%[90]" by Joseph Stiglitz.

New rules for the game

There are three elements to the needed new rules for the game.

1. There needs to be some system for achieving a more equitable ratio between executive and worker pay.
2. We need to tax the wealthiest among us more heavily to create real jobs and improve the nation's infrastructure and public services.
3. We must pay workers a living wage.

Why it won't happen – Money and Power:

The existing governmental partisan gridlock cannot even do the easy things, so doing something as important but difficult as rewriting the rules and leveling the economic playing field does not stand a chance. The power of money creates a gridlock and makes implementing any changes problematic. The people with large amounts of money have an extraordinarily strong hold on the politicians.

---

90. https://www.wnyc.org/story/121224-stiglitz-american-inequality/

Why it could happen – People:

Countless ideological issues arise in every election cycle that divide the electorate and allow the moneyed players to control the outcomes. If enough Senate and House candidates would push the ideological issues to the side and focus on this single issue like a laser, they might win. The public is looking for a change and this concept could be it. The uber-wealthy only represent 1% of the population. That leaves us – the other 99%. Ninety-nine percent is an incredibly significant number. If candidates would commit to a program of economic fairness and jobs as the single most important issue – regardless of party affiliation – they could draw support from all voters, not just their own party.

Why it might happen – Moderate Populists:

The moderates have a toehold in Congress in the form of a few visionary moderate populists (a member of a political party seeking to represent the interests of ordinary people) – from both parties. They get it! If we can convince the average citizens to be independent thinkers, gullibility for the false rhetoric that has put us in the present situation will not be an issue. Then they will elect populist representatives regardless of the large sums of money spent to convince them to vote otherwise.

Why it must happen – True Prosperity:

Fixing the economy and achieving true prosperity for most of our citizens is the single most important issue facing the country. If a parent cannot afford to provide a home or food for the family, then national security is just that – providing for the family. That is their idea of security. Yes, we have national security interests around the world, but the biggest security interest is right here at home. If we fix the economy and achieve low unemployment rates and living wages, that will take care of most of the other socio-economic issues. In that environment, we can have a more rational and informed debate over the other issues. Historically, when the economy has been in good shape, the government made good decisions on other issues.

One of the major factors contributing to the 2008 financial crash was the number of bad mortgages – mortgages where the amount owed exceeded the value of the property used as collateral. It was not just the mortgages themselves. Some Wall Street geniuses bundled up packages of bad mortgages and resold them to other institutions. When this financial house of cards came tumbling down, we – the taxpayers – stepped in and bailed out the banks. We paid off the bad debts to keep the banks solvent. However, many of the poor homeowners whose mortgages were suddenly upside down (The mortgage debt was more than the value of the house.) lost their homes and more. We bailed out the bankers, but not the borrowers. Why didn't we (the federal government) take the money we gave to the banks, and force the banks to write down the mortgages to bring them above water and immune from foreclosure? Same amount of money going to the same banks but passing through a process to relieve the pressure on the homeowners! Could it have anything to do with the fact that the lobbyists for the banks have much more power than the poor homeowners do?

The Economic Policy Institute report titled, "Income Inequality in the United States", dubbed the U.S. the "Unequal States of America" due to the size of the wealth gap. America's wealth inequality is even more gaping than its income inequality. (Income is the amount earned each year. Wealth is the accumulated assets over many years.) According to The New York Times, the richest one percent in the United States now own more wealth than the bottom 90 percent. According to Common Dreams and the Institute for Policy Studies, the three wealthiest Americans have more wealth than the bottom

50% of the country combined. Every year, the current income inequality rate compounds the wealth distribution inequality, making it exponentially worse.

A reasonable level of inequality will exist as long as we have an innovation system that rewards excellence and entrepreneurship. There are a couple of problems with that statement, and the way our present system works. We have gone far beyond the reasonable level of inequality, and the people reaping the greatest rewards are not necessarily the innovators and entrepreneurs.

At today's levels, the concentration of wealth is inhibiting the overall economy. The disproportionate concentration limits the overall amount of growth, and at the same time means that growth fails to benefit most of the people. Consolidation of so much wealth and capital in so few hands is inefficient because it depresses demand, a point made famous by Henry Ford[91] and more recently billionaire Nick Hanauer in his much-discussed TED talk[92] and magazine articles[93]. As Hanauer puts it, *"There quite simply is a limit to how many luxury yachts a person could want or own."* Even billionaire Education Secretary Betsy DeVos only has ten.

The economists cannot agree about the possible harm the concentration of wealth may cause – or not. I am not advocating eliminating all the concentration of wealth, but we can take some of the 1% wealth to eliminate poverty. We must. If Congress created regulations to distribute wealth across the population then it would

---

91. https://www.npr.org/2014/01/27/267145552/the-middle-class-took-off-100-years-ago-

    thanks-to-henry-ford

92. https://www.ted.com/talks/

    nick_hanauer_beware_fellow_plutocrats_the_pitchforks_are_coming

93. https://www.politico.com/magazine/story/2014/06/the-pitchforks-are-coming-for-us-

    plutocrats-108014

give more people more spending power, which in turn would drive up growth and drive down inequality. The top 100 billionaires added $240 billion to their wealth in 2012 – enough to end world poverty four times over[94].

> *"According to the latest release on the distribution of wealth in the US from the Federal Reserve, as of the second quarter of 2021, the top 1% of Americans by income had an aggregate net worth of $36.2 trillion, edging out the aggregate net worth of the middle 60% of $35.7 trillion. That's the first time the total wealth of the top 1% has been higher than the middle 60% since the Federal Reserve began tracking this data[95] in 1989."*

Growth in more equal countries is much more effective at reducing poverty. Oxfam research shows that because wealth is so unequal in South Africa, even with sustained economic growth, a million more people will be pushed into poverty unless action is taken.

Poor people are envious of wealthy people, but that is not the issue. If the government could magically transform poor people into comfortable, prosperous middle-class citizens, they would not care how much money the wealthy have. However, when they are working hard at two or three low-paying jobs and still just scraping by, it is hard not to be resentful of that lady with all the yachts.

Paul Graham is a wealthy and successful entrepreneur, a programmer, writer, and investor. In 1995, he and Robert Morris started Viaweb, the first software as a service company. On his blog site[96], he says:

---

94. http://www.preda.org/world/top-100-billionaires-could-end-world-poverty-four-times-over/

95. *https://www.businessinsider.com/top-1-have-more-money-than-the-middle-class-2021-10*

"Since economic inequality per se is not bad, we should not attack it. Instead, we should attack the bad things that cause it. For example, instead of attacking economic inequality, we should attack poverty."

I disagree with his statement on three counts. First, I do not agree that economic inequality is not bad. Second, asking the uber-wealthy to pay for programs to reduce poverty is not an attack. Third, poverty is not the cause of income inequality; it's the effect. It is a logical outcome of a thorough analysis of needs and means. Society has a serious need to alleviate poverty. The hoarded wealth of the uber-wealthy can provide the means to address the need.

It is not just the have-nots who think wealth inequality is a problem for the country. Many billionaires also feel that way. Fortune Magazine[97] quoted seven of them. Here is a sample.

Paul Tudor Jones II – Estimated net worth: $4.7 billion[98] – Occupation: Tudor Investment Corporation Founder, Co-Chairman, and Chief Investment Officer. What he said:

"This chart is corporate profit margins going back 40 years as a percentage of revenues, and you can see that we're at a 40-year high of 12.5 percent. Now, hooray if you're a shareholder, but if you're the other side of that, and you're the average American worker, then you can see it's not such a good thing," Jones said in a TED talk. "Now, higher profit margins do not increase societal wealth. What they actually do is they exacerbate income inequality, and that is not a good thing. However, intuitively, that makes sense, right?

---

96. http://paulgraham.com/slm.html

97. http://fortune.com/2015/11/28/billionaires-income-inequality/

98. http://www.forbes.com/profile/paul-tudor-jones-ii/

> *Because if the top 10 percent of American families own 90 percent of the stocks, as they take a greater share of corporate profits, then there's less wealth left for the rest of society[99]."*

They are concerned on economic and ethical grounds.

Let's examine the commonly stated argument that the rich deserve their wealth because they earned it. In the vast majority if not all the cases, the uber-wealthy earned and deserve a lot of money. The question for me is, "Did they earn all of the money they have, or did they take a disproportionate share of the profits that were earned by many people?" I do not know if it is greed, or ego, or what motivates them to amass such obscene amounts of money while paying the people who helped them earn the money as little as they can get away with. How does a person with billions of dollars justify the situation where less than 100 miles from wherever they are there is a person suffering from many of the painful effects of poverty, without taking deliberate and sustained actions to fix the problem? If the uber-wealthy either will not or cannot figure out how to use their largess for the benefit of society as a whole, then it is time for the government (whose responsibility is to provide security for all citizens) to assist the richest among us in making an impact with their money.

There is a need for government spending. It is the economic engine that drives the rest of the economy. I am not talking about the government competing with, managing, or owning companies. I am talking about the government contracting with companies for goods and services. When the government spends money, it does not just benefit the person or company they initially paid for delivering something. That person spends the money so another person

---

99. *https://www.ted.com/talks/paul_tudor_jones_ii_why_we_need_to_rethink_capitalism/*

   transcript?language=en#t-145410

benefits. If a portion of that wealth were taken from the rich in the form of taxes and spent on infrastructure and public service jobs, then the people who earned money from those programs would have money to spend, initially on essential expenses, and eventually on discretionary non-essential things like vacations, recreation, entertainment, home improvements, and hobbies. In addition to being happier, the people would feel less stress and anger, and perhaps less inclined to commit crimes. Economists call this phenomenon 'the multiplier effect'. The multiplier effect leverages every federal dollar spent. In today's economy, the uber-wealthy hoard wealth or play financial games with their money that do not produce anything but more money for the owner.

The following describes the multiplier effect of infrastructure-spending programs, but it applies to all government spending.

Example of How the Multiplier Effect Works[100]

- If the government spent an extra $2 billion on infrastructure, this investment would cause salaries/wages to increase by $2 billion; therefore, national income will increase by $2 billion.

- With this extra income, workers will spend at least part of it in other areas of the economy.

- For example, if they spent 75% of the extra income (statistically, middle, and low-income earners spend close to 75% of their pay) there would be another $1.5 billion injected into the economy. (E.g., shopkeepers would earn money from increased sales.)

---

100. http://www.businessinsider.com/infrastructure-economic-multiplier-2012-11

- This extra spending would cause an increase in manufacturing to meet the demand created by the spending; therefore, firms would employ more workers and pay higher salaries.

- These workers will also increase their spending. This spending will lead to another injection into the economy, causing higher real GDP.

- In other words, if we increase spending on infrastructure, it is not just infrastructure workers who benefit from higher incomes. Related industries and service industries also benefit.

America is facing a form of tyranny by the rich. Thomas Jefferson feared this possibility and even forecast it in 1779.

> *". . . experience has shown that even under the best forms (of government), those entrusted with power have, in time, and by slow operations, perverted it into tyranny."*

Unless you are one of the top 1%, you probably agree that wealth inequity is a problem. Class warfare is not just something the poor may decide to wage on the rich. It is something that has been going on for decades and the poor have already lost the war. Our government spends all its time arguing about political differences concerning peripheral issues instead of putting a laser focus on the single most important issues – eliminating poverty, rebuilding America's middle class, and restoring the American Dream. In addition to infrastructure jobs, the country needs to reinvest in its public-service jobs like education, police, firefighters, universal healthcare, etc. All of these are real jobs that improve the quality of life for everybody. The people in those jobs will spend their discretionary income on entertainment, recreation, and other mom-and-pop enterprises.

Congress has been grossly ineffective at doing anything because the people with money control Congress. The super-rich wrote the bills and regulations through lobbyists and think tanks and paid the elected representatives to pass them. Now that the rules favor the fat cats and allow them to amass huge wealth, it is in their interest for Congress to do nothing – so it does. The system is broken. There are many well-meaning people in Congress, but the structure and policies they must follow allow the minority to prevent the majority from doing anything. I do not believe it is the fault of either just the Republicans or the Democrats. Both sides have some legitimate concerns and ideas. The problem is that the rich and powerful control enough votes to prevent anything from happening. Who wins when Congress does nothing? Those who created and like the rules just the way they are!

The conservative response to calls to tax the uber-wealthy more heavily has recently been some version of, "In America, we don't punish success." That is true. If someone does something well, they should be rewarded, not punished (assuming what they did was a good thing). But wait a minute! Since when is a multimillion-dollar salary or profit punishment? The income inequity problem arises when the person being rewarded has control over how the rewards are distributed. In far too many cases, the workers whose efforts contributed significantly to the boss's success, get a ridiculously small share of the benefits from their efforts. If 'punish' is the right word, we are not talking about punishing success; we are talking about punishing excess. These uber-wealthy have unilaterally changed the rules on compensation to allow themselves a grossly disproportionate share of the profits created by their companies. Then they compound this inequity by creating loopholes in the tax code to enable them to reduce the amount they contribute for the common good.

So, Yes! Punish excess! Put in place better controls over executive salaries to ensure the workers can make a living wage and America can rebuild its vibrant middle class. Make the uber-wealthy pay more in taxes to fund infrastructure jobs and social programs. Even after implementing this type of program, the uber-wealthy will still have unimaginable amounts of money. I really do not understand why some people think this type of program would be a punishment for anyone.

"We all do better when we all do better."

Paul Wellstone – MN Senator

The question for corporate executives should not be 'Can we get people to work for less?' The question is 'Should we?' The current economic system allows (actually encourages) management to pay their workers as little as they can to get the work done. At the same time, the management team pays obscene salaries to the executives. According to CNBC, the top five most highly paid CEOs in the US and their annual salaries (not accumulated wealth – annual salaries) as of 2017 were[101]:

- Marc Lore, Walmart U.S. E-commerce - $236,896,191 (Just to put that in perspective, that is about **$450 per minute – or $27,000 per hour**, 24 hours per day, 365 days a

---

101. https://www.cnbc.com/2017/05/11/highest-paid-ceos-in-america.html

year. Meanwhile, Walmart's **average** salary (not minimum) for a full-time retail employee is **$13.60 per hour** – only paying for time on the clock.) Lore makes $27,000 per hour (24 hours a day). The employee makes $28,288 per year (Total).

- Tim Cook, Apple - $150,036,907

- Sundar Pichai, Google - $106,502,419

- Elon Musk, Tesla - $99,744,920

- Ginni Rometty, IBM - $96,764,750

Those numbers are their salaries – not including bonuses.

Updated for 2020:

Highest Paid CEOs and Executives in 2020[102]

---

102. https://www.bloomberg.com/graphics/2021-highest-paid-ceos/

Rank	Name	Breakdown
1	**Elon Musk** CEO	$6.7B
2	Mike Pykosz CEO	$359.7M
3	Trevor Bezdek Co-CEO	$496.8M
4	Douglas Hirsch Co-CEO	$496.8

In America's booming economy, companies are making good profits, the company owners are making huge salaries, and shareholders are seeing their share values rising. Meanwhile, the hard-working employees' wage increases are barely keeping up with inflation – if they are at all. Despite their conscientious hard work, the employees' wages are stagnating while the cost of living is rising. Income inequality is a major cause of poverty in America. If that is not enough reason to pay a living wage, then consider the evidence that paying a living wage is good for business and the country. Countless articles that make this point. Some of the benefits include:

- Employees are happier, more productive, and loyal to the company.

• Employees remain with the company longer, becoming more productive.

• Employees are less likely to shirk if they value their job more.

• Better pay results in better job applicants. (Higher IQ, better personalities, more productive, and more highly motivated.)

• Reduced customer churn – more customer loyalty.

• Higher revenue per customer.

• Greater profit margins.

• Reduced need for social safety-net programs.

• Greater buying power for each employee creates additional jobs for others.

• Reduced turnover saves training costs (estimated at $4,000 per employee in many industries).

• Fewer disciplinary problems.

• Reduced supervisory costs.

• People with a sense of financial stability show less signs of stress and act less compulsively or improperly.

• Reduced stress leads to healthier (and therefore more productive) employees.

• Fewer conflicts between employer and employees.

- Better reputation with customers (e.g., Costco vs Walmart)

These effects interact so that the whole is greater than the sum of its parts. We have heard the contrary idea many times: "Industries must pay workers a minimum wage to keep their prices low and profits high." The argument goes that if companies are required to pay employees more, there will be fewer jobs available, or prices will have to go up. That is simply not true.

A *2016 National Employment Law Project study*[103] looked at job growth trends every time the federal minimum wage increased (since it was first established in 1938). It found no correlation between federal minimum wage increases and lower employment levels. Instead, the data suggests that employment actually increased about 68% of the time in the year after a minimum wage increase. This improvement is because when companies increase wages, workers spend their additional earnings, increasing demand. This demand increases business, creating jobs and innovation[104].

Companies that treat and pay their employees well consider their workforce not as a cost to be minimized but as a strategic asset to be valued and managed. With this attitude, they invest in their employees and are usually rewarded with improved productivity and profitability. However, one of the barriers to companies making investments in their employees is the time delay between making the investment and seeing the return (the results from that investment hitting the bottom line). Business leaders must emphasize sustainability over profit maximization within everything they

---

103. *http://www.nelp.org/content/uploads/NELP-Data-Brief-Raise-Wages-Kill-Jobs-No-Correlation.pdf*

104. http://www.upworthy.com/5-successful-corporations-show-what-can-happen-when-employees-are-paid-a-living-wage

create. They must balance the need for profit with the need to create a business that can survive in the long term. Paying a living wage is a critical part of that sustainability strategy.

One common concern regarding raising the minimum wage to a living wage is that it will drive up costs to the consumer. It's true, but it's negligible. "... estimates suggest that a minimum wage of $15 per hour would only lead to a 4 percent hike in prices[105], raising the cost of a cup of coffee at Dunkin' Donuts from around $2 to $2.08. The effects on prices and profits would be minimal because increased costs can be offset by increased productivity due to greater effort, lower turnover (which can save employers $4,700 per employee[106]), and higher sales."

The living wage is more than just what happens at the bottom of the scale. It also applies to the middle-income earners. From the early 1900s up into the 1970s, increases in productivity resulted in increases in workers' pay.

But that doesn't happen anymore. Real wages have declined for most Americans, despite huge gains in productivity over the last several decades. Look at this chart based on research from the Economic Policy Institute, which shows this problem clearly.

Productivity Growth vs. Income Growth

105. http://www.peri.umass.edu/fileadmin/pdf/research_brief/PERI_fast_food_wages.pdf

106. http://www.peri.umass.edu/fileadmin/pdf/working_papers/working_papers_351-400/
   WP373.pdf

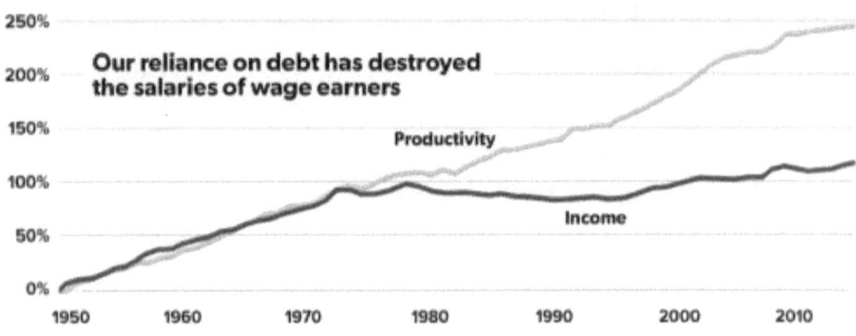

What is going on here?

It's not that computers are destroying our jobs, or that we have moved jobs overseas.

Back in Henry Ford's days and decades after, productivity—a measure of how efficient we are at producing goods and services—and income gains moved hand in hand."

Then, something happened. As the Economic Policy Institute States:

> *"From 1973 to 2016, net productivity rose 73.7 percent, while the hourly pay essentially stagnated—increasing only 12.5 percent over 43 years... This means although Americans are working more productively than ever, the fruits of their labors have primarily accrued to those at the top and to corporate profits, especially in recent years[107]."*

These major increases in productivity created enormous increases in wealth, but due to income inequality, that wealth was not evenly distributed. Meanwhile, the cost of most consumer goods has risen significantly. When compared in terms of spending power, the average worker has lost ground, while the owners, executives, and

---

107. *https://www.epi.org/productivity-pay-gap/*

shareholders have become very wealthy. Tell your elected representatives to make the minimum wage a living wage.

What happened when Seattle raised the minimum wage to $15 per hour? A new report from the University of CA at Berkeley says it had a positive impact across a range of criteria.

A couple of excerpts tell the tale.

- The study found that since the new law went into effect, wages have increased, unemployment has decreased and the total number of hours worked is up, meaning employers are not cutting hours to account for the higher minimum wage.

- The study found that instead of the new minimum wage making it harder for businesses to find low-skill employees; it's causing surrounding communities to raise their wages to compete with the new opportunities for workers in Seattle. It turns out companies struggle when they are not paying their workers enough, not the other way around.

- In Seattle, as the minimum wage has increased, more people are working, they're working more, and they're being paid more, all of which is great for the overall health of the economy.

- All the dire warnings from conservatives about businesses closing and widespread unemployment simply did not come to fruition.

- The broader takeaway here is that Seattle's $15-per-hour experiment is working. It is already showing tangible benefits that suggest raising the minimum wage a reasonable amount relative to the cost of living has broad economic benefits and generally improves people's lives.

Two of the biggest factors in the decline of manufacturing jobs are technology and automation. Any repetitive task can be automated, and the automated processes make fewer errors and can work faster and longer than the humans that they replace. This applies not just to manufacturing jobs. Grocery stores replace cashiers with self-checkout kiosks. ATMs replace bank tellers. Voice recognition takes your order at the drive-thru. You can probably list several additional examples. As this trend continues, it has a direct impact on people being able to earn a living. Robert Reich presents[108] an interesting futuristic look at what might happen. The solution is called Universal Basic Income.

"Why we will Need a Universal Basic Income

Imagine a little gadget called an i-Everything. You can't get it yet, but if technology keeps moving as fast as it is now, the i-Everything will be with us before you know it.

A combination of intelligent computing, 3-D manufacturing, big data crunching, and advanced bio-technology, this little machine will be able to do everything you want and give you everything you need.

There is only one hitch. As the economy is now organized, no one will be able to buy it, because there will not be any paying jobs left. You see, the i-Everything will do ... everything.

---

108. http://robertreich.org/post/151111696805

We're heading toward the i-Everything far quicker than most people realize. Even now, we're producing more and more with fewer and fewer people.

Internet sales are on the way to replacing millions of retail workers. Diagnostic apps will be replacing hundreds of thousands of health-care workers. Self-driving cars and trucks will replace 5 million drivers.

Researchers estimate that almost half of all U.S. jobs are at risk of being automated in the next two decades.

This is not necessarily bad. The economy we are heading toward could offer millions of people more free time to do what they want to do instead of what they have to do to earn a living.

But to make this work, we'll have to figure out some way to recirculate the money from the handful of people who design and own i-Everythings, to the rest of us who will want to buy i-Everythings.

One answer: A universal basic income – possibly financed out of the profits going to such labor replacing innovations, or perhaps even a revenue stream off of the underlying intellectual property."

Reich raises some interesting issues. The frightening thing is that the underlying question is not if it will happen, but when.

"The genie is out of the bottle," he said. "We need to move forward on artificial intelligence (AI) development, but we also need to be mindful of its very real dangers. I fear that AI may replace humans altogether."

Elon Musk and Bill Gates have also weighed in on this issue and expressed similar sentiments.

> *"Musk is a supporter of a universal basic income, claiming that it will be "necessary" as automation increases. Gates has advocated for a tax on robots that take jobs. "Right now, the human worker who does, say, $50,000 worth of work in a factory, that income is taxed, and you get income tax, social security tax, all those things," he said in an interview with Quartz[109]. "If a robot comes in to do the same thing, you'd think that we'd tax the robot at a similar level.""*

> *"These Towns Are Trying Out A Basic-Income Scheme and It's Already Changing Lives[110]*

> *Ontario's basic income program, launched in April 2017, is currently operating in three towns — Thunder Bay, Lindsay, and Hamilton. The scheme has enrolled more than 4,000 low-income people living on less than CA$34,000 (US$29,500) individually, or CA$48,000 as a couple. This includes those who are working, in school, or living on financial assistance.*

> *For three years, single participants will receive up to CA$17,000 a year and couples will receive up to CA$24,000. Those earning any money will see their basic income amounts reduced by 50 cents for every dollar they make. Participants with disabilities are eligible for another CA$6,000 annually — although they do need to wave*

---

109. https://www.fastcompany.com/4030576/elon-musk-says-automation-will-make-a-universal-basic-income-necessary-soon

110. https://www.huffingtonpost.com/entry/ontario-basic-income_us_5aeac0e0e4b06748dc8fb7a5

goodbye to state disability support, which can work out to more money.

A third-party research team will evaluate the effects on people's physical and mental health, food security, stress and anxiety, housing stability, education, and employment. Their responses will be compared against a control group — low-income participants who won't receive the basic income but will fill out surveys about their life and well-being.

Universal basic income, or the idea of giving people money without any conditions, is not new. However, it is gaining fresh momentum globally as inequality worsens[111] and swaths of jobs are at risk from automation and other factors. Ontario joins a handful of other places in the world to test out some sort of guaranteed basic income, including the Dutch city of Utrecht[112], a village in Kenya[113], the city of Stockton, California[114], and Finland, although Finland doesn't currently have plans[115] to extend its pilot program past its scheduled end in December. This experiment is worth keeping an eye on as a possible strategy in the war on poverty."

Raising wages does not kill jobs!

111. https://www.theguardian.com/business/2018/apr/07/global-inequality-tipping-point-2030

112. https://www.huffingtonpost.ca/2015/07/10/utrecht-basic-income_n_7770648.html

113. http://www.businessinsider.com/kenya-village-disproving-biggest-myth-about-basic-income-2017-12

114. https://www.npr.org/2018/01/29/581674763/in-california-stockton-experiments-with-guaranteed-basic-income

115. http://www.wired.co.uk/article/finland-universal-basic-income-results-trial-cancelled

Zero empirical evidence!

It's not a law of economics. It's a con job!

Trickle-down economics does not work. Money doesn't trickle either up or down. Money is earned. The 'trickle' factor comes into play when it comes time to divide the results from the earnings. Looking at the ratio of workers' earnings to executives' earnings leads to the conclusion that money trickles down but gushes up. Elsewhere in this book, Nick Hanauer provides a more comprehensive explanation of the unjustified promotion of the trickle-down concept. If the goal is to eliminate poverty by raising the amount of money in the hands of the lowest paid workers, then pay them more directly. Do not pay more to the people who already have a lot of money and hope they find a way to pass it along to those less fortunate. We have already tried that. It is how we got to our present deplorable and untenable condition.

For our democracy to thrive, the economy must thrive. We must manage the income and wealth system to eliminate poverty.

Fixing the infrastructure will concurrently reduce poverty and fix the economy. We need to upgrade and add to our existing roads and bridges, improve our public water supply, treatment, and distribution system, improve the power and communications grids, and improve public transportation. All these programs will create thousands of long-lasting, well-paying jobs – not to mention make America a better place to live and keep up with the rest of the industrialized world. Most of the money spent on infrastructure cannot be outsourced to a foreign cheap-labor country, so it means jobs for Americans.

America's infrastructure is failing[116]. According to a Fortune.com, article titled, "Here's How Bad U.S. Infrastructure Has Become":

● More than two out of every five miles of America's urban interstates are congested, and traffic delays cost the country $160 billion in wasted time and fuel in 2014.

● One out of every five miles of highway pavement is in poor condition and our roads have a significant and increasing backlog of rehabilitation needs.

● After years of decline, traffic fatalities increased by 7% from 2014 to 2015, with 35,092 people dying on America's roads.

● Similar issues exist for America's bridges, water and sewer mains, water treatment plants, municipal buildings, schools, state and federal parks and recreation areas, and more.

Government spending on infrastructure can be a vital infusion into the economy with the multiplier effect playing a role in leveraging the investment. To pay for a grand and comprehensive infrastructure program, the local, state, and federal governments need to collect more revenue. That money must come from the citizens and businesses through taxation. There are a couple of ways to accomplish that. We could decide to tax the wealthy more heavily to pay for it, or we could find a way to fix the income inequality issue, or we can do both. If we pay the average workers more, then they will pay more taxes. The combined way is appealing because it feels more like everybody is pitching in to improve the country.

---

116. *http://fortune.com/2017/03/30/infrastructure-spending-funding/*

America cannot afford to pretend it is the only economy in the world. We are at the center of the global economy and have to compete with other countries. The global economy is a complex collection of difficult issues, but at their heart, most Americans are in the center regarding what we want.

- Most Americans want a good job that pays a living wage, with reasonable opportunities for promotion and growth based upon effort and ability.

- We want our children to have a better life than we do.

- We do not mind if some people make a lot more money than we do as a reward for their efforts and excellence.

- We do resent it if they make an obscene amount more than the rest of us just because they have the power to write the rules that enable them to do it.

- We recognize that we live and trade in a global society where other countries have different rules and standards than we do.

- We want rules that protect our jobs and companies while at the same time promoting global trade.

Unscrupulous politicians and others use gaslighting to confuse and mislead the public about what is in their best interest. Because of the distorted fringe packaging of the information we get from the politicians, we are not sure how to get what we want. Extremists use terms like "Free Trade", "Fair Trade", and "Open Borders" to divide us, not inform us. We are smart enough to know that total isolationism is neither desired nor an option. In general, the American people are in the political center regarding what we want, while being fed extreme positions as a part of partisan posturing from elected (or trying to be elected) politicians.

Who represents America's working class? Who fights for better pay and fringe benefits? It used to be the labor unions. In America's current economy, unions have lost their role. Owners and management make all the decisions regarding the sharing of the revenue generated by the company. One of the results of this disparity of power is the disproportionate distribution of company revenue. Workers' wages have declined or stayed the same while executive salaries and shareholder values have skyrocketed. The clearly visible evidence of the consequences from this situation is the shrinking of the middle class, increasing wealth and income inequality, and the growing poverty problem. Under current conditions, non-union employees have no means of fighting for better wages and working conditions. Management has all the power and makes all the rules. Corporations have successfully lobbied for rules and regulations that have made it difficult for workers to organize into unions.

When and where unions have thrived, they have had a positive impact on wages and working conditions for both union and non-union workers. The unions tend to mitigate the power of management and result in a more equitable distribution of the company's revenue. Unions tend to be the only entity working in support of the lower income workers. They affect more than just wages. Where there are unions, workers have better working conditions and fringe benefits such as paid vacations and holidays, sick days, health care plans, and retirement plans with company matching.

Most people living in poverty in America have jobs. They are called 'the working poor', people who have jobs but do not earn a living wage. As the economy has moved away from manufacturing to retail and service jobs, unions have lost membership. Lacking unions to fight for them, many workers' wages have stagnated or decreased.

Progressive and conservative think tanks continue to produce conflicting reports regarding the benefits or harm associated with labor unions. Just by observing the empirical evidence, it is apparent that over the last four decades, the influence of labor unions has decreased while poverty and income inequality have increased. It may be a coincidence, but not likely!

The connections between jobs, the economy, and poverty are obvious. Given that our democracy depends on a strong economy, eliminating poverty is essential.

Safety, Security, and Criminal Justice

Mass incarceration was an agenda to control the minority population and to establish severe poverty amongst its people! There, I said it! It was another form of slavery that included harsh free labor, to hold control, produce financial gain to people in power, to beat men of all color senselessly, and to reduce household income and sustainability. Whether you've done a criminal act or innocently done nothing wrong, you're convicted and held in imprisonment until proven otherwise. At that point, even being initially arrested is viewed as a permanent punishment within your community. But what if you get the labels ``Offender", "Felon ""Criminal" on your background? The labels alone undeniably create a mindset that "You cannot be trusted", "You do not deserve these opportunities given to you because of what you've done", and "even if you get hired, I am going to give you hell." These are the realitics that men, women, and children face on a daily basis.

America is not safe and secure, not just for those who come in, but for those who have been living here. Domestic terrorism is at an all-time high. From school shootings, to gun violence in our neighborhoods, to the children who are able to obtain weapons and shoot their teachers, to the music industry promoting the lifestyle of a thug and how to be affiliated in a gang, to the doctors who have provided illegal drugs to their patients, to the police who have uncontrollably used force to savagely kill those they are to protect, and to the government who doesn't want to provide aid to its state based off the political affiliation. America has got to do better. Consider the question, "How do we insure domestic tranquility, if we kill our own?"

If we include providing a nice neighborly place to live in our definition of democracy, (and we should) then safety, security, and criminal justice are essential elements. Sadly, people living in poverty would seldom describe their conditions as safe, secure, and crime-free. That might be the view from the clouds, but the closer you get to the ground level the more frightening and dangerous poverty becomes. You may wonder why our leaders and politicians allow it to continue. Politicians and their donors/owners use crime, terrorism, and military threats to distract us from poverty and other important issues. The three combine to form one of the biggest industries in the world. It's a perfect fit. The people making the money are gaslighting from up in the clouds where they are least threatened but most profitable.

We've turned our backs on each other due to the jealousy, greed, fake news media, racism, discrimination, white supremacy, self-hate, depression, etc.; resulting from the gaslighting. The harm we have done to our urban and impoverished brothers and sisters has made us target one another (domestic violence, one-parent household, homelessness, bullying, black on black crimes, and police brutality that kills black youth). There are literally bodies dying in the streets. This creates satisfaction for parties who want to see that cohort of society destroyed, and sadly, the victims feed into the narratives every time.

On one hand, you have gangs and street gangsters in the community that seek to run and display some kind of power. With power comes gun violence and fear into their hoods. Teenagers have stopped "boxing it out" or handling their situations like grown men and women. They are using guns to make their problems go away, not realizing that their actions leave them with a death sentence.

On the other hand, you have innocent victims (black men, women, and children) being gunned down by police following their racial profiling tactics; believing that someone with a different skin color is deemed more of a threat. They pull their trigger because that hairbrush or cellphone might be a gun. They pull their trigger because they are concerned that they are being disrespected, revealing their inferiority to the minority they are accosting.

The US has the largest military and the most guns of any country in the world. Given those two factors, we must be the safest country on Earth. We are not. We are in the middle of a "War on Terrorism!" We must be winning the war because the number of American civilians who died worldwide in terrorist attacks last year was eight. For comparison, lightning killed 29 people. More relevant, we had 38,000 suicides and 22,000 murders – both of which can be connected to poverty. If it's not terrorists, what are the causes of deaths in the USA? (The following table represents pre-Covid conditions.)

Cause	# of deaths
All causes	2,500,000
Diseases and illnesses (Medical issues)	1,800,000
Accidents	125,000
Suicide	38,000
Homicide	22,000
All others	478,000

According to a CNN report, *Using numbers from the Centers for" Disease Control and Prevention; we found that from 2001 to 2013, .406,496 people died by firearms on U.S. soil"* Remember how many citizens terrorists killed last year? Eight! How much money do we spend on the War on Terror? Since it is the only War we are fighting right now, let us assume that the US military budget (DoD) is the number - $610 billion. (This does not consider the DOJ, DHS, DEA, CIA, etc.) We spend $610 billion to protect ourselves from terrorists and others who would do us harm while we allow our own citizens to kill about 60,000 of us (murders and suicides) and we will not allow the National Institutes of Health or the CDC to do any research on the issue of gun violence in America. That's right! Congress passed the Dickey amendment and has inserted language into subsequent spending bills prohibiting such research. Congress is not protecting the average citizen. They are protecting the gun industry. Ironically, guns are not the cause of the problem. Gun use is a symptom of the anger, frustration, impotence, and desperation caused by poverty, racism, and white supremacy in America. Gun violence is the predictable consequence of the feelings of anger, frustration, and desperation caused by poverty, racism, and white supremacy.

Americans do not feel safe. We occasionally worry that if certain things happen, our cozy world could crumble. Just because a foreign power has not invaded the US, does not mean that the average citizen feels safe and secure. National security is much more than being safe from a military or terrorist attack. **'Safety'**denotes being physically safe from bodily harm. **'Security'**is a broader category. Security includes safety, a job, food, a place to live, heat in the winter, and low poverty rates. The US has the second highest poverty rate[117] among the wealthy countries.

- low infant mortality rates (US ranks 178th),

- high life expectancy (US ranks 49th),

- quality education (US ranks 25th),

- a reasonable retirement income, (available for some but not for all)

---

117. https://qz.com/879092/the-us-doesnt-look-like-a-developed-country/

- good health, and other basic creature comforts and necessities (a dream, but not a universal reality).

Over the past few decades, the average American's security level has been declining. Politicians emphasize our safety from military invasion and allocate hundreds of billions of dollars to our national defense. At the same time, millions of citizens lack the true security defined above.

We've turned our backs on each other due to jealousy, greed, lack of confidence, fake media, racism, discrimination, white supremacy, self-hate, depression, etc. The harm we have done to our brothers is a combination of poverty and what has happened over the recent years to make us target one another (domestic violence, one-parent household, homeless, bullying, black on black crimes, police brutality, sentencing young black men, and black bodies dying in the streets). These conditions create satisfaction for parties who want to see black communities destroyed. Sadly, the communities feed into the narratives every single time.

When will we say, "Enough is enough!", and change our ways? It starts by looking in the mirror and realizing we're all a human race, and that the more we target our own by killing each other the more we deteriorate our own culture.

Issue #10 - We spend too much on defense and not enough on safety and security.

America has a WAR ON TERRORISM and a minor skirmish against violent crime. This is absurd when we consider that there has been more domestic terrorism than foreign terrorism. The response does not reflect the demand. There have been fewer than 50 deaths in the United States since 9/11/2001 that can arguably be attributed to international terrorism dating back to and including 9/11. During that same period, we have experienced over 165,000 murders, nearly 1,000,000 reported forcible rapes, and about 9,000,000 robberies. (Rape is the most underreported crime in America. The 1,000,000 forcible rapes only count those that get reported.) Most of the documented terrorist attacks were committed in a perverted interpretation of some otherwise peaceful religious doctrine. They represent a minuscule part of the problem. The murderers, rapists, and robbers did not tell us why they did what they did. We can probably blame some of them on rage, jealousy, mental illness, and greed, but there is a simpler, more prevalent cause. It comes down to Maslow's hierarchy of needs. The following graphic presents the concept very well.

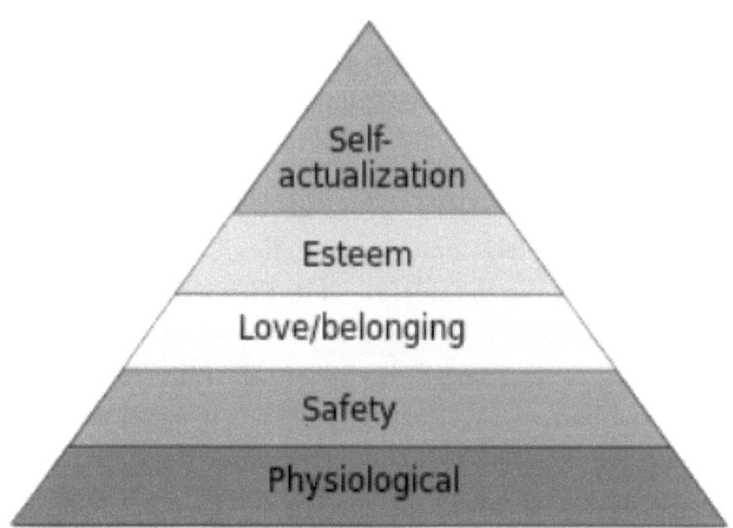

Hierarchy implies that you must achieve the lower level before you can proceed to the next higher level. We only need to grasp an understanding of the lowest two levels to comprehend what is causing these trying times. Physiological needs represent the requirements for human survival like enough food to eat, and shelter from the elements. Safety includes physical and psychological factors including good health, emotional, and financial safety. There are far too many American citizens stuck in the bottom two levels of the pyramid, lacking physiological needs and personal safety.

People at these bottom levels may feel helpless, hopeless, and angry. They often believe they are working hard and getting nowhere. They are sure their current condition is not their own fault (and to a large extent, they are correct), so they look for someone else to blame. Who is actually to blame? Is it those with wealth and power who are to blame? The Latin phrase "Qui bono?" meaning "To whom is it a benefit?" might be in play here. The people at the top of the hierarchy benefit by creating and enforcing policies, institutions, and regulations that strategically cause damage to a targeted group of its own citizens? We need a defense from those attacks.

There is enormous wealth in this country – more than enough for every person to live reasonably above the bottom two levels of the pyramid. Unfortunately, some people with great wealth have used that wealth to rewrite the rules to allow themselves to accumulate even more wealth – at the expense of people with less wealth. (The old, "It's a dog-eat-dog world" mentality). The issues for the people living on the bottom two levels of Maslow's pyramid are survival and safety. The best path to attaining these two things and moving up to the next level on the pyramid is getting a job that pays a living wage. Many economists say that the most effective way for the government to enable this is by creating a major infrastructure program and funding more public-service jobs. They do not recommend welfare as the first solution, but only as a social safety net for those unable to engage in the job market for any number of valid reasons.

The country would pay for this or any other program through taxes. Here is where greed becomes an issue. Whom would we tax? Let's start with who has the money. In this instance, the wealthy will be required to pay because they have the wealth. The people on the bottom obviously do not have it. The people in the middle cannot afford it and still stay in the middle. That leaves the people at the top. Why should the wealthy have to pay? Because they have fixed the current rules to enable them to pay themselves a disproportionate share of their companies' revenue. Many of the wealthy are generous citizens who recognize their good fortune, contribute to, and invest in programs that create quality employment opportunities. Unfortunately, others use their wealth to avoid paying for programs that do not immediately increase their wealth. I am not talking about stripping them of their wealth. They can afford to pay for major programs and still be staggeringly wealthy. We should tax them more because they gaslight to deflect attention away from themselves and encourage us to blame others for our problems, and they pay lobbyists to convince elected officials to leave the rules the way they are. We can fight the gaslighting with education and truthful messaging.

There are two variations on how poverty and crime link together. Unemployment leads to more property crimes – stealing to survive. Inequity leads to crimes against individuals out of a sense of outrage. The evidence is overwhelming that poverty is the major cause of crime in the United States. We get all outraged and call Homeland Security whenever we have a rare activity that we can classify as terrorism, but we have daily violent crimes all over the country that don't get treated at the cause. We treat the symptoms and continue to suffer the consequences. We spend billions on a criminal justice system, incarcerate millions of citizens for minor crimes, and destroy the lives of millions of individuals and their families. Sadly, all these activities do nothing to make us any safer from harm. We must stop treating the symptoms and put the emphasis on fixing the root causes of the problem – poverty and inequity. When we call the problem terrorism, no cost is too great to combat it. We need to have the same attitude about fighting poverty, pay, and wealth inequality.

The goal of any civilized society is to provide its citizens with a place to live in peace, prosperity, and harmony. To achieve that, the citizens pass laws that everyone has to live by and provide a criminal justice system to enforce those laws. Individuals who violate the laws are punished. But America has a disgraceful criminal justice problem that targets one group of people more harshly than any other group. We incarcerate more of our citizens than any other country in the world. The War on Drugs is a large reason why incarceration increased; however, a major part of the problem is simply people committing a crime to survive. People living in poverty will do whatever it takes to survive. At the same time there is an insidious effort to keep prisons full because it is profitable to the Prison Industrial Complex. The criminal justice system, including incarceration and recidivism, costs billions of dollars every year. Reducing poverty will greatly reduce crime. The money saved by reducing crime will balance the money spent reducing poverty.

Years ago, politicians were convinced that imposing more draconian punishments for all crimes would reduce the crime problem. They competed to be perceived as Tough On Crime. This misinformed belief led America to become the most punishing country in the world by a wide margin. The Brennan Center for Justice has done research on this belief in severe punishment and their findings are disturbing.

*Some have argued that despite the immense social and"
economic costs of America's mass incarceration system, it has
succeeded at reducing crime," saidreport co-author Dr.
Oliver Roeder[118]. The data tells a different story: if reducing"
crime is the end goal of our criminal justice system, increased
"incarceration is a poor investment*

*This report amplifies what many on the left and the right"
have come to realize in recent years: mass incarceration is
.not working It simply isn't necessary to reduce crime," said
Inimai Chettiar, director of the Brennan Center's Justice
Program and author of the executive summary. The prison"
.explosion has been very expensive A better use of public
resources would be improving economic opportunities,*

*supporting 21st century policing practices, and expanding
treatment and rehabilitation programs, all of which have
proven records of reducing crime without incarceration's
high costs."*

Once again, partisan politics, spurious arguments, and deliberate
deception have exacerbated the problem – abetted by a large dose
of Prison Industrial Complex (PIC) lobbyists' money. America's
enthusiasm for incarceration created a completely new problem,
referred to as the Prison Industrial Complex. Washington University
in St. Louis produced a report titled, "The Economic Burden of
Incarceration in the U.S.,[119]" Their research revealed that the real
total cost of incarceration in the U.S. is more than $1 trillion or
6% of GDP. "We find that for every dollar in corrections costs,

---

118. https://www.brennancenter.org/press-release/virginia-increased-incarceration-had-limited-
effect reducing-crime-over-two-decades

119. https://ijrd.csw.fsu.edu/sites/g/files/upcbnu1766/files/media/images/publication_pdfs/
Economic_Burden_of_Incarceration_IJRD072016_0_0.pdf

incarceration generates an additional $10 in social costs," said Pettus-Davis, director of the Concordance Institute for Advancing Social Justice and co-director of the Smart Decarceration Initiative.

The US could eliminate most crime in the country if we eliminated poverty. Money spent on eliminating poverty produces many benefits to society. Incarceration produces almost none!

How big is the incarceration problem? The American criminal justice system holds more than 2.1 million people in 1,719 state prisons, 102 federal prisons, 901 juvenile correctional facilities, 3,163 local jails, and 76 Indian Country jails as well as in military prisons, immigration detention facilities, civil commitment centers, and prisons in the U.S. territories. The incarceration rate of the US is by far the highest in the world. The United States represents about 5% of the world's population, but we house around 25% of the world's prisoners. The table below, showing the number of prisoners in each country, illustrates how out of scale America's incarceration rate is. If you look at the issue on a per-capita basis, America is still off the scale.

1 United States of America 2,145,100

2 China 1,649,804

3 Brazil 668,914

4 Russian Federation 605,955

5 India 419,623

6 Thailand 322,634

7 Indonesia 233,620

8 Turkey 229,790

9 Iran 225 624

10 Mexico 208,689

Recidivism (people returning to prison) is a major factor in America's unacceptable incarceration problem. Recidivism facts[120] from the Bureau of Justice illustrate the severity of the problem.

- About 66% of prisoners released across 24 states in 2008 were arrested within 3 years, and 82% were arrested within 10 years.

- The annual arrest percentage among prisoners released in 2008 declined from 43% in Year 1 to 22% in Year 10.

- About 61% of prisoners released in 2008 returned to prison within 10 years for a parole or probation violation or a new sentence.

People who are living in the upper levels of Maslow's Hierarchy are not committing violent crimes. Spending money and creating policies to reduce poverty are the best ways to improve safety and security.

Issue #11 – Being poor is a crime.

Not really, but it might as well be. When a person is arrested, the judge looks at the situation and decides whether to allow bail and the amount of bail after considering things such as:

- Flight risk – If the judge releases the accused, what is the likelihood that he or she will show up for trial.

---

120. https://www.bjs.gov/index.cfm?ty=pbdetail&iid=4986

- Danger to Society – If released, is the accused likely to hurt somebody?

- Severity of the crime – From vandalism to multiple murders.

- Previous criminal record (repeat offender)

- Ties to the community.

Seems fair, right? Not so much! Consider two people accused of a crime they did not commit. They are equal in every way when it comes to the criteria listed above. The only difference is that one of them is wealthy and the other is poor. The judge fairly applies her sentencing criteria and sets equal bail requirements for both of $10,000. Usually bail bonds are 10% of the set bail so an accused offender with a $10K bail must put up a $1K bond. You can see where this is going. The wealthy person pays the bond and goes home to live a normal life while awaiting trial, eventually gets exonerated and no harm done. The poor person sits in jail, possibly loses his job because he can't show up, and spends the months awaiting trial housed with other prisoners, some of whom are guilty of violent crimes. This experience alone is traumatizing. Most have families to return to. If the accused is a single father or one who is paying child support who is innocently imprisoned, they are traumatized by the effects and impact it will have if they aren't able to be there to support their family.

Once again, poverty rears its ugly head. An innocent under caste (a lower caste of individuals who are permanently barred by law and custom from mainstream society) a poor person spent months in jail while a wealthy person moved on with little hardship. The impact of the time in jail is compounded when the poor person is released and cannot find a job that pays as well as the one he lost. At this point, some form of recidivism becomes an apparent solution due to the need to provide a stable income. The only reason people who have not been convicted are sitting in jail is that they have no savings in the bank and cannot make bail, or family members choose to not support. For example, if there is a black man who is sitting in jail and makes calls to his family to help him out, he typically has two options, both leading to a negative outcome. Option one, he has no money saved, so he cannot help himself. Option two, he calls his family, but they have bills and no savings so they cannot give help with bail; so, they can't help. There is no option three, so they sit in jail awaiting trial – innocent until proven guilty doesn't provide much comfort.

Unless the underlying crime is so severe or there is some other reason to deny or set a prohibitively high bail, people with financial resources make bail and continue to live their normal lives. Truly innocent until proven guilty.

Housing prisoners is a profitable business, so the prison industrial complex lobbies for stiffer bail requirements (spuriously in the name of protecting citizens) to generate more profits.

Poverty also plays another role. The wealthy accused can afford to hire an experienced lawyer. The less fortunate must rely upon an overworked, underpaid, and typically inexperienced public defender. This scenario is not the exception, it is the rule. The headline of the following graphic is frightening.

"70% of people in local jails are not convicted of any crime!"

"This graph originally appeared in Mass Incarceration: The Whole Pie 2017[121] is a pie chart showing the number of people locked up on a given day in the United States in jails,

---

121. *https://www.prisonpolicy.org/reports/pie2017.html*

> *by convicted and not convicted status, and by the underlying offense, using the newest data available in March 2017. (We've also updated this graph for 2018[122].)*
>
> *The "not convicted" population in American jails is larger than most other countries' total incarceration populations[123]."*

This is a systemic outrageous fact! This is totally inconsistent with who we want to believe we are and the values we share. Under these conditions, these innocent receive worse treatment than those who are actually guilty. Let's go back to Jim Crow Laws from the early 1890's and how they were established to provide racial order. Let's see how the Ku Klux Klan was organized to violently lynch, kill, and dismantle coloreds from 1865 on. *Mass incarceration operates as a tightly networked system of laws, policies, customs and institutions that operate collectively to ensure the subordinate status of a group defined largely by race[124].*

'Innocent until proven guilty' doesn't have the same lofty meaning when we realize how many innocent people are incarcerated. Black people represent under 14% of the U.S. population, but they account for 53% of all the people in this country who were falsely convicted of a serious crime and then freed after serving at least part of their sentence[125].

If you are an average middle-class American and you get arrested for something you did not do, it is an inconvenience, but no big deal.

---

122. *https://www.prisonpolicy.org/graphs/pie2018_jail_detail.html*

123. *https://www.prisonpolicy.org/graphs/pie2017_jail_detail.html*

124. *https://newjimcrow.com/*

125. https://www.npr.org/2022/09/27/1125442683/wrongful-convictions-disproportionately-affect-black-americans-report-shows

Right? Wrong! Look closely at the graphic below. Of the 443,000 not convicted people in jail, only 140,000 of them are accused (not yet proven guilty) of a violent crime. That means that nearly 300,000 (INNOCENT) people accused of non-violent crimes are waiting in jail for trial. People are innocent until proven guilty. That means that 300,000 innocent people are in jail indefinitely, awaiting trial. Actually, there is one more criterion that applies – 'poor' – too poor to afford bail. So, people are in jail because they are poor. With them in jail or prison are people accused and guilty – not a good influence on the innocent there with them and providing profits to the prisons/jails. That leads them into deeper poverty when they are finally acquitted and released and lose their job because they were in jail.

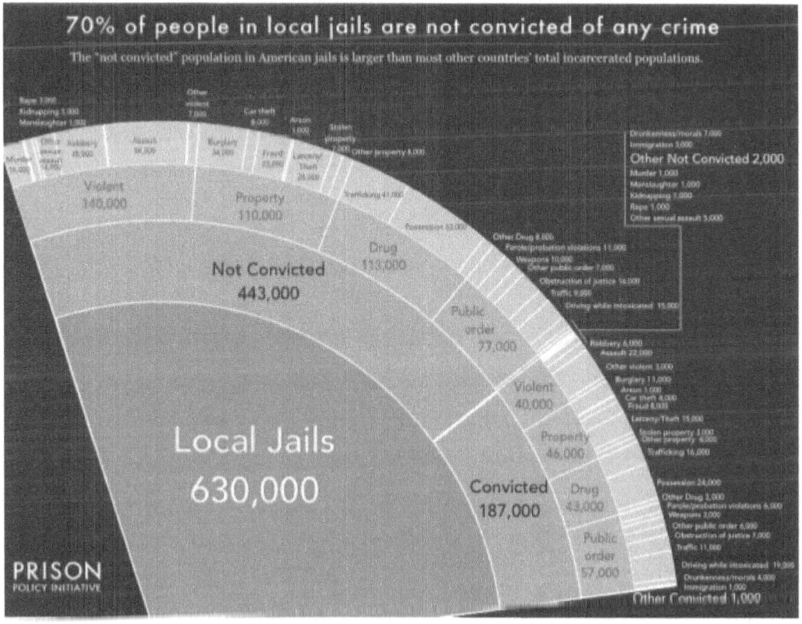

Given the backlog in many courts, some people wait for weeks or months before going to trial. In New York City, it costs $168,000 per year to house an inmate. Surely, there is a better use for that money than housing people accused of non-violent crimes. Poverty is the reason some people commit crimes; poverty is sometimes the result of someone committing a crime, and sometimes poverty is the result of someone simply being unjustly accused of a crime. It is a vicious circle that we must break[126].

> *Black people are 13.6% of the American population but 53% of the 3,200 exonerations listed in the National Registry of Exonerations. Judging from exonerations, innocent Black Americans are seven times more likely than White Americans to be falsely convicted of serious crimes.*

I said people sometimes wait for weeks or months to go to trial. For some it is worse than that[127].

> *"Incarcerated for Years Without Trial: Chicago police missed more than 11,000 court dates since 2010, causing months or years of unnecessary delays for inmates awaiting trial."*

> *Although no court documents indicate that the state had any physical evidence linking Robinson to the gun, a judge denied his request for electronic monitoring and set his bond at $7,500—the amount he'd have to pay to be released from jail and resume work and school as he awaited trial. It was a sum neither Robinson nor his family had at their disposal. Robinson's family set out on the first of numerous failed*

---

126. https://www.law.umich.edu/special/exoneration/Documents/
    Race%2520Report%2520Preview.pdf

127. https://www.theinvestigativefund.org/investigation/2016/11/16/incarcerated-years-
    without-trial/

attempts to raise the money while Robinson stayed in jail waiting for his case to be resolved.

As Robinson reacclimated to life behind bars, he noticed something that dismayed him: a few of the inmates he'd met during his first spate in jail as a teenager were still there now, awaiting trial.

"There were guys there still fighting their cases from when I first came to the county in 2007," Robinson said. "These guys were in there for six, seven years."

He didn't yet know it, but Robinson was about to join their ranks. Although formally innocent in the eyes of the law, he would spend 1,507 days in jail—more than four years—awaiting trial for the weapon-possession charges."

Read the complete article in the link provided. It raises many other compelling issues. Robinson served four years in jail because his family could not pay $7,500 in bail. For many innocent accused citizens, 'taking a plea' is deemed a better option. Innocent people will plead guilty to some crime to avoid waiting in jail for a trial. In the warped system, the police and prosecutors look good because they caught and 'convicted' the person. Everybody is playing by the rules, but the rules do not work for everybody – especially if you are poor. Jails are just one portion of the US incarceration problem.

"If jails are for criminals, why are there still so many people behind bars after decades of declining crime[128]? The answer is both surprising and disturbing.

According to the most recent data[129] from the Bureau of Justice Statistics[130], the number of U.S. jail inmates rose from

---

128. *https://www.bjs.gov/index.cfm?ty=pbdetail&iid=5804*

621,000 in 2000 to 744,600 in 2014. But as the lower part of each bar in the chart shows, this increase was not driven by the jailing of more convicted criminals. Instead, jails are now overflowing with people who are awaiting trial (upper part of each bar). These individuals, who may be innocent of the crime they're charged with, account for 95 percent of the growth in the jail population over the past 15 years."

"In October 2013, the incarceration rate of the United States of America was the highest in the world, at 716 per 100,000 of the national population. While the United States represents about 4.4 percent of the world's population, it houses around 22 percent of the world's prisoners[131]."

There are all kinds of shameful disturbing statistics about where America stands in the world concerning the percentage of our population we keep in prison – especially young black males. This includes many articles about the impact the failed "War on Drugs" has had on our prison industry's growth. The articles provide a clearer understanding of the issues.

For America to have so many prisoners, they must have broken the law – and they did. Then why is there a problem? Because many of the laws were sponsored by the congressional representatives who were bought by the prison industry for the specific purpose of filling

---

129. https://www.washingtonpost.com/news/wonk/wp/2017/04/24/were-jailing-way-more-people-whove-been-convicted-of-exactly-nothing/?utm_term=.dc39d3b5cb0c

130. https://www.bjs.gov/index.cfm?ty=pbse&sid=38

131. https://www.google.com/search?rlz=1C2CHZL_enUS740US740&source=hp&ei=CB0DW4i4FqH85gLynYzABQ&gs_ivs=1&q=incarceration+rates&oq=incarceration+rates&gs_l=psy-ab.18...3745.4628.0.5019.10.7.0.0.0.0.78.422.7.7.0....0...1c.6.64.psy-ab..3.7.421.0..0j0i20i264k1j0i131k1j0i20i263k1.0.UpXIrsNSOlc#tts_43ec3e5dee6e706af7766fffea512721_0

prisons to improve the profits of the companies who own and operate them.

> ***"How for-profit prisons have become the biggest lobby no one is talking about[132]:***

> *The Justice Policy Institute identified the private-prison industry's three-pronged approach to increase profits through political influence: lobbying, direct campaign contributions, and building relationships and networks. On its website[133] CCA states that the company does not lobby on policies that affect "the basis for or duration of an individual's incarceration or detention." Still, several reports have documented instances when private-prison companies have indirectly supported policies that put more Americans and immigrants behind bars – such as California's three-strikes rule[134] and Arizona's highly controversial anti-illegal immigration law[135] – by donating to politicians who support them, <u>attending meetings with officials who back them</u>, and*

---

132. https://www.washingtonpost.com/posteverything/wp/2015/04/28/how-for-profit-prisons-have-become-the-biggest-lobby-no-one-is-talking-about/?utm_term=.1b75965bfe7c

133. https://urldefense.proofpoint.com/v2/url?u=http-3A__www.cca.com_investors_corporate-2Dgovernance_political-2Dlobbying-2Dactivity&d=BQMFaQ&c=RAhzPLrCAq19eJdrcQiUVEwFYoMRqGDAXQ_puwStYjge&r=5SH8Pfo-WfSu0lIoF4k9UO9B1Vs0qMYeyezk4qdJZSc&m=VLjsbgcLTyGmdpAVNR9wEvMw639MoWC6y_zzjebegn0&s=Z0ht3qQylhTpCSbkEgijqTXkwaI_TByqo-HbSvMhaXg&e=

134. https://urldefense.proofpoint.com/v2/url?u=http-3A__inthesetimes.com_article_6084_corporate-5Fcon-5Fgame&d=BQMFaQ&c=RAhzPLrCAq19eJdrcQiUVEwFYoMRqGDAXQ_puwStYjge&r=5SH8Pfo-WfSu0lIoF4k9UO9B1Vs0qMYeyezk4qdJZSc&m=VLjsbgcLTyGmdpAVNR9wEvMw639MoWC6y_zzjebegn0&s=xuFzLvaCfdd-yaR6wfrG9YXrpk0NI-ngcOqOA71SsOQ&e=

> *lobbying for funding for Immigration and Customs Enforcement.*[136] *Showing just how important these policies are to the private prison industry, both GEO Group and Corrections Corporation of America have warned shareholders that changes in these policies would hurt their bottom lines."*

A year after the War on Drugs was created by then President Nixon in 1971, politicians decided to 'get tough on crime', making the drug issue "public enemy number one". Lobbyists for the prison industry pushed their congressmen to take this tough approach that coincidentally meant big profits for the industry. This incarceration issue was an intentional consequence that has gained momentum and become a major problem within urban communities. In her book entitled "The New Jim Crow", Michelle Alexander states that "The Reagan administration hired staff to publicize the emergence of crack cocaine in 1985 as part of a strategic effort to build public and legislative support for the war." By 1998, "The CIA admitted that guerilla armies it actively supported in Nicaragua were

---

135. *https://urldefense.proofpoint.com/v2/url?u=http-3A__www.npr.org_2010_10_28_130833741_prison-2Deconomics-2Dhelp-2Ddrive-2Dariz-2Dimmigration-2Dlaw&d=BQMFaQ&c=RAhzPLrCAq19eJdrcQiUVEwFYoMRqGDAXQ_puw5tYjg&r=5SH8Pfo-WfSu0lIoF4k9UO9B1Vs0qMYeyezk4qdJZSc&m=VLjsbgcLTyGmdpAVNR9wEvMw639MoWC6y_zzjebegn0&s=iknSHLW9rK9CjqMe5eICF41jYf2UDgsOfv57PASAa-U&e=*

136. *https://urldefense.proofpoint.com/v2/url?u=http-3A__www.justicepolicy.org_uploads_justicepolicy_documents_gaming-5Fthe-5Fsystem.pdf&d=BQMFaQ&c=RAhzPLrCAq19eJdrcQiUVEwFYoMRqGDAXQ_puw5tYjg&r=5SH8Pfo-WfSu0lIoF4k9UO9B1Vs0qMYeyezk4qdJZSc&m=VLjsbgcLTyGmdpAVNR9wEvMw639MoWC6y_zzjebegn0&s=Ed28F-XKMdH1COtCJjZIPIMwngW2Ub1Ns_PfDGS8w_A&e=*

smuggling illegal drugs into the United States–drugs that were making their way onto the streets of inner-city black neighborhoods in the form of crack cocaine." From 1970-1985 the U.S. prison population increased to 306,078 inmates due to drug possession. According to the Federal Register, the average annual cost to house a federal prisoner is about $28,893.40.

Based on the knowledge of how corrupted the U.S. Justice system can be, and the subsequent consequences on the lives that were lost or destroyed in prison because of the push of the war on drugs, the close connection to our losing the war on poverty must not be ignored. We cannot begin to estimate the lost revenue from all the people in jail who could be working and paying taxes. As a very conservative wild guess, let's add $9,000 per prisoner per year for a total of about $37K.

If you were listening to a panel on incarceration and recidivism, at this point the presenter typically compares this cost to what it would cost to provide these people with a good education – making the point that most people in prison did not graduate from high school. If we had spent more on educating them, (average per-pupil annual cost is $11,153), it would provide a second chance to those reentering society, it would add value to their potential of establishing employment above their original standard, it would alleviate and reduce recidivism significantly, and it would eventually cause the mass incarceration rate to plummet by two-thirds. The question is, how do we get there? How do we push inmates to want to do better? How do we prevent a population of people from going to prison in the first place?

There are several flaws in this approach. Most of these offenders did not do well in school, and therefore they are not interested in another opportunity to fail. Education is only one small link in the chain of services and resources that must be provided, delivered, and managed for the client to be successful. If any link fails, the client fails. The clients need a well-designed and managed suite of services, customized for each individual, and a job that pays a living wage.

If we created a program that paid each non-violent prisoner in the program a living wage to work on infrastructure, public sector, and community service projects, it would cost about the same amount as we are paying to keep them in prison. I am not suggesting we give people money for nothing, and I am not suggesting we treat them as slaves. I am suggesting we create a national fund for state and municipal governments to apply for to implement infrastructure, public sector, and community service programs that people convicted of a crime are sentenced to participate in – and get paid for their work. If we do this program, we will greatly reduce crime because people who can make a living are not forced to take a living. Moreover, they would be paying taxes, contributing to the economy, not taking from it. They would be living at home and being responsible parents. They would spend the money they earn, creating jobs for others. A program like this would emphasize OSHA training and certification, teach them about money management, and the importance of quality education.

In addition to all these benefits, America would improve its infrastructure and provide better public services. This program could employ inmates even before they are out of prison, allowing them to establish a nest egg to bridge them while they reenter society. I can imagine some conservatives complaining that those lazy out-of-work freeloaders don't deserve a job. Would they prefer the alternative; their living in poverty or committing crimes to survive? Using this approach, everybody benefits from better infrastructure and public services, and we infuse the overall economy with additional capital. Paying people to do work that is productive to society is much better than paying for keeping them in prison. Everybody wins and nobody loses. The rich person may feel like he is losing, but that is a matter of choice – how they choose to perceive it. They could also perceive it as investing in making the world a better place. And by the way, those lazy out-of-work freeloaders primarily exist in people's gaslit imagination.

There are humane things we can do to address a lack of security. Incarceration is inhumane, racially biased, and ineffective. If most criminals had a job that paid a living wage and allowed them to feel safe and secure, they would have less motivation to commit a crime. We need to invest in infrastructure projects that have the double benefit of improving our infrastructure while also creating jobs that pay a living wage. We need to change the way we think about "National Security". It is much more than military defense.

This concept is a far better return on investment than the current incarceration model that statistically results in about 70% of the people who complete serving their prison sentences committing another crime within five years of their release and repeating the cycle. This recidivism is particularly tragic for people whose first offense was a minor non-violent victimless crime. After serving their initial sentence, their criminal record is an anchor dragging them back into the criminal justice system. We need to fix the outrageous drug laws that send non-violent offenders off to prison. The additional benefit of changing the drug laws and decreasing the crimes associated with drug use is that it would make the country safer for the average citizen who might otherwise be the victim of a crime.

I am not talking about a program that would cost additional money and require more taxes. We already spend the money to house prisoners. There might be some incremental cost when we first implement the program, but over time, the cost would go back down as the number of prisoners goes down.

Issue #12 - Incarceration is bad for democracy.

Incarceration is expensive, ineffective, racially biased, anti-democratic, and inhumane; and yet the United States incarcerates more of its citizens than any other country in the world. You are probably familiar with most of these issues, but 'anti-democratic' may not have been on your list. Many states take away a convicted felon's right to vote while they are serving their sentence. A few of them take it away for life. Given the statistical reality that more poor and minority citizens than middle- and upper-class citizens are incarcerated, and that those demographics are more likely to vote Democratic, denying the felons their voting rights can have an effect on an election outcome. Follow the trail. If a person is poor, they are more likely to commit a crime than middle- and upper-class citizens. If they are convicted felons, they lose their right to vote. This penalty falls disproportionately on voters likely to vote Democratic. Completing the circle, Poverty is bad for democracy.

We have ex-offenders walking around whose constitutional rights have been violated. Those who re-enter society after serving time in prison for possession of marijuana are prevented from voting and are discriminated against. It's outrageous that they're still labeled for their "crime" as the same states that took their rights from them have legalized or decriminalized the sale and use of marijuana and established and profited from medicinal marijuana farms and stores to help those in society dealing with depression, insomnia, anxiety, and other mental disorders. Just imagine that you're getting out of prison and you see stores and institutions that sell "medicinal weed and mushrooms" by the gram and ounce, but you served 10 years for possession of less than 5 grams of marijuana. Now you can't vote, you're discriminated against, underpaid, harshly treated, and labeled for life a "felon or offender." Now think about how unjust this is.

Another example of how constitutional rights have been trampled is restoring voting rights to ex-offenders. Those who re-enter society after serving time in prison for possession of marijuana are considered felons, prevented from voting, and are discriminated against. For example, when Barack Obama was campaigning for president, Millions of black ex-offenders could not vote for him because of their felony conviction. It's true. The same restriction applied to brown and white citizens, but the evidence is overwhelming that the War on Drugs disproportionately impacted black citizens. Further evidence of this unfairness was the Republicans legislators fighting a Virginia bill that would have restored voting rights to ex-offenders, admittedly for political reasons. Whenever it appears that the candidates are choosing the voters instead of the voters choosing the candidates, something is wrong.

If incarceration is not the answer, what is? What are the alternatives? Many states and local criminal justice programs have implemented diversion or alternative sentencing programs. These programs provide a variety of options for law enforcement. They prescribe a collection of counseling, job training and placement, housing, transportation, legal, and family support services. Satisfactory completion of the prescribed program removes (expunges) the crime from the individual's record. This seemingly minor last step makes a world of difference because it enables the person to reintegrate into society without a criminal record. Diversion programs and alternative sentences are typically only an option for non-violent minor crimes.

The program is easy to implement. The arresting officer who feels the offender and society may be better served by a diversion program typically initiates it. The offender is handled outside the usual criminal justice process. Instead of going through being charged, tried, and convicted (at significant monetary and societal cost), the offender admits guilt and accepts placement in an alternative sentencing program. If the offender fails to complete the program, the judge re-invokes the guilty plea, and the offender serves a prison sentence.

An Alternative Sentence follows an individual's trial and conviction. It is a judicial sentencing option that enables the judge to allow the convicted offender to avoid spending time in prison. As with the Diversion program, if the offender completes the alternative sentence, the criminal record is expunged. If he or she fails to follow through and complete the conditions of the alternative sentence, the judge re-invokes the conviction, and the offender does prison time. Both programs have strong incentives for the offender to successfully complete the program.

Despite the positive potential for the Alternative program, some minors seemed terrified of the possible outcome. Every two months they have to be evaluated to determine their compliance with their sentence and completion of the tasks assigned to them, as well as to take a drug test. This really puts some of them on edge. The Alternative Program also provides them the privilege to live in their community amongst their peers. In many cases this is a good and bad thing. For one, they are able to work and be around their family and friends. However, because of their previous presence in the environment, there is a risk that they will be drawn back into their bad habits of drugs, drinking, violence, and getting into trouble; making it difficult to complete their process. Alternative programs rely on a strong mentor or sponsor program to support the ex-offender. Evidence has demonstrated that the single most important factor in the success of an alternative program is having a good working relationship with a dedicated mentor.

The Justice Policy Institute produced a report titled Treatment or Incarceration[137]? that explores the efficacy of diversion and alternative sentencing programs for drug crimes. The study focused on treatment for minor drug offenses, but the same logic applies to comprehensive alternative sentencing or diversion programs for minor non-violent crime first offenders with any criminal behaviors. Their findings include: (Excerpted for brevity)

> ***Finding 1: Treatment can be less expensive than a term of imprisonment.*** *Reports by government agencies, centrist and center-right think tanks, and surveys of programs in Maryland show that treatment is a much less expensive option than incarceration for handling substance-abusing offenders.*
>
> *[...] the evaluation found that the average cost of placing a participant in Drug Treatment Alternative Program (DTAP), including the costs of residential treatment, vocational training and support services was $32,974—half the average cost of $64,338 if the participant had been sent to serve the average term of imprisonment for participants, 25 months.*

---

137. http://www.justicepolicy.org/uploads/justicepolicy/documents/

   04-01_rep_mdtreatmentorincarceration_ac-dp.pdf

Finding 2: Treatment can be cost effective. Other studies that used a cost-benefit analysis—a broader measure of how money spent on treatment alternatives compares to money spent on prisons in terms of crime rates and other societal benefits like employment and tax revenues—have shown that, dollar for dollar, treatment reduces the societal costs of substance abuse more effectively than incarceration does.

[...] Drug treatment in prison—such as in-prison therapeutic community programming, or that same program with community aftercare after the person leaves prison—yields a benefit of between $1.91 and $2.69 for every dollar spent on them. By contrast, therapeutic community programs outside of prison—typically work release facilities—yielded $8.87 of benefit for every program dollar spent. The reason for the difference versus in prison treatment programs was mainly due to higher program completion rates and lower recidivism.

Finding 3: Treatment can reduce substance abuse and recidivism while building communities. Beyond saving money and being more effective, a variety of different research entities have shown that treatment may work better to reduce substance abuse. Along with reduced drug addiction and recidivism, many treatment programs are community builders, helping people facing severe challenges become productive parts of their families and neighborhoods. Brooklyn's DTAP graduates are three-and-one-half times more likely to be employed than they were before arrest—92% were working after they completed the program.

Many states have implemented reentry programs designed to assist ex-offenders with the transition from prison to a successful career. Despite the excellent services that these programs provide, an unacceptably large percentage of ex-offenders end up back in prison. One of the biggest negative factors mitigating against the ex-offender's success on the outside is the fact the person spent time in prison and the label that they are an "ex-offender" and "felon". Those notions alone add discrimination and stereotyping no matter the race, age, orientation, person. An alternative sentence does not include a criminal conviction on the individual's permanent record or extended time in crime school – a.k.a. jail/prison. For more information about keeping people out of prison, I recommend "Keep Out of Jail Those Who Don't Need to Be Locked Up[138]" - Feb. 26, 2015. The author, Julia M. Stasch, is the president of the John D. and Catherine T. MacArthur Foundation.

More than half return to prison.

- Over 2,000 prisoners per day are released from US prisons.
- Over 1,000 former prisoners per day return to prison.
- The average 5-year cost for each returning prisoner is over $200,000.
- Those who don't return face challenging obstacles to their success.

---

138. http://www.nytimes.com/roomfordebate/2015/02/26/would-we-be-safer-if-fewer-were-jailed/keep-out-of-jail-those-who-dont-need-to-be-locked-up

Have you heard about America's Plantation Prisons? What do we call it when a person is denied any rights, has to live where his master tells him to, do what his master tells him to do, create wealth for his master and in return gets a place to live, clothes to wear, and food to eat? We used to call it 'Slavery', but in the 21st century, we call it 'Incarceration'. Today's private prison industry is remarkably similar to the 19th century plantation economy. The difference is that slaves were almost entirely black. Prisoners are disproportionately black, but not as exclusively. However, the vast majority are from poverty-stricken communities and demographics.

Incarceration is morally reprehensible, and then we make it worse. Prisons sign contracts with companies to manufacture products at extremely low costs – because the labor costs are essentially slave wages. It is time society got angry about this situation. Prisoners make a wide assortment of products[139], including military protective gear, McDonald's uniforms, furniture, etc. We are buying the products of these 21st century slaveholders just like the textile mills bought the cotton from the plantations. Support reform of the criminal justice system! To better understand the veracity, importance, and magnitude of this issue, watch Michelle Alexander's Ted Talk The future of race in America: Michelle Alexander at [140]TEDx Columbus[141]

The Center for Research on Globalization published an article titled, "The Prison Industry in the United States: Big Business or a New Form of Slavery?[142]" The opening paragraph captures the problem.

---

139. https://www.thrillist.com/gear/products-made-by-prisoners-clothing-furniture-electronics

140. https://www.youtube.com/watch?v=SQ6H-Mz6hgw

141. https://www.youtube.com/watch?v=SQ6H-Mz6hgw

142. https://www.globalresearch.ca/the-prison-industry-in-the-united-states-big-business-or-a-new-form-of-slavery/8289

"Human rights organizations, as well as political and social ones, are condemning what they are calling a new form of inhumane exploitation in the United States, where they say a prison population of up to 2 million – mostly Black and Hispanic – are working for various industries for a pittance. For the tycoons who have invested in the prison industry, it has been like finding a pot of gold. They do not have to worry about strikes or paying unemployment insurance, vacations, or comp time. All of their workers are full-time, and never arrive late or are absent because of family problems; moreover, if they don't like the pay of 25 cents an hour and refuse to work, they are locked up in isolation cells."

It is bad enough that they pay prisoners a pittance, but the impact is broader than that. Prison labor is replacing manufacturing jobs in the economy. Hard-working Americans are losing their jobs to prisoners here in the US. I am not saying that the prisoners should not keep busy and, if possible, be productive. However, if they are doing the work, the prison corporations should pay competitive wages. The prisoner's money could be saved, invested, and provide them with a much-needed financial base to live on when they are released.

Ex-offenders are the most dangerous group of people in America. According to the FBI's crime statistics, approximately 4% of Americans commit a serious crime. People who commit crimes have some common characteristics, but on average, from the whole population, it is about 4%. If we look at specific subgroups, then the numbers change. What identifiable and targetable subgroup is most likely to commit a crime? We cannot name "Drug Dealers" or other known criminal groups because by definition they are already committing a crime. The answer is, "ex-offenders," people who have already been convicted of a crime and have served their sentence. The numbers vary from state to state, but the statistics show that between 50% - 70% of ex-offenders will commit a crime and be back in prison within five years of being released. So, if we are interested in reducing crime and improving public safety, invest in reentry programs that improve the likelihood that an ex-offender will be able to succeed in the outside world.

It is also a good economic policy. It costs an average of $40,000 per year to incarcerate a prisoner. The average sentence in state prison is 5 years. (Federal sentences are longer.) At $40K per year, that means that each prisoner costs the taxpayer over $200K. Recidivists, (people who go back to prison) typically serve longer sentences, so their cost is even greater.

Then there is the moral issue. A vastly disproportionate percentage of prisoners are black men – many of whom began their criminal careers as young men in poverty-ridden circumstances. For them, committing a crime was a matter of survival. They had no job, no father, no education, no home, and no hope. When they are released from prison, what do they have to go back to? How can they survive? It is morally and ethically unacceptable that society does not do more to ensure this whole class of young men is not so unfairly disadvantaged.

According to the National Institute of Justice[143], among state prisoners released in 30 states in 2005:

• About two-thirds (67.8%) of released prisoners were" arrested for a new crime within 3 years, and three-quarters .(76.6%) were arrested within 5 years

• Within 5 years of release, 82.1% of property offenders were arrested for a new crime, compared to 76.9% of drug

---

143. *https://www.nij.gov/topics/corrections/recidivism/pages/welcome.aspx*

offenders, 73.6% of public order offenders, and 71.3% of violent offenders.

• More than a third (36.8%) of all prisoners who were arrested within 5 years of release were arrested within the first 6 months after release, with more than half (56.7%) arrested by the end of the first year.

• A sixth (16.1%) of released prisoners were responsible for almost half (48.4%) of the nearly 1.2 million arrests that occurred in the 5-year follow-up period.

• Within 5 years of release, 84.1% of inmates who were age 24 or younger at release were arrested, compared to 78.6% of inmates ages 25 to 39 and 69.2% of those age 40 or older."

Keeping people in prison is profitable for companies in the PIC but not for the rest of society. The PIC industry's incentives are upside down. If the prisons do well in facilitating a prisoner's successful return to society, the prisons get no further revenue from that individual. On the other hand, if they do poorly and the ex-offender commits another crime and returns to prison, they profit from their failure. The incentives are rewarding the wrong outcomes. Besides the financial cost of recidivism, there is the public safety cost. When ex-offenders get desperate and commit crimes, there is at least one victim involved. Because the ex-offenders spent time in prison (sometimes called 'crime school'), they are better criminals, so they may commit several crimes, with multiple victims, before the police catch them.

Efforts by the Brennan Center for Justice and the Vera Institute paid off a few years ago and state and federal prisons instituted programs to reduce their prison populations. As the research has raised awareness of and outrage over the incarceration problem, the Prison Industrial Complex has insidiously evolved into The Treatment Industrial Complex. Essentially, they rebranded their programs from incarceration to treatment and carried on business as usual. Their incentives are still upside down. They make money by keeping people in their programs. They lose money if their facilities are not kept full. The Politico article, "Stop the Treatment Industrial Complex[144]", describes the problem in frightening terms.

The PIC lobbies for stiffer sentencing and maintaining criminal status for many otherwise victimless drug offenses. Money presently being spent on incarceration produces extraordinarily little benefit to society. Politicians must take immediate steps to reduce spending on incarceration and to use the money on programs that reduce poverty and in turn reduce crime and improve public safety.

Issue #13 – Our government is killing people in our name.

The Death Penalty – aka Capital Punishment: There is no nice way to say it. The death penalty is cold-blooded, premeditated taking of a person's life – sometimes called murder in the first degree. The people who are committing this murder are the citizens whose government carries out the penalty – you and me. The criminal being penalized (murdered, or as we euphemistically refer to it – executed) was convicted of committing an egregious offense, typically in some deranged state of mind. We the citizens, on the other hand, are hopefully not in a deranged state. We have deliberately, with malice-aforethought, decided to kill someone. The trial process is

---

144. https://www.politico.com/agenda/story/2016/03/stop-the-treatment-industrial-complex-000061

flawed and sometimes convicts, condemns, and kills innocent people[145].

> *As of January 2020, the Innocence Project has documented* "
> *over 375 DNA exonerations in the United States.*
> *Twenty-one of these exonerees had previously been sentenced*
> *to death. The vast majority (97%) of these people were*
> *wrongfully convicted of committing sexual assault and/or*
> *murder."*

The United Nations Office of the High Commissioner on Human Rights reports[146]:

> *If you are poor, the chances of being sentenced to death are* "
> *immensely higher than if you are rich. There could be no*
> *greater indictment of the death penalty than the fact that in*
> *practice it is really a penalty reserved for people from lower*
> *socio-economic groups."*

People are not executed for being poor but being poor statistically increases their risk. What makes this situation even more tragic is

---

145. https://innocenceproject.org/

146. https://www.ohchr.org/en/press-releases/2017/10/death-penalty-disproportionately-affects-poor-un-rights-experts-warn#_853ae90f0351324bd73ea615e6487517__4c761f170e016836ff84498202b99827__853ae90f0351324bd73ea615e6487517_text_43ec3e5dee6e706af7766fffea512721__0bcef9c45bd8a48eda1b26eb0c61c869_25E2_0bcef9c45bd8a48eda1b26eb0c61c869_2580_0bcef9c45bd8a48eda1b26eb0c61c869_259CIf_0bcef9c45bd8a48eda1b26eb0c61c869_2520you_0bcef9c45bd8a48eda1b26eb0c61c869_2520are_0bcef9c45bd8a48eda1b26eb0c61c869_2520poor_0bcef9c45bd8a48eda1b26eb0c61c869_252C_0bcef9c45bd8a48eda1b26eb0c61c869_2520the_c0cb5f0fcf239ab3d9c1fcd31fff1efc_from_0bcef9c45bd8a48eda1b26eb0c61c869_2520lower_0bcef9c45bd8a48eda1b26eb0c61c869_2520socio_0bcef9c45bd8a48eda1b26eb0c61c869_252Deconomic_0bcef9c45bd8a48eda1b26eb0c61c869_2520groups

that the death penalty does not work. Go to the Amnesty International website and click on "Death Penalty Facts."

"Know the Facts About Capital Punishment[147]

Capital punishment does not work. There is a wealth of mounting evidence that proves this fact.

The death penalty, both in the U.S. and around the world, is discriminatory and is used disproportionately against the poor, minorities, and members of racial, ethnic, and religious communities. Since humans are fallible, the risk of executing the innocent can never be eliminated.

Furthermore, the astronomical costs associated with putting a person on death row – including criminal investigations, lengthy trials and appeals – are leading many states to re-evaluate and re-consider having this flawed and unjust system on the books."

There are so many things wrong with this situation. We need to do away with the death penalty.

Issue #14 –The vast majority of the voters want more effective gun regulations, but the politicians won't even discuss it.

Gun safety is not some mysterious problem with no known solution. On the contrary, we know exactly what the problem is and how to fix it. So, why haven't we done it? Because the rules of our democracy allow a minority of the elected officials to have veto power over

---

147. *https://www.amnestyusa.org/issues/death-penalty/death-penalty-facts/*

the legislation, and the gun lobby owns enough senators to block meaningful gun safety legislation.

It keeps happening! A deranged teenager with an assault weapon killed seventeen innocent teens at the Marjory Stoneman Douglas High School in Parkland Florida, and another nut killed ten and wounded ten at San Antonio High School in Texas. It took legal intervention to block the plans for untraceable 3D-printed guns from being disseminated on the open Internet. However, no laws have been changed to prevent gun manufacturers from continuing to make money selling dangerous military-grade guns. Lost in the outrage over the children are the additional 96 people killed and 190 wounded by guns every day in America. Our elected officials immediately consoled everyone with their 'thoughts and prayers'. No action – just thoughts and prayers.

After many mass murders, the evidence is clear. Thoughts and prayers do not stop bullets. The NRA pays our elected officials to placate us and ignore our pleas to fix the problem. The citizens elected the politicians, but corporate big-money supporters own them. A survivor student from Douglas High School had a truly clear message for us, *!We're children" You're the adults, so do something!"*

The following post showed up on my friend's FB page 1/24/18 (just 24 days into the new year)

Warning! – The following is unedited and contains profanities. If you are more offended by the profanities than the violence – wake up!

This is Bailey Holt. Yesterday (1/23/2018), she went to high school for a normal day and was gunned down. Look at her.... GOD DAMMIT LOOK AT HER! Her name was Bailey Holt.

Stare at this fucking picture of a perfectly innocent, perfectly great 15-year-old who was doing everything right and was murdered for no reason...when you are done, when you can't take any more, reply to this post and tell me that there is nothing that we can do to stop the gun violence in our country. Please tell me. Because this enrages me. This could be your daughter. Your sister.

A 15-year-old, white male (and yes most mass shootings are done by white males) killed 2 and wounded 19 yesterday.

There have been 11 school shootings in 2018. Fucking 11 shootings at a school in 23 days. That is way beyond unacceptable. That is a national crisis. The assholes in Washington are playing political games over a stupid fucking budget and our babies are being murdered. This is an outrage. Look at that picture!! Her name was Bailey Holt.

There have been 11 school shootings in 2018. Fucking 11 shootings at a school in 23 days.

"In January, more than 1,170 people were killed by guns. Nearly double that number were wounded, according to data collected by the Gun Violence Archive and provided to HuffPost on Tuesday. While not a perfect comparison, almost 20 years ago, it took two weeks before the New York Times went to print without a story on the Columbine High School massacre on page one.

Once rare, mass shootings have become commonplace[148], accepted as part of contemporary American life. They do not inspire protests, or command wall-to-wall media coverage."

Update: According to Forbes magazine[149], as of early April 2023, we have had more that 200 mass shootings

If you are hung up on whether the number 11 is accurate, wake up! One shooting used to draw national attention for weeks, then days. Now, we have had eleven school shootings in twenty-three days and the mainstream media barely mentions it. How did we allow ourselves to become so accepting of this situation? Read:

• The NY Times article titled, "School Shooting in Kentucky Was Nation's 11th of Year[150]. It Was Jan. 23." Or read,

---

148. https://www.huffingtonpost.com/entry/public-outrage-mass-shootings_us_5a70dbf6e4b0a6aa487424be?ncid=inblnkushpmg00000009

149. https://www.forbes.com/sites/brianbushard/2023/04/10/over-200-killed-in-us-mass-shootings-so-far-this-year-a-decade-long-high/?sh=4274432bf0e7

150. https://www.nytimes.com/2018/01/23/us/kentucky-school-shooting.html

- "Columbine Shocked the Nation. Now, Mass Shootings Are Less Surprising[151]."

People do not typically shoot people just because they own a gun. They shoot people because they are angry and frustrated with their situation and feel a need to punish someone. However, if they couldn't get a gun so easily, then the shooting might not have happened. Granted, there are other ways to kill people, but guns make it way too easy.

America leads the world in firearm ownership. Should we have the right to keep and bear arms? What does this question mean? Which arms do we have the right to keep and bear? This debate has been going on for decades, and cogent arguments exist on both sides. However, I think it is within reason to assume that high volume ammunition clips, automatic weapons, and 'cop-killer' bullets should be included in that debate.

Some people believe that they need a gun to protect themselves and others. Not so! A Scientific American article proves the point.

"More Guns Do Not Stop More Crimes, Evidence Shows.

More firearms do not keep people safe, hard numbers show. Why do so many Americans believe the opposite?[152]"

"Most of this research—and there have been several dozen peer-reviewed studies—punctures the idea that guns stop

---

151. httpoi//www.nytimes.com/2017/11/10/us/columbine-texas-mass-shooting.html?action=click&contentCollection=U.S.&module=RelatedCoverage®ion=EndOfArticle&pgtype=article

152. *https://www.scientificamerican.com/article/more-guns-do-not-stop-more-crimes-evidence-shows/*

violence. In a 2015 study using data from the FBI and the Centers for Disease Control and Prevention, for example, researchers at Boston Children's Hospital and Harvard University reported that firearm assaults were 6.8 times more common in the states with the most guns versus those with the least. Also in 2015, a combined analysis of 15 different studies found that people who had access to firearms at home were nearly twice as likely to be murdered as people who did not. [...]

More than 30 peer-reviewed studies, focusing on individuals as well as populations, have been published that confirm what Kellermann's studies suggested: that guns are associated with an increased risk for violence and homicide. "There is really uniform data to support the statement that access to firearms is associated with an increased risk of firearm-related death and injury," Wintemute concludes. Gun advocates argue the causes are reversed: surges in violent crime led people to buy guns, and weapons do not create the surge. But if that were true, gun purchases would increase in tandem with all kinds of violence. In reality, they do not."

This is one of the most comprehensive and compelling articles I found on the topic of gun violence. If you are interested in this topic, take time to read it.

Consider this proposal. Require every gun owner to buy insurance for owning a gun. The insurance companies would do an actuarial study to measure the risk and determine what it would cost. Most people would not be able to afford the insurance. If someone can't afford car insurance, they can't drive a car. Same for gun ownership! If you can't afford the insurance, you can't own the gun. It's not a practical solution, but it makes us think a bit differently about the risk.

Next, we need to examine who the victims of gun violence are. Occasionally, there is an outrageous event like the massacre at Sandy Hook Elementary School in Newtown, Connecticut. A gunman with an automatic rifle and a high-capacity ammo clip killed over 20 first graders and their teachers. However, it is important to note that mass murders are only a small portion of the violent gun deaths. Carnage is a daily event all over the country. Murder is the leading cause of death for young black men. As with the drug and incarceration problem, the most vulnerable citizens, and therefore the most at-risk members of society, are poor, young, minority males in major cities.

Guns do not examine the race, the social class, or ethnic group before they fire the bullet. It's the people behind the gun that evaluate who to shoot to kill. The issue of the matter is, the one who bears arms can be mentally incompetent to handle and understand the effects and impact of owning one. Back in the civil rights era, there were police officers who racially killed unarmed black men and women based on skin and hatred. They were mentally incompetent to handle the ownership and responsibility of possessing a gun and the position to protect the lives of others. Mass shooter Dylan Roof killed nine African Americans. His lawyers emphasized that he lacked the "mental capacity" due to his mental illness. In most states, no assessment is taken into consideration when obtaining a gun. The evaluation that is assessed is if you have the proper finances to obtain the firearms.

The same analysis goes for African American males who ferociously kill their peers because of gang affiliations, jealousy, money, and envy. Their mental incompetence initiates from the lack of love in the household, street politics, and education; but the underlying cause comes from poverty, environmental, and mental illness.

The firearms industry is making huge profits selling guns in this country. Ironically, tighter gun laws and tighter narcotics laws, result in more people being incarcerated for longer periods, and another predatory industry makes more money. When we listen to zealots debating this issue from either side, we seldom hear about the corporate financial profits being made at the expense of a generation of inner-city youth.

Most Americans, including NRA members, believe in the right to bear arms and support some reasonable regulations regarding background checks and closing some glaring loopholes in the existing rules. According to a CNN poll after the Orlando Pulse Nightclub shooting killed 49 people in July 2016, public support for background checks[153] and other related measures debated in the senate was over 90%. If we listen to the politicians, one side tells us the other side wants to get rid of the Second Amendment and the other side claims the NRA is in charge. Let's start the conversation from where we agree, not out on the fringes. At a point where over 90% of the American people supported more effective gun control legislation, Congress could not get a majority to vote for it. They didn't even bring a bill to the floor for a vote because they did not want to be on record for voting for or against it. The few extremists (generously paid by the gun lobby) called the shots over the majority. Politicians need to pay for this disregard of the will of the people.

"'The Time Is Now.' This New Coalition of Celebrities and Activists Just Pledged to Take on the NRA – (04-22-2018)

---

153. http://www.cnn.com/2016/06/20/politics/cnn-gun-poll/

> *A new coalition of celebrities and activists[154], including actor Alyssa Milano and Parkland student[155] David Hogg, announced plans Friday to take on the National Rifle Association and elected officials who accept money from the powerful gun advocacy group.*

> *In an open letter to NRA Executive Vice President Wayne LaPierre, which was first obtained by TIME, the more than 100 members of the newly formed NoRA Initiative — short for No Rifle Association — pledge to reduce the NRA's influence in American politics through a series of voter registration drives, nationwide art campaigns, demonstrations, and boycotts.*

> *"Your time signing checks in our blood is up," the letter says. "We're coming for your money. We're coming for your puppets. And we're going to win."*

Massachusetts has The Toughest Gun Law In America[156]. Read the article to see what they are doing and how it is working.

This discussion is not a battle over the right to bear arms. That is only the red herring used to deflect our attention from the gun manufacturers profit motives. If we take the 'right to bear arms' out of the discussion and focus instead on the 'need to bear arms', then the evidence plays a more important role.

How bad is the problem? According to the FBI website, the United States has averaged over 16,000 violent deaths per year in the years

154. https://www.hollywoodreporter.com/news/general-news/alyssa-milano-alec-baldwin-amy-schumer-launch-anti-nra-campaign-1104304/

155. http://time.com/collection/most-influential-people-2018/5217568/parkland-students/

156. https://www.huffingtonpost.com/entry/toughest-gun-law-america_us_5aeb27a9e4b041fd2d23d3f7

since the invasion of Iraq by the US led coalition forces. On the other hand, between March of 2003 and March of 2008, the following is an accounting of the casualties in Iraq.

- Coalition forces   4,415

- Iraqi Military   8,387

- Iraqi Civilians   42,455

- Total   55,257

If we count from March 2003 to March 2008, that is five years. At 16,000 murders per year, the total number of murders in the US was about 80,000. The point is not to trivialize the sacrifice of the people who have died in Iraq. The point is that the country is not more outraged at the number of violent deaths in the US. Of those 16,000 murders per year, the perpetrators used guns to commit over 12,000 of them.

The arms manufacturing companies heavily subsidize the NRA and similar groups to feed us patriotic-sounding arguments in defense of the right to bear arms. The NRA is one of the most effective lobbying groups in the country. Many rational and responsible gun owners are also NRA members. Unfortunately, the leadership appears to be disconnected from its membership and closely held by the arms manufacturers. They portray themselves as speaking for gun owners, but their real bosses are the arms manufacturers. If politicians funded a project to propose the most effective possible set of laws and regulations for reducing gun violence in the US, it would result in some highly informative discussions and research – resulting in some much better-informed votes on the issue.

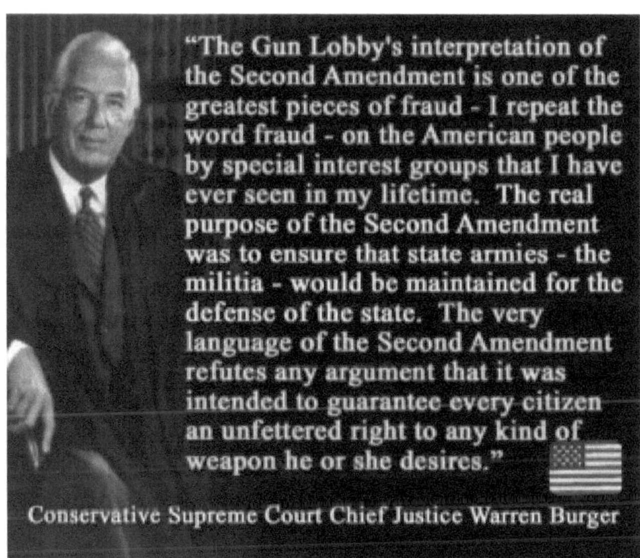

Conservative Supreme Court Chief Justice Warren Burger

The "right to bear arms" debate is beyond absurd! Let's begin with the constitutional issue. The law does not allow people to carry bazookas, automatic weapons, or other military armament. Sane, rational people have agreed upon that for years. As for a well-regulated militia, four bubbas in a club-cab Ford 150 with AR-15s do not equal a militia.

The right to bear arms is not intended to allow citizens to protect themselves from their government. The government has a full-fledged military, with planes, bombs, tanks, and ships. Good luck with that! Taking up arms against the government is treason.

Owning a gun for self-defense must be for protection from other armed citizens. Except for a few very isolated incidents, that very seldom happens. The availability of guns is far more likely to get an innocent person killed than to protect one.

If we want to know how bad the problem is or what works to fix it, sorry. The Center for Disease Control (CDC) cannot do the research because the NRA got legislation passed forbidding the CDC from funding research that might result in gun controls. The <u>Dickey Amendment</u>[157] is a provision first inserted as a rider[158] into the 1996 federal government omnibus spending bill[159] which mandated that *"none of the funds made available for injury prevention and control at the Centers for Disease Control and Prevention[160] (CDC) may be used to advocate or promote gun control[161]."* Well, we don't really have to do the research; all we need to do is look at other countries that have solved this problem. Prior to the Orlando shootings, citizens with guns had killed more people in the US than terrorists. (The shooter in Orlando was not a member of ISIS and did not really have any jihadist reasons for his actions. He was just a nut with a gun!)

Automobiles used to kill many people, so we passed regulations requiring manufacturers to make them safer, we required people to be licensed to use them, owners must register them, and people must wear seat belts. Deaths from automobiles dropped dramatically. If we are injured in a car because of a manufacturer's defect, we can sue the carmaker. Not so with gun makers. The gun lobby got Congress to pass laws making manufacturers immune. Politicians continue to allow gun manufacturers to dictate zero tolerance for any form of

---

157. https://en.wikipedia.org/wiki/Dickey_Amendment

158. https://en.wikipedia.org/wiki/Rider_(legislation)

159. https://en.wikipedia.org/wiki/Omnibus_spending_bill

160. *https://en.wikipedia.org/wiki/Centers_for_Disease_Control_and_Prevention*

161. *https://en.wikipedia.org/wiki/Gun_control*

gun control. Don't talk about the 'good guy with a gun'. It's BS! We have too many guys with too many guns.

If we heard that some country had killed over 16,000 American citizens last year, we might rightly assume that we had launched a counter-attack and wiped out the menace, but we would be wrong. The 16,000 victims were killed by their fellow citizens, living right in their communities. There is no military or even criminal justice solution to that problem. The only way to reduce that number effectively is to eliminate the root cause – hopelessness, typically combined with poverty. A person who has a reasonably safe and secure life is much less likely to commit a violent crime than a person living in poverty and hopelessness and forced to commit a crime just to survive. There are around 16,238 murders per year in the United States: this total averages out to around 44 murders per day. (Suicides are not included in this total.) "United States has ranked globally in the top 11[162] for violent crime murder rate since 2001." We spend billions on our military to defend us from attack. Perhaps we need to redirect their attention. We have fewer than 30 deaths per year classified as foreign attacks. However, we have over 16,000 deaths and countless violent attacks from our fellow citizens every year.

"The Police Executive Research Forum brought together police chiefs from across the country and asked their opinions as to developing crime issues, thus the list below reflects the perceptions of law enforcement leadership.

Top 10 Factors Identified as Contributing to Violent Crime.

1. *Gangs 82 %*
2. *Juveniles / youth crime 80 %*
3. *Economy / poverty / unemployment 74 %*

---

162. http://www.nationmaster.com/country-info/stats/Crime/Violent-crime/Murder-rate

4. *Impulsive violence / disrespect issues 74 %*
5. *Release of offenders from correctional institutions 69 %*
6. *Drugs-Cocaine 67 %*
7. *Poor parenting 63 %*
8. *Increased availability of guns 55 %*
9. *Reduced cooperation from witnesses / victims 37 %*
10. *Educational system-increasing dropout rates 36 %"*[163]

I see the list differently. I see it as a list of the symptoms of a larger and more critical problem – hopelessness. All the issues on the list are problematic, and we address all of them to some degree within this book. There is one item on the list that we have the strongest objection to. Item #3 on the list (Economy / poverty / unemployment) does not belong within the list. It belongs with hopelessness as a cause of the rest of the issues. Start by asking, "Why?" Why do people join gangs? Why do juveniles commit crime? Why do people turn to drugs? Why do we have seemingly impulsive violence and disrespect? Take a moment to contemplate each of these questions. When we did the exercise, we always ended up with poverty and hopelessness as some part of the answer for every question. We realize the solution is sounding redundant, but I warned you; fixing poverty is a critical part of the solution to most of America's problems.

"On Tuesday (5/24/2022), the Federal Bureau of Investigation released a report titled "Active Shooter Incidents in the United States in 2021[164]*," which logged sixty-one mass shootings last year. The deadliest of these was at a supermarket in Boulder, Colorado, where ten people were killed, a death toll that was matched ten days ago, at a supermarket in Buffalo, New York, and then exceeded,*

---

163. *https://www.crimeinamerica.net/top-10-factors-contributing-to-violent-crime/*

164. *https://www.fbi.gov/file-repository/active-shooter-incidents-in-the-us-2021-052422.pdf/view*

at Robb Elementary School, in Uvalde, Texas, where an eighteen-year-old shot and killed nineteen children and two adults. Early reports indicate that he used a handgun and a rifle. Families who gathered at the local civic center, which was used as a reunification site, were asked for DNA swabs to assist investigators in identifying their loved ones. The shooting began around eleven-thirty in the morning; as darkness fell, many families were still waiting outside the civic center, without word of their children.

This is the second-deadliest K-12 school shooting in U.S. history, after the December, 2012, massacre at Sandy Hook Elementary School, in Newtown, Connecticut, where twenty children and six educators were killed. Eventually, Sandy Hook also came to be seen as the graveyard of the gun-control movement: in 2013, a new assault-weapons ban, and also a bill to require universal background checks for firearm sales, failed in the Senate. If an entire classroom of dead first-graders could not spur even remedial action in Congress on gun control, nothing would. And nothing has[165]."

Two gun safety bills (H.R. 8 and H.R. 1446) were passed by the House of Representatives in 2021, but were not even put on the Senate's calendar for debate and passage until after the massacre in Uvalde, Texas (05/25/2022). The bills have overwhelming public support (as high as 90% for HR 8), but because of the gun lobby's influence, nothing is expected to pass! If our elected officials cannot be relied upon to do what the vast majority of their constituents want, democracy is not working.

---

165. *https://www.newyorker.com/news/daily-comment/seeing-america-again-in-the-texas-elementary-school-shooting*

Australian comedian Jim Jeffries provides a humorous[166] but well-grounded look at America's outrageous approach to gun control. Click the link in the footnote to get an ironic laugh over a very serious topic.

On January 26, 2018, the Virginia House of Delegates defeated in committee on a straight party-line vote a bill to ban bump stocks that enable legal guns to perform like illegal machine guns – just like the ones used in the Las Vegas massacre. The lame excuses given by the Republicans who defeated the proposed bill included:

> • *Del. Thomas C. Wright Jr., R-Lunenburg, said "... evil can move people to use anything to cause mayhem, "whether they use trucks, cars, box cutters, knives or whatever. Regardless of what laws we pass, until the evil in men's hearts change, it's not going to solve the problem," [*He blamed the problem on evil – not poverty. Wrong!*]

---

166. https://www.youtube.com/watch?v=0rR9IaXH1M0

● *Pro-gun representatives from the National Rifle Association and the Virginia Citizens Defense League argued that the state should not act because the federal government is already reviewing bump stocks.*

It is difficult to believe that responsible representatives can give such lame excuses for not doing the will of the people who elected them. It is easy to understand the NRA position. They have become a highly effective lobbying group for gun manufacturers. The NRA pays to elect and subsequently own their representatives. Meanwhile, the average citizen lives in fear of potentially being an innocent victim of the next nut with a gun in his hand and mayhem on his mind.

The following provides an interesting approach to the problem of gun violence[167].

"To get a gun in Japan, you first have to attend an all-day class and pass a written test which are only held once per month. You also must take and pass a shooting range class. Then head over to a hospital for a mental test and a drug test (Japan is unusual in that potential gun owners must affirmatively prove their mental fitness.), which you'll file with the police. Finally, pass a rigorous background check for any criminal record or association with a criminal or extremist groups, and you will be the proud owner of a shotgun or an air rifle. Just don't forget to provide police with documentation on the specific location of the gun in your home, as well as the ammo, both of which must be locked and stored separately. And remember to have the police inspect the gun once per year and to retake the class and exam every three years.

---

167. http://www.bbc.com/news/magazine-38365729

*Japan had 11 gun deaths in 2008, the US had 12,000. …
Any other shitty arguments?"*

There is a consistent and unacceptable congressional response to these mass shootings.

- December 23, 2015 – Fourteen people were shot and killed at a disability center in California.

  o Typical politician's response, "We need to fix our mental illness laws."

  ▪ Result – Nothing was done.

- June 12, 2016 – Forty-nine people were shot and killed at a nightclub in Florida

  o Typical politician's response, "It's horrifying to see so many innocent lives cut short by such cowardice."

  ▪ Result – Nothing was done.

- October 3, 2017 – Fifty-eight people were shot and killed at a concert in Las Vegas.

  o Typical politician's response, "Right now we're focused on passing our budget."

  ▪ Result – Nothing was done.

- November 6, 2017 – Twenty-six people were shot and killed at a church in Texas.

  o Typical politician's response, "The right thing to do at a time like this is to pray."

▪ Result – Nothing was done.

● February 15, 2018 – Seventeen people were shot and killed at a high school in Florida.

o Typical politician's response, "Right now, we need to take a breath."

▪ Result – Nothing was done.

The behavioral response pattern is completely predictable and totally unacceptable. In addition to threatening our individual physical safety, the apparent acceptance of violently killing people lowers people's fear of criminal justice response to the shootings and makes violence an option for people pursuing insurrectionist attacks on our democracy.

The statements and data about mass shootings were all accurate when we wrote them over the past few years, but recent events require us to update the carnage report. The following article from the <u>May 8th edition of *The Hill*</u>[168] captures the situation.

> *"Seven shootings over the weekend, including a massacre at a Dallas-area outlet mall, brought the total number of mass shootings in the U.S. this year over 200, according to the nonprofit Gun Violence Archive[169] (GVA).*
>
> *This year, according to GVA's tracker, there have been 202 incidents in which four or more people — other than the attacker — were shot.*

---

168. https://thehill.com/blogs/blog-briefing-room/3993604-u-s-passes-200-mass-shootings-this-year-nonprofit/

169. *https://www.gunviolencearchive.org/*

In the past two years, the U.S. crossed 200 mass shootings[170] in mid-May and, in 2020 and 2019, didn't reach 200 until mid-to-late June. Between 2016 and 2018, the country passed 200 mass shootings in late July.

The GVA tracker logged three shooting incidents Saturday, including the incident at Allen Premium Outlets[171] in Texas, where a gunman killed eight people and injured seven others before being fatally shot by police. One person was killed in a mass shooting in California and another in Ohio, and several others were injured in both states that same day.

Another four mass shooting incidents were recorded Sunday, killing five people total and injuring a dozen others in California, Missouri, New Jersey and Maryland.

The Texas shooting Saturday was the second-deadliest shooting this year, after the shooting in Monterey Park, Calif.,[172] where 11 people were killed. President Biden[173] has decried the recent spate of shootings[174] and urged Congress to act on gun control.

Last year, the GVA tracker recorded 647 total mass shootings in the U.S., for a total of 20,200 "willful, malicious or accidental" gun-related deaths and nearly 40,000 injuries."

---

170. *https://twitter.com/GunDeaths/status/1655302689058869249?s=20*

171. *https://thehill.com/homenews/state-watch/3992995-officials-identify-suspect-in-texas-mall-mass-shooting/*

172. *https://thehill.com/homenews/3825529-police-identify-deceased-72-year-old-suspect-in-monterey-park-mass-shooting/*

173. *https://thehill.com/people/joe-biden/*

174. *https://thehill.com/homenews/administration/3953759-outrageous-and-unacceptable-biden-slams-gop-for-standing-with-nra-in-wake-of-alabama-kentucky-gun-violence/*

For more information, read the April 10, 2023 Forbes magazine article titled: "Over 200 Killed In U.S. Mass Shootings So Far This Year—A Decade-Long High[175]"

To sum it up concisely, the problem is horrific and getting worse, while our elected leaders continue their partisan bickering over solutions - assuming they talk about the issue at all.

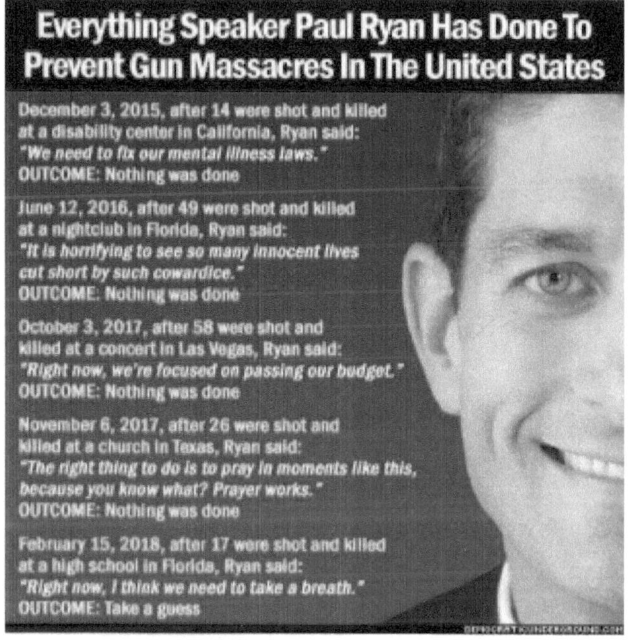

Let's get rid of assault rifles. Confiscating assault weapons is a non-starter but consider this. No more assault weapons can be sold. People who own an assault weapon can keep it, but they cannot sell

---

175. https://www.forbes.com/sites/brianbushard/2023/04/10/over-200-killed-in-us-mass-shootings-so-far-this-year-a-decade-long-high/?sh=4274432bf0e7

it or give it away. When they die, its ownership passes to the state (possibly for some compensation). Assault weapons are not part of a person's estate and cannot be inherited. After a few years, this simple process will remove all assault weapons from legal private ownership.

Continuing to examine safety and security, Post-Traumatic Stress Disorder (PTSD) does not just afflict the Military. Read Laura Hillenbrand's book, <u>The Unbroken</u>, about Olympic Runner Louie Lamperini, whom the Japanese shot down, captured, and tortured during WWII. It is a remarkable story of courage and determination for the first two-thirds of the book. The last third details the psychological impact of his inhumane experiences. There are many parallels with the situation in America today. While the torture may not be as brutal or as intense as that of a POW, people living in some neighborhoods in America are under an unending constant threat to their safety and success.

First, let us acknowledge that we have many military veterans who have returned from fighting with a heavy psychological load. If we need evidence of this burden, consider that an average of 22 veterans a day commit suicide. If that many commit suicide, we can only imagine how many more are so stressed that they consider it. However, they are not the only citizens suffering from PTSD. We also need to look at civilians living in poverty in urban neighborhoods. Let's consider the litany of traumatic stresses they may face. Lack of a job leads to:

- Homelessness

- Hunger/starvation/lack of proper nutrition

- Inability to provide for the family.

- Criminal behavior (both as the victim and the criminal)

- Anger at the "System"

- Anger with "The Man"

- Constant sense of physical danger from:

  - Drive-by shootings
  - Gang territorial fights
  - Drug-dealers' turf wars

- Driving while Black

- Etc.

The risks and associated stresses may be different from what our military faces, but unlike military dangers that end when they leave the war zone, these people live in the war zone – so there is no relief in sight. Given these conditions, it becomes easier to understand why large crowds of protesters assemble to voice their dissatisfaction with their environment.

PTSD can manifest itself in many ways. The deep psychological trauma from constant or intense stress can cause the victim to behave in seemingly irrational ways. Irrational implies there is no apparent reason for the person's actions. In the mind of the suicidal vet or the persecuted black youth, there are logic paths we may never imagine. The reasons may not be rational using our standards, but the youth involved have experienced a major standards reset.

As a society, we must stop sending our troops off to fight wars we cannot win. On the home front, we must get serious about putting people to work at jobs that pay a living wage. All this talk about gun control, thoughts and prayers, love, interracial harmony, and understanding will not fix the problems. If we really want to make neighborhoods safe, put people to work. People cannot hang out on a street-corner if they are at work. More to the point, they will not want to be hanging out on the street corner, because that is where the losers hang. Given a choice, most people will choose peace and prosperity over crime and violence. Let's make sure they get to make that choice. If our elected officials had half the courage and determination that Louie Lamperini had, they would fix this problem immediately!

The US could eliminate most crime in the country if we eliminated poverty. Money spent on eliminating poverty produces many benefits to society. Incarceration produces almost none!

Gun Safety, PTSD, homeless veterans, and Plantation Prisons are all illustrative of a democracy in need of reform. Tribal partisan politics are preventing meaningful debates and actions to solve problems.

Issue #15 - The opioid epidemic is not a healthcare issue. It's a public safety menace that must be fought and destroyed.

Once again, Poverty is a major contributing factor in a national problem that politicians are unable or unwilling to address. A Robert Wood Johnson Foundation report cites job uncertainty and personal finances among the major causes of suicide in middle-aged Americans. As I look at the opioid epidemic, I cannot help wondering if many of the deaths associated with that issue are a form of unintended suicide. Poverty leads its victims to depression and persistent poverty leads them on to suicidal thoughts. Opioids relieve depression, but in large doses it is lethal – deliberately or coincidentally.

"Opioid addiction is often described as an "equal opportunity" problem that can afflict people from all races and walks of life, but while true enough, this obscures the fact that the opioid crisis has particularly affected some of the poorest regions of the country, such as Appalachia, and that people living in poverty are especially at risk for addiction and its consequences like overdose or spread of HIV. The Centers for Disease Control and Prevention (CDC) considers people on Medicaid and other people with low-income to be at high risk for prescription drug overdose[176]."

The CBS News report that Drug overdoses killed more Americans[177] last year than soldiers died during the Vietnam War puts the opioid epidemic in perspective.

"The latest numbers from the Centers for Disease Control and Prevention show that 64,070 people died from drug overdoses in 2016. That's a 21 percent increase over the year before. Approximately three-fourths of all drug overdose deaths[178] are now caused by opioids[179] — a class of drugs that

---

176. *https://archives.drugabuse.gov/about-nida/noras-blog/2017/10/addressing-opioid-crisis-means-confronting-socioeconomic-disparities*

177. https://www.cbsnews.com/news/opioids-drug-overdose-killed-more-americans-last-year-than-the-vietnam-war/

178. *https://www.cbsnews.com/news/overdoses-are-leading-cause-of-death-americans-under-50/*

179. *https://www.cbsnews.com/news/ex-dea-agent-opioid-crisis-fueled-by-drug-industry-and-congress/*

includes prescription painkillers[180] as well as heroin[181] and potent synthetic versions like fentanyl[182].

A new report from Police Executive Research Forum (PERF), an independent research organization that focuses on "critical issues in policing," puts those numbers into context.

According to the report, more Americans died from drug overdoses in 2016 than the number of American lives lost in the entirety of the Vietnam War, which totaled 58,200.

<u>Ex-DEA agent: Opioid crisis fueled by drug industry and Congress[183]</u>

The group says it is focusing its efforts on the opioid epidemic because "despite the groundbreaking work that police and other agencies are doing, the epidemic is continuing to worsen. Rannazzisi ran the DEA's Office of Diversion Control, the division that regulates and investigates the pharmaceutical industry. Now in a joint investigation by 60 Minutes and The Washington Post, Rannazzisi tells the inside story of how, he says, the opioid crisis was allowed to spread – aided by Congress, lobbyists, and a drug distribution industry that shipped, almost unchecked, hundreds of millions of pills to rogue pharmacies and pain clinics providing the rocket fuel for a crisis that, over the last two decades, has claimed 200,000 lives."

---

180. *https://www.cbsnews.com/news/opioids-prescription-painkiller-safety-addiction-risk/*

181. *https://www.cbsnews.com/news/heroin-use-in-u-s-reaches-alarming-20-year-high/*

182. *https://www.cbsnews.com/news/fentanyl-what-you-need-to-know-about-deadly-opioid/*

183. *https://www.cbsnews.com/news/ex-dea-agent-opioid-crisis-fueled-by-drug-industry-and-congress/*

The 10/17/2017 report also showed that the year's 64,070 drug fatalities outnumbered:

- *The 35,092 motor vehicle deaths in 2015.*

- *AIDS-related deaths in the worst year of the AIDS crisis, when 50,628 people died in 1995.*

- *The peak year for homicides in the U.S., when 24,703 people were murdered in 1991.*

- *Suicides[184], which have been rising in the U.S. for nearly 30 years and totaled 44,193 in 2015.*

The data also shows that overdoses of synthetic drugs[185], such as fentanyl[186] — that is 50 to 100 times stronger than the painkiller morphine — are driving the sharp increases in opioid overdose deaths.

The CDC identified 15,466 deaths from heroin overdoses in 2016, while 20,145 deaths were caused by fentanyl or other synthetic opioids."

The Newsweek article titled, "HOW TO CURE AMERICA'S OPIOID EPIDEMIC[187]" makes an important point.

"Unlike many other chronic diseases, addiction is entirely preventable. Too few are talking about or spending time on stopping the problem before it starts. We must save every life we can, but to focus exclusively on treatment and recovery

---

184. https://www.cbsnews.com/news/us-suicide-rates-climb-higher/

185. https://www.cbsnews.com/feature/synthetic-drug-surge/

186. https://www.cbsnews.com/news/fentanyl-what-you-need-to-know-about-deadly-opioid/

187. http://www.newsweek.com/how-cure-americas-opioid-epidemic-630346

at the expense of prevention is like building prosthetic limb stores on shark-infested beachfronts. We need to warn people not to swim in those waters and we need to kill the predatory sharks."

BBC News provided a frightening comparison[188] that highlights the seriousness and magnitude of the situation.

"Opioid crisis linked to two-year drop in US life expectancy.

US life expectancy fell last year for a second year running for the first time in more than half a century, reportedly driven by the worsening opioid crisis.

Life expectancy in 2016 fell 0.1 years to 78.6, according to the National Center for Health Statistics.

It was the first consecutive drop since 1962-63. The last two-year decline before that was in the 1920s.

The previous fall in overall US life expectancy was a one-year drop in 1993, at the height of the Aids epidemic."

On average, there are 121 suicides per day in the US. White males accounted for seven of ten suicides in 2015. Twice as many women attempt suicide as men, but four times as many men die by suicide as women. The reason for the seemingly illogical difference is in the means. Women typically use poison and many of them are rescued. Men use firearms, and no rescue is possible.

Why are 70% of suicides white males? "These are being called "deaths of despair." Harvard public policy professor Robert D. Putnam[189], told the BBC,

---

188. http://www.bbc.com/news/world-us-canada-42452733

"This is part of the larger emerging pattern of evidence of the links between poverty, hopelessness, and health." Veterans are often one of the largest segments within this group. According to a 2014 Veterans Affairs (VA) report, 20 commit suicide each day; 65% of them are age 50 or older."

As always, when trying to understand why something that is happening is counterintuitive, ask yourself the question, "Cui bono?" (literally "to whom is it a benefit?") It always makes sense to follow the money. The cost of a single 500mg acetaminophen caplet is about $.01 (a penny). NSAIDS cost about $.04 per pill. Legal opioids cost about $1.50 per pill. It is easy to see where the profits for Big Pharma lie.

The NY Daily News[190] targets the cause of the problem.

"Perhaps we have to reexamine our view of addiction and, by extension, how we treat it and all of the misguided notions of the "war on drugs." As we are discovering more and more, addiction is less about the substances and more about a person's need for the substances. Thus, the opioid epidemic is less about opiates and more a byproduct of certain very complex social, cultural, biological, and economic factors that make a person vulnerable to the addictive escape of pain pills.

Unless we address those underlying causal factors, we will never make a meaningful dent to the opiate crisis because we will have effectively been looking at the telescope through the wrong end. We can analogize it with heart disease: Is

---

189. https://bigthink.com/politics-current-affairs/this-may-be-responsible-for-the-high-suicide-rate-among-white-american-men/

190. http://www.nydailynews.com/opinion/fix-opioid-epidemic-address-article-1.3404116

it the heart attack that kills someone or the lifestyle and hereditary predispositions that led to the heart attack that are the ultimate culprit?"

Poverty is the hidden assassin in the opioid epidemic. The Brookings Institute proposes[191] six steps to address the opioid epidemic.

"Un-burying the lead: Public health tools are the key to beating the opioid epidemic

Among the six recommended next steps to address these social determinants of the opioid crisis, Matthew suggests policymakers:

1. *Utilize Medicaid to reimburse supportive housing programs that co-locate employment, education, and health services.*
2. *Promote and finance two-generation, family-centered treatment, and support for children under foster and kinship care.*
3. *Involve community leaders in designing preventive systems for younger children to promote healthy behaviors, social skills, community opportunities, and pro-social involvement.*
4. *Broaden public health-based approaches to rebuild workforce capacity among victims of past drug epidemics.*
5. *Extend the benefits of public health-based interventions to individuals who were burdened by criminal justice rather than public health approaches to the disease of addiction during America's earlier opioid crisis.*
6. *Strengthen supports for public housing providers to avoid*

---

191. https://www.brookings.edu/research/un-burying-the-lead-public-health-tools-are-the-key-to-beating-the-opioid-epidemic/?utm_campaign=Economic%2520Studies&utm_source=hs_email&utm_medium=email&utm_content=60319611

eviction when residents are amenable to treatment for opioid addiction."

Poverty and the prescribing of opioids for pain relief are the two major contributing factors to the opioid crisis – both of which can be corrected. Because people are suffering and dying from opioid abuse, we must continue to treat the symptoms in the near term. At the same time, we need to have our elected representatives begin immediately fixing the root causes.

We do need to focus on prevention. However, the Brookings article fails to address the underlying issue that will have the biggest impact on prevention. Nobody takes drugs to get somewhere. They take drugs to escape from where they are; and where they are is typically a close neighbor to hopelessness. Continuing to follow the trail of clues, they arrived in neighborhoods of hopelessness on a bus called poverty. The long-term solution to suicide and the opioid problem is to reduce poverty.

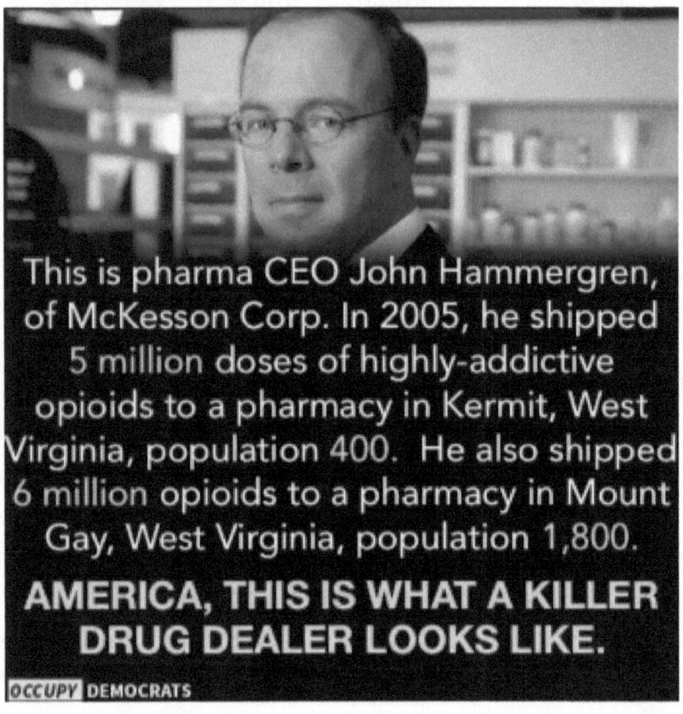

The opioid epidemic is a bit of an exception from the traditional DEA challenge. Many of the addicts started out simply trying to manage physical pain caused by an injury. Normally happy and healthy people suffer some form of pain-inducing injury, and their doctor prescribes pain medication. WHAM! Wow! That feels good. I want to feel like that some more. Okay, maybe I should stop. Ouch. Stopping hurts. And just like that, an addict is born.

There is another option. According to a report from the National Safety Council,

> *"Opioids have been used for thousands of years in the treatment of pain and mental illness. Essentially everyone believes that opioids are powerful pain relievers. However,*

recent studies have shown that taking acetaminophen and ibuprofen together is actually more effective in treating pain. [...] Since the development of acetaminophen, medical professionals have had the choice of three different classes of medications when treating pain. Those decisions are usually made by considering the perceived effectiveness of each medicine and its side effects along with the physical status of the patient. For example, acetaminophen should not be taken by someone with advanced liver damage, Nonsteroidal Anti-Inflammatory Drugs[192] (NSAIDs) should not be given to an individual with advanced kidney disease or stomach ulcers, and opioids pose a potential risk to anyone with a personal or family history of addiction.

Although many have long... believed that opioids are the strongest pain medications and should be used for more severe pain, scientific literature does not support that belief. There are many other treatments that should be utilized for treating pain. Studies have shown NSAIDs are just as strong as opioids[193]." [NSAIDs include Aspirin, Ibuprofen, and Naproxen.]

We may wonder, given the alternatives and potential negative consequences, why do doctors still prescribe opioids. There is no acceptable explanation for that. For some people, managing chronic pain is a major issue; and for them, opioids may be a significant part of the solution. However, the majority of people who are prescribed opioids receive it to relieve pain caused by some physical trauma like surgery. Saving opioids as the pain reliever of last resort[194] seems like

---

192. *https://www.medicinenet.com/nonsteroidal_antiinflammatory_drugs/article.htm#what_are_nsaids_and_how_do_they_work*

193. *https://www.nsc.org/getmedia/8ecdc0e5-ae58-43e8-b98b-46c205e1c2b2/evidence-efficacy-pain-medications.pdf*

a reasonable first step in reducing the number of people introduced to opioids in the first place.

> *"The evidence for opioids treating chronic pain is very weak (despite their effectiveness for acute pain), while the evidence that opioids cause harm in the long term is very strong. And a recent study found that doctors can wean some chronic pain patients off opioids and actually improve their pain outcomes. More research is needed in this area, but the current evidence suggests that the risks of opioids might not be worth the gains, if there actually are any, for most chronic pain patients."*

Prosperity, Safety, and Security need to be the first priority of our elected officials. Here's the problem. They do not elect themselves. We, the citizens and voters must do our jobs better and elect statesmen who act in the best interest of the country, not petty partisan politicians who vote the party line.

---

194. https://www.vox.com/science-and-health/2017/11/9/16622922/opioids-ibuprofen-acetaminophen-acute-pain-study

Healthcare

Healthcare costs are a major contributor to poverty in America. The costs are too high, and the way we pay for them exacerbates America's poverty issues.

Issue #16 - America's healthcare system is failing most Americans.

America's healthcare system is frequently a major contributor to a person's poverty status. What does socioeconomic status have to do with a person's access to affordable healthcare? In every other developed country in the world, the answer is, "Nothing!" In the US, the answer is, "Everything!"

The poor in America cannot afford healthcare insurance. Surely, that cannot be true. The US provides everyone with police and fire protection, and we have the world's largest military protecting us. However, when it comes to healthcare, many of our low to middle-income families are on their own for routine healthcare. If they do not have healthcare insurance, they can go to the emergency room for critical care needs. Just stop for a moment and think about that. Poor people cannot afford healthcare insurance. That typically means they cannot afford to go to the doctor's office for annual wellness checkups or when a poor health symptom first occurs, and the treatment is minor and inexpensive. Instead, the system forces them to wait until the condition becomes intolerable, driving them to turn to the nearest trauma center or emergency room where it is vastly more expensive to get treatment.

One of the biggest causes of personal bankruptcy in the US is catastrophic medical bills. All too often, the resulting bankruptcy leads directly to poverty for that whole family. The looming risk of imminent poverty from some healthcare related event in the family places a psychological burden on the parents, and a subconscious resentment against those who do not have to worry about it. That resentment adds fuel to the fiery political/tribal disputes and racism issues we face.

In the debates over the Affordable Care Act, petty partisan politics, driven largely by the money from lobbyists representing the health insurance and pharmaceutical industries, prevailed over care and compassion. Providing affordable quality healthcare should not be a partisan issue. Regardless of which party constituents are in, they want quality affordable healthcare. This is yet another outrageous example of our democratically elected representatives not responding to the will of the people.

Given the huge financial risks, why would anyone not have healthcare insurance? Simply stated, because it costs too much. The average citizen cannot afford to be without insurance and cannot afford to buy it. Ouch! I believe that is called being between a rock and a hard place. For example:

> *Average premiums and deductibles nationwide[195] unsubsidized shoppers:*

> *● Premiums for individual coverage averaged $321 per month while premiums for family plans averaged $833 per month.*

---

195. *https://resources.ehealthinsurance.com/affordable-care-act/much-health-insurance-cost-without-subsidy*

- *The average annual deductible for individual plans was $4,358 and the average deductible for family plans was $7,983.*

For a low to middle income family, spending about $1,000 per month is not an option. The median US income is about $52,000 per year. That means that over 23% of their income would go to health insurance. If a person is in one of the successful groups with an average family income of around $250,000, the healthcare insurance drops to about 4%. Once again, the people at the lower end of the socioeconomic spectrum are the big losers, and their representatives ignore their cries for help.

Now let's consider an alternative. Everyone needs and deserves healthcare, but do they need healthcare insurance? Do we really need health insurance companies? According to a Forbes Magazine article titled, "Why Spend $900 Billion On Health Insurance?[196]"

> *"The health insurance industry operates on the spread between what it charges the consumer and what it allows providers to spend. Having said that, history shows that they have only taken risks when forced to do so but add considerable cost to the system in the process. Obamacare exacerbates that problem. The insurance companies are raising prices rapidly (Kaiser Family Foundation), but they are lowering payments to providers as quickly as they can. Hospitals and doctors are assuming more of the risk but have little control of the pricing. Despite claims to the contrary, the insurance policies that are being offered do not reward outcomes. Instead, the policies want to push patients to the low-price provider without concern to the actual patient care*

---

196. https://www.forbes.com/sites/michaelbell/2013/02/19/why-spend-900-billion-on-health-insurance/#b5b2ede27bf8

> *provided. Health insurers want to be paid no matter what coverage is offered and how well it works (kind of like mortgage brokers)."*

From what I can discern, health insurance companies are no more than big administrative organizations that collect money, spend a lot on marketing and claims processing and ultimately pay for delivery of approved services. The US projects spending about $3.2 trillion this year on healthcare. Some of that is paid for by the government (e.g., VA, Medicare, and Medicaid) and most of it flows through healthcare insurance providers. I cannot find a reliable source detailing how much flows through the private insurers, so for the sake of illustration, I have chosen to estimate half of it or $1.6T. If everybody was covered for everything, we would not need the insurance companies. We would still need to pay some organization to pay the providers for their services, but it would be far less than $320B. Heck, I'll do it for only 1% of that and save the country $316.8B per year. (And I would still make $3.2B!) If we centralized the management and structure of the system, we could improve incentives for wellness and create rewards for outcomes, not procedures. That would reduce the number of people forced into poverty by catastrophic medical bills and be a major improvement in personal security for every American.

Lobbyists for the healthcare insurance industry spend millions of dollars trying to convince us how bad healthcare is in other countries that have implemented some form of universal healthcare. Put simply, the worst of them is better than what we have. We need to thoroughly investigate the programs in other countries, learn from them, and implement a national program specifically designed to meet our conditions and needs.

Consider universal healthcare in Japan.

- 100% of Japanese people have health coverage, regardless of their income.

- They get to choose their own doctors and see them twice as often as we do.

- They have the world's longest life expectancy and second lowest infant mortality rate in the world.

- 95% of Japan's healthcare is non-profit.

- The Japanese government caps fees for medical services and pharmaceuticals.

We can have better healthcare at lower costs and eliminate the crushing burden for American citizens of worrying about a catastrophic medical event.

In 2017, more than 11.3% of Americans did not have healthcare insurance[197]. Back in 2009, as Congress negotiated to solve the problems associated with the cost and availability of healthcare, the Republicans in Congress had pledged not to let President Obama pass any meaningful legislation – on anything. There was a proposal for providing universal health care, a single-payer system with the government managing the payments. This type of system is in place in many developed countries around the world. Healthcare insurance and major pharmaceutical companies who did not want to lose any income fueled and funded the Republican obstruction to the program. The resulting compromise solution based upon former Republican Governor Mitt Romney's program in Massachusetts (a Republican solution that still met strong resistance from Republicans) was called the Affordable Care Act (ACA). The Act

197. https://www.cnbc.com/2017/04/11/the-number-of-americans-without-health-insurance-rose-in-first-quarter-2017.html

contained several provisions that have proven greatly beneficial and have created broad public support for the Act at the consumer level. Massachusetts Executive Office of Health and Human Services (EOHHS) lists the following ten benefits[198] from their program.

.10"Creates new protections to ensure your insurance plan covers you when you need it. Massachusetts already has strong insurance protections. The Affordable Care Act (ACA) enhances these protections by eliminating limits on the amount of benefits you can receive.

9. Expands coverage for young adults. Under the ACA, young adults are able to stay on their parents' coverage until age 26.

8. Strengthens the primary care system and supports community health centers. The ACA has already provided more than $130 million to community health centers in Massachusetts to strengthen their programs while expanding access to primary care for community members.

7. Reduces childhood obesity and tobacco use. The Department of Public Health is using ACA grants to improve emergency medical services for children, reduce childhood obesity and encourage tobacco cessation.

6. Rewards quality of care, rather than quantity. The ACA supports the goals of the Commonwealth's 2012 cost containment law by promoting the formation of Accountable Care Organizations that reward quality and efficiency of care rather than the quantity of care.

---

198. https://www.mass.gov/orgs/executive-office-of-health-and-human-services

5. Makes prescription drug coverage more affordable for seniors. *The ACA closes the "donut hole" in Medicare prescription drug coverage. Nearly 60,000 Massachusetts seniors saved an average of $667 each on prescription drugs in 2012 and will save more as the donut hole is closed completely.*

4. Covers preventive health services with no copay. *Thanks to the ACA, most health plans must now cover preventive services like shots, smoking cessation and cancer screenings at no cost to the consumer. This will help increase access to critical preventative care in the short term and save lives in the long run.*

3. Provides tax credits to small businesses and increased coverage for employees. *The ACA establishes tax credits for certain small employers to make it more affordable to cover their employees, which can be combined with additional wellness rebates through the Health Connector. Very low-income employees who cannot afford their employer's coverage will become newly eligible for MassHealth, without any penalty for employers.*

2. Provides billions in additional federal dollars for Massachusetts. *The ACA streamlines state health insurance programs while providing additional federal reimbursement for people already covered. The ACA also provides grants to help states protect taxpayers from excessive premiums.*

1. Ensures affordable coverage for more middle-income families. *The ACA extends health subsidies to those with incomes from 300% up to 400% of the federal poverty level* *(approximately $46,000 for an individual), making health insurance affordable for more low-and-middle-income families.*

Despite the resulting public support, the ACA continues to be the target of intense partisan political battles. When the American people elected President Obama, Senate Republican Leader Mitch McConnell publicly stated that the goal of his party was to block everything the President tried to do and limit him to one term. That declaration still reverberates in the halls of congress as issue after issue runs into partisan name-calling and a lack of substantive discussion or debate. The ACA is not perfect, but improving or replacing it makes sense, not eliminating it."

The ACA has several problems that make it not viable as it stands for a long-term solution, but it needs to be improved or replaced, not repealed. If we were to take a clean slate approach to designing a perfect healthcare system for the whole country, what would be the criteria or goals we should start with? A perfect healthcare plan would:

- Ensure every person in the country has access to quality healthcare. (Make healthcare a part of the security services everyone gets – just like military, FEMA, fire, and police protection.)

- Ensure the doctor and patient involved, not the government or private insurance companies, make the decisions about treatment.

- Place a major emphasis on prevention and wellness.

- Ensure fair and equitable pricing for drugs and procedures.

- Control costs – Ensure nobody faces financial ruin for medical cost reasons and the national budget does not take a major hit.

- Reward excellence. Devise a financial compensation system for medical professionals that rewards excellence and fiscal responsibility.

- Reduce administrative costs.

- Improve epidemiological data gathering and usage while maintaining individual privacy.

- Increase medical research funding.

- Manage and coordinate collaborative research efforts. (Reduce cutthroat competition for big drug payoffs in return for more collaborative efforts for earlier and better outcomes.)

- Differentiate necessary and elective services. Make the patients pay for most elective services. [Not sure about this one. What do you think?]

Americans spend far more than the citizens from other developed countries do for similar outcomes. That is why US Doctors Call For Universal Healthcare: "Abolish the Insurance Companies[199]"

---

199. https://www.occupy.com/article/us-doctors-call-universal-healthcare-abolish-insurance-companies#sthash.FObX9SUY.dpbs

The traditional function of health insurance companies is to share the risk and reduce uncertainty about the potentially harmful financial impact of a health issue – and to make a profit. As presently mandated by law, the insurance companies must spend 80% of all the money that they collect on healthcare costs and quality improvement programs[200]. That means the subscribers are paying the insurance provider about 20% of their premiums for administrative, marketing, and overhead costs. If the government caps insurance companies' share of revenue at 20% of what they collect, then the only way they can increase their profits is by raising the premiums. If they raise premiums to increase their 20% share, then that means they must spend more to use up the 80% share. That is not an incentive to bring down healthcare costs. It's an incentive to spend more. How does that affect the individuals? Many patients will not see any significant change in what they pay because they will get a subsidy or rebate to offset the increase. However, at the national level, it keeps the total cost to provide healthcare rising instead of falling.

During the debates over the ACA, there was much rhetoric about keeping the government out of making decisions about an individual's healthcare. At first glance, that seems like a reasonable idea. As usual, the Devil is in the details. The ACA was supposed to allow people to keep their previous doctors; however, the political discussion did not explain that instead of the government, the for-profit insurance companies would be making the decisions. Oops! The ACA tried to allow people to keep their previous doctors. However, if we have coverage by an insurance plan, we can only go to doctors in our network. Instead of the government, the insurance companies are making healthcare decisions for individuals regarding which doctors the patients can see and what treatments they get. If we remove the decision-making issue by providing healthcare to

---

200. https://www.healthcare.gov/health-care-law-protections/rate-review/

everyone with the government as the single payer, then decisions about which doctors and which treatments go back to the individuals and their doctors, and there is no more financial or medical uncertainty. In the larger view, there is no need for health insurance – just healthcare.

The next big, obvious flaw with the ACA is the size of the risk pool. For the system to work, everyone must be in the pool – high, middle, and low risk people. If everyone participates, then the money is available to cover everybody, while all the participants share the risk and cost equally. The ACA tried to build a sustainable model based on this principle, but it had a fatal flaw. If the distribution of enrollments skewed towards more high risk and fewer low risk subscribers, then the costs would also skew higher. To be a sustainable program, everyone must be in the pool. The best way to get everyone in the risk pool is with a single payer system. The ACA is not that.

Some people may wonder, why should the healthy young people pay the same amount for their minimal care as the older people who are heavier users. (Citizens would pay for healthcare as a part of federal taxes at a nearly universal rate.) The answer is that everyone pays a flat rate for life, so the extra money paid during the healthy younger years is available during the older more costly years – assuming Congress does not treat the money as a slush fund and rob it.

The only way the universal healthcare economics can work is to cover everyone and have everyone pay for the service. We have examples of this single universal service provider model already in place and serving the population very well. They include the military, police, and fire departments, highway departments, and FEMA. Healthcare is similar. An individual may be healthy for long periods, may experience occasional minor ailments, and on a rare occasion, have a major health problem. Just as everyone can drive on our roads and is eligible for FEMA assistance, everyone should be eligible for healthcare. Notice, I did not say health insurance.

From what I can see, if we go to a universal healthcare single-payer system, there will no longer be a need for healthcare insurance companies. With universal healthcare, everyone is in the pool, sharing the risk and getting the services they need. By providing preventive care, wellness, early diagnosis, and care for ailments, the cost can come down while health in general should improve. Although the politicians could not pass a single-payer system, nearly sixty percent of Americans want it as the solution[201] (including many Republicans). Big Pharma and the Healthcare Insurance providers through their lobbyists own our elected representatives and continue to prevent any consideration of a single-payer solution.

America has some of the absolutely best doctors and hospitals in the world. On the other hand, America has remote and economically depressed areas where access to quality healthcare is problematic. Unfortunately, America also has people living within fifty miles of an excellent hospital, staffed by outstanding doctors, who, for financial reasons, might as well be living in a remote community when it comes to accessing excellent healthcare. Universal healthcare will ensure that all Americans have equitable access to quality essential healthcare.

If national security is more than just being physically safe from foreign attack, then the definition should also include being safe from the catastrophic financial impact of a medical emergency and the provision of lifesaving healthcare. The following quote from an article titled, "18 Ridiculous Statistics about The HealthCare

---

201. https://www.washingtonpost.com/news/the-fix/wp/2016/05/16/most-americans-want-to-replace-obamacare-with-a-single-payer-system-including-a-lot-of-republicans/

Industry That Will Make You Tear Your Hair Out[202]" captures the situation very well.

> *"Today, virtually every single American is one really bad day from financial ruin. Did you know that medical bills are the number one reason for bankruptcy in the United States? Did you know that the vast majority of people that go bankrupt due to medical bills actually have health insurance?*
>
> *Meanwhile, there are a significant number of people becoming fabulously wealthy in this system. Our "health care industry" has turned large numbers of doctors, lawyers, health insurance company executives, and pharmaceutical company executives into multi-millionaires. The healthcare industry in the United States has been so corrupt and so greedy for so long that we do not even remember what a legitimate medical system looks like anymore.*
>
> *A recent study found that medical bills are the root cause behind more than 60 percent of all personal bankruptcies in the United States each year. The same study found that three-fourths of people that go bankrupt because of unpaid bills actually have insurance.*

From all I can see, healthcare insurance companies add major costs and do not add any value. Even if they could be made extremely efficient, they add no value. To quote management guru Peter Drucker, *"There is nothing quite so useless as doing with great efficiency something that should not be done at all."* I cannot think of any good reason for paying a lot for nothing. There are countless references

---

202. http://www.businessinsider.com/statistics-about-the-health-care-industry-2011-

2?op=1/#recent-study-found-that-medical-bills-are-the-root-cause-behind-more-than-60-

percent-of-all-personal-bankruptcies-in-the-united-states-each-year-1

discussing ways to control or regulate the healthcare insurance industry. Because I am recommending eliminating them altogether, I will not discuss any of those here.

That brings us to the public option. Under that model, the government would provide another insurance plan that would compete with the private healthcare insurance companies; the theory being that providing a public option as competition would bring the cost down, and it probably would. But, to what end; getting a better price for something that adds no value? Who needs that? If we replace healthcare insurance companies with universal healthcare, then there is no need for a public option. Everybody receives access to quality healthcare. They all share the cost in the same way that we all share the cost of other government services. Our elected officials must be held accountable for ensuring every citizen has access to affordable quality healthcare. Part of our challenge as citizens will be to work together to refine the system to enable our elected officials to serve the people who elected them, not those who pay for their re-election.

When it comes to women's health, we talk the talk, but do not walk the walk. As Americans, we love and revere mothers. They are the backbones of our families. We protect them in every way. Oops! I was doing pretty well up until that last statement. The good news is that infant mortality rates in the US have dropped to historic lows. The bad news is, according to a PBS report[203]:

> *"The United States has the highest rates of maternal mortality in the industrialized world. Women are twice as likely to die from complications of pregnancy or childbirth in the U.S. than in Canada or the United Kingdom. For*

---

203. https://www.hsph.harvard.edu/deans-office/2022/05/19/the-crisis-of-maternal-mortality/

women of color, especially, the risk is infuriatingly, heartbreakingly, unforgivably high."

The rate at which rural women die of pregnancy-related complications is 64% higher than the rate for women in large cities. Sadly, about 700 women die each year in the United States because of pregnancy or delivery complications – most of their deaths are preventable. In addition to the deaths, many mothers and newborns suffer permanent medical complications.

One major factor is that 54% of rural counties lack hospital obstetric services. Of the 83 rural hospitals that have closed since 2010, three-quarters of them were in states that did not take advantage of the Affordable Care Act (ACA) and accept Medicaid. Republican governors made the conscious and callous political decision to reject the ACA Medicaid funding. Further adding to the outrage, maternal mortality rates among black women are more than triple the rates among white women.

Providing rural maternity healthcare is never going to be profitable. As a country, we must decide that saving rural mothers' lives is worth whatever it costs. It may not mean opening hundreds of rural OBGYN and delivery clinics. It may be more cost-effective to develop a comprehensive medical trauma transport system that includes helicopters as needed. The first step is committing to saving mothers' and babies' lives. America must be among the best in the world in this area, not the worst.

Issue #17 - A woman's choice

Through a long and persistent process, a powerful minority of the voters manipulated the system into a situation where they were able to get the Supreme Court to overturn Roe v. Wade and enable states to pass and/or enforce restrictive anti-abortion laws. Several recent public opinion polls indicate a majority of voters support women's choice. That is not the way a democracy is intended to function.

Due to pressure from the anti-abortion zealots, there are very few facilities available in some areas where a woman can get a legal abortion. Wealthy women can afford to travel to a clinic. Poor women cannot. They have to go through government agencies like Medicaid to receive any governmental assistance; making it harder to receive coverage. Either they get an illegal (and sometimes unsafe) abortion, or they have the baby – and another baby is born into poverty. Abortion and poverty are intricately connected. According to an article published by the United States Conference of Catholic Bishops:

> **"Poverty and Abortion: A Vicious Cycle**
>
> *"My boyfriend Jimmy and I had been going from shelter to shelter just to stay warm as winter's chill coursed through us. I was with Jimmy and pregnant."*
>
> *– Anna**
>
> *"On several occasions we had to deal with homelessness.I can remember sleeping on a park bench and sleeping at bus stops... In 2009 I discovered I was pregnant with my daughter Mia. And prior to being pregnant with her I had been pregnant before. I had an abortion... So, this time around I wanted to do things the right way. I wanted to choose life."*
>
> *– Jacqueline**

Anna and Jacqueline describe a plight that is too common. If anything, surveys indicate that low-income women are more against abortion than other women. Yet economic realities pressure many to act against their convictions. This has been a disturbing reality for a long time and is getting worse.*

In a 2005 study, 73% of women undergoing an abortion said not being able to afford a baby now was a reason for the abortion. That number rose to 81% for women below the federal poverty line' (L. Finer et al. in Perspectives on Sexual and Reproductive Health, Sept. 2005, pp. 110-118 at 115.) *And while the abortion rate for American women declined by 8% between 2000 and 2008, among poor American women it increased by 18%."* (R. Jones and M. Kavanaugh, in Obstetrics & Gynecology, June 2011, pp. 1358-1366 at 1362)

Anti-abortion equates with pro-poverty[204].

"... if poorer women had the same access to contraception as more well-off women, it would cut the birth rate for single women living in poverty in half. Doing the same for abortion would also have a dramatic impact, reducing the birth rate from 72 births per 1,000 women to 49. Of course, the real solution would be to make both contraception and abortion accessible to lower-income women, which would probably result in their unintended birth rate coming close to what it is for higher-income women."

---

204. http://www.slate.com/blogs/xx_factor/2015/03/02/

poor_women_have_more_abortions_even_though_middle_class_women_abort_more.html

Abortion has become a poster child for demonstrating the disproportionate impact a single issue can have on politics. The Huffington Post article, "Why U.S. Politics Is Obsessed With Abortion[205]" describes the issue very well.

> *"For no issue in American life is more emotional, divisive and personal — and therefore easier to manipulate by cynical politicians[206] of all parties and ideological affiliations.*
>
> *This is even though — or rather because — most Americans don't view the issue as a priority to debate in this or any other election. It is an obsession at the edges of politics, but it is the passion of the edges that controls U.S. public life. [...]*
>
> *It's a perfect fundraising and theatrical opportunity for both parties, even though most voters will find the spectacle outrageous. [...]*
>
> *In other countries, legislatures are forums for debate and compromise. But in America, the power — as opposed to the theater — is in the courts. As a result, legislators are free to be irresponsibly extreme, knowing that in the end they won't, in fact, decide the final outcome.*
>
> *Abortion is a cause and symbol of the ruination of American politics. It was the first shot in a culture war that has turned the two-party system into a fractured mess."*

In 2022, the conservative Supreme Court overturned a 50-year-old ruling on abortion and threw the country into a partisan crisis.

---

205. https://www.huffingtonpost.com/entry/
     us-politics-abortion_us_565e66f1e4b072e9d1c40a72

206. *http://www.realclearpolitics.com/articles/2008/04/quarrelsome_nation_the_thirtee.html*

Within a month of the decision, a 10-year-old girl who was impregnated by her rapist was forced to endure public shaming and travel out of her home state to terminate the unwanted and undeserved pregnancy. State legislatures across the country are racing to pass unqualified, restrictive anti-abortion laws. Unqualified means there are no reasonable exception to the laws like the health of the mother, rape, and incest.

A slight majority of Americans describe themselves as pro-choice, but what does that mean? If we add in any qualifiers, such as 'in the first 20 weeks of pregnancy', the number shifts. "Survey after survey shows that most American voters don't rank abortion as a crucial issue. It isn't on most radar screens; climate change, income inequality, and education are." Despite this fact, Abortion continues to be a major litmus test in making many political decisions.

Does abortion really affect the way people vote? According to a Pew Research Center report titled, "The Complicated Politics of Abortion[207]":

> *"Far more opponents than supporters of legal abortion view this as a very important voting issue. Fully 73% of those who say that abortion should be illegal in all cases rate abortion as a very important voting issue; 55% of those who say abortion should be illegal in most cases also rate it as very important.*
>
> *By contrast, just a third of those who favor legal abortion in all cases, and just 22% who say it should be legal in most cases, rate abortion as very important to their vote. About four-in-ten voters in each group (44% legal in all cases, 42%*

---

207. http://www.people-press.org/2012/08/22/the-complicated-politics-of-abortion/

legal in most) say abortion will be not at all important in their decision about whom to vote for. [...]

Among opponents of legal abortion, large majorities of both women (64%) and men (59%) say the issue will be very important to their vote. But among supporters of legal abortion, more women than men say it will be very important (34% vs. 19%)."

Nationally, more than 63% of citizens favored leaving the Roe v. Wade decision as it was. Despite this majority level of support, proponents of overturning the decision are pushing for electing people who will approve appointments of justices who will vote to restrict access to abortion.

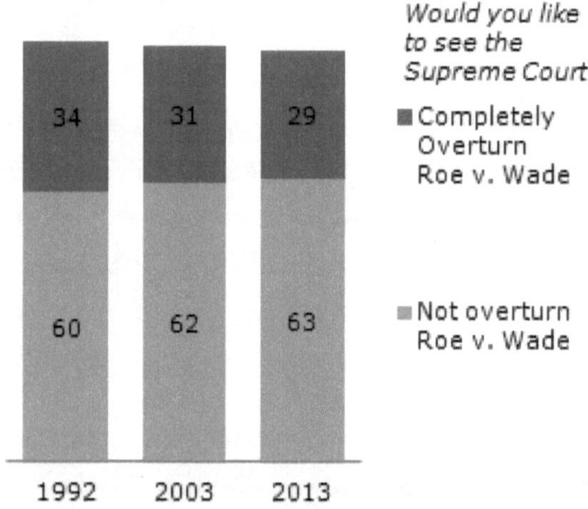

"Most Americans — Democrats and Republicans[208], men, and women, pro-choice and pro-life — all share a mistaken belief about abortion: that it's rare. Twenty-seven percent of Americans think fewer than 10 percent of women will have an abortion in their lifetime; 51 percent say it's fewer than 20 percent, a new Vox poll of 1,060 registered voters conducted by communications firm Perry/Undem shows. This turns out to be a significant underestimate. The best data available suggests that about 25 to 30 percent of American women will terminate a pregnancy at some point in their lives. [...]

Americans also overestimate the safety risks for women who have abortions, our poll shows. Most people think abortion is either "less safe" or "about as safe" for women as giving birth. But that's not true. Bearing a child causes more serious complications and deaths for mothers than abortion does.

Abortion is a common medical procedure. There are hundreds of thousands[209] more abortions each year in the US than either appendectomies or hysterectomies."

There is also an insidious element to the politics of abortion. People who are strongly pro-life may vote for a candidate based solely on that single issue, even though their candidate is likely to vote against their interests on a wide range of other issues.

At his Supreme Court confirmation hearing, Brett Kavanaugh was asked by Kamala Harris, "Can you think of any laws that give the government the power to make decisions about the male body?" He could not.

---

208. http://www.pewforum.org/2013/01/16/roe-v-wade-at-40/

209. https://www.vox.com/a/abortion-statistics-opinions-2016/poll

Emboldened by changes in the Supreme Court under the Trump administration, anti-abortion activists have launched a major campaign to make it nearly impossible[210] for women to get a safe, legal abortion.

2021 was a pivotal year for abortion laws in America - A half century of abortion *rights for American women faltered this year.*

"For half a century, American women have had the right to choose to end a pregnancy at any point before a fetus is viable outside the womb. If 2021 saw that freedom start to crumble, 2022 could see it more widely wiped away.

"I think this is the time," said an anti-abortion rights activist from Hattiesburg, Mississippi, who declined to share her name this fall while outside the state's only remaining abortion clinic in Jackson.

Mississippi, which has asked the Supreme Court to end constitutional protection for abortion, appears likely to at least win affirmation of its 15-week ban on the procedure—more than two months earlier than the current standard allows.

MORE: How unprecedented the Texas abortion law is in scope of history

Texas, which now forbids abortions after six weeks, has become the first state to effectively eliminate most procedures statewide since Roe v. Wade was decided in 1973. SB8, which has been in effect for nearly four months, has defied

---

210. https://abcnews.go.com/US/2021-pivotal-year-abortion-laws-america/story?id=81860784

repeated legal challenges with its novel enforcement mechanism that pits citizen against citizen."

Poverty is a critical component of the abortion issue. Zealots and fanatics are willing and working to subvert democracy to achieve their goals. Abortion is a volatile, partisan, divisive, and shifting issue that is contributing to the political infighting that threatens our democracy.

Issue #18 - We continue to incarcerate people for marijuana use.

Some people still think that people fighting for the legalization of medical marijuana are a bunch of stoners looking to get high. Not so. There are two major groups fighting against legalization.

1. Criminal Justice industries – Enforcing marijuana laws is a large and lucrative business[211]. *"On a national level, national criminal justice expenditures for enforcing marijuana laws are $7.6 billion per year with $3.7 billion being allocated to police, $853 million to the courts, and $3.1 billion to corrections".*
2. Pharmaceutical companies – Big Pharma would lose billions of dollars if marijuana was legalized for medical and recreational use.

The Brookings Institute produced a video that captures one family's determined story to improve their daughter's life using medical marijuana.

---

211. https://www.prisonpolicy.org/scans/jfa/marijuana_report.pdf

"The Life She Deserves[212]" profiles the difficult choices the Collins family faced and explores what many patients and families sacrifice to get medical relief. Whether it is for a child with epilepsy, a young woman battling breast cancer, an Iraq War veteran with PTSD, or an elderly woman with chronic arthritis, accessing medical cannabis often requires weighing steep costs against the benefits."

"The Brookings Institution[213] is proud to present "The Life She Deserves," a new documentary short film that is an intimate portrait of Jennifer Collins and her family's struggle to find a treatment to control her debilitating epilepsy and their fight to change medical marijuana laws."

Take twenty-one minutes and watch this video (linked in the footnote). If you have any doubts about the medical use of marijuana, this will answer your questions and, hopefully, activate you to support changing the laws.

---

212. *https://www.brookings.edu/the-life-she-deserves-medical-marijuana-in-the-united-states/*

213. *https://www.brookings.edu/blog/fixgov/2018/04/19/documentary-short-human-side-of-medical-cannabis-policy/?utm_campaign=Brookings%2520Brief&utm_source=hs_email&utm_medium=email&utm_content=62246644*

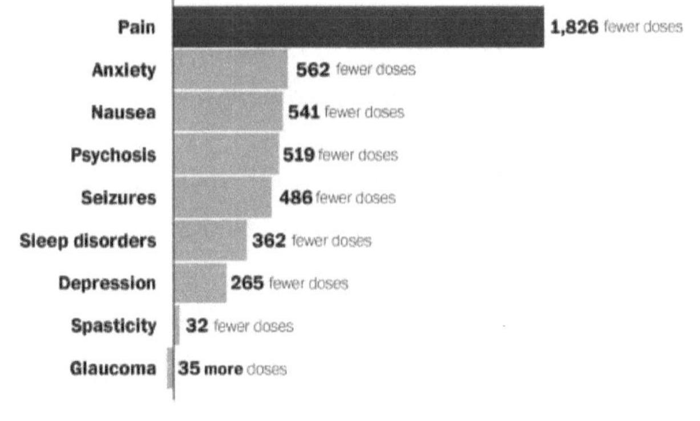

The quality of America's healthcare products, devices, and services is among the best in the world. Due to costs and other factors, large numbers of Americans do not have access to them. The government needs to do a better job of working with Big Pharma to encourage the development of new cures while also keeping costs down. Ironically, as I was writing this book, the Senate confirmed President Trump's nominee, Alex Azar, as the new Secretary of Health and Human Services. As the head of Eli Lily, Azar led the company to increase the price of Insulin from $21 to $255 a vial. Trump did NOT drain the swamp! He brought in his own alligators to run the swamp. Some general thoughts on the prescription drug issue in America include:

- Generics have the potential to greatly reduce the cost of drugs.

- The government must do a better job of regulating and inspecting the production of generic drugs.

• We need tighter specifications about how closely generics must match their branded equivalents.

• We need to reduce the cost of bringing generic drugs to market while also ensuring their quality.

• Brand-name drug makers can still make a profit even after the generic competition comes to market.

• We need a mechanism for managing the price of life-saving and chronic condition drugs so that people do not have to make life-or-death decisions about buying the drugs they need.

• Drug-makers are working aggressively to lock up international trade deals that allow them to control pricing of drugs globally. We must look closely at the Trans-Pacific Partnership (TPP) to ensure drug pricing does not go out of sight. Policy-makers need to address this TPP complication as a major part of the overall solution to controlling drug prices. Many of these trade deals originate as programs for third-world countries, but they eventually work their way into more global deals that end up affecting drug prices in the US.

• Having a single payer system would enable the payer to negotiate with the drug companies to get the best pricing.

• The Federal government must open its mind to the potential medical benefits of marijuana.

In this healthcare chapter, I have raised many questions and answered some of them. Each question raised has the potential to be a complete book on its own. My goal in mentioning them is to raise awareness of them and their impact on cost, because the cost of healthcare has a direct connection with poverty. The price of healthcare and life-saving drugs can drive a family into poverty, or if they are already poor, the drugs may be beyond their ability to pay. If we had universal healthcare, then the cost would not be crushing to the individual, and everyone would have access to the life-saving drugs they need. Universal control would also allow us to reduce the overall costs.

The International Federation of Health Plans publishes a list of prices for common drugs and services. The results paint a painfully clear picture – everything costs much more in the US. Things are out of control and our government is not taking any significant steps to fix the problem. To advocate for lower drug prices, we need to have a better understanding of what is driving the current pricing models.

Have you ever heard that "Black people" do not go to the doctor because they do not trust what the doctor has prescribed them nor the information provided? Despite long records of racism and unfair treatment that doctors have performed against black people since the early 1900's, black people have now started to gain some trust back into the doctors' hands. A study in 2020 by the Kaiser Family Foundation and The Undefeated[214], showed that *A majority of" African Americans have low levels of trust in the healthcare system, expressing much less confidence in doctors and hospitals than white "people* In this study it states that "only 6 of 10 Black adults said they trust doctors to do what is right most of the time compared with 8 of 10 white people." So what happens to the other 4 Black adults who have no trust at all in the healthcare system? They use marijuana as their everyday type of prescription to heal the body. For pain, nausea, anxiety, sleep disorders, for treating anorexia; even for

214. https://www.kff.org/racial-equity-and-health-policy/report/kff-the-undefeated-survey-on-race-and-health/

mental disorders like autism. Most people believe that it has to be a dire emergency for them to even consider engaging with medical hospitals.

Issue #19 – The pricing of prescription drugs resembles a protection racket.

Paying for prescription drugs (even just the co-payment) can be financially devastating for low-income families or individuals. The cost of prescription drugs in America is another example of unregulated capitalism allowing conditions that are good for the top 1%, but debilitating, if not destructive, to everybody else. Sovaldi is the drug that cures Hepatitis C. A 12-week regimen is required. In India, the cost is $4 per pill. In the US it costs $1,000 per pill. Our government does nothing to protect its citizens from this abuse. We can't allow big pharma lobbyists to own our politicians. Politicians have to represent their constituents.

The profiteering greed illustrated by the 1,066 % increase in the retail price of the EpiPen during the leadership of EpiPen CEO Heather Bresch created anger and resentment throughout the U.S., among those needing this critical emergency drug and beyond. Bresch was far from alone in her price gouging tactics. Read A Decade Marked By Outrage Over Drug Prices[215] for more examples of corporate greed leading to individual poverty.

Drug Companies' Primary Mission Has Shifted From Finding Cures To Making Money.

There are major problems with the cost of drugs. They include:

---

215. https://www.npr.org/sections/health-shots/2019/12/31/792617538/a-decade-marked-by-outrage-over-drug-prices

• Drug companies claim they need to charge high prices to cover their cost of research into new cures. As a simple statement, this is true. However, much of what they include in their 'research' category might better be labeled marketing, acquisitions, and operations.

• Government policies prevent the government from bargaining to get the best possible pricing as other countries do. (Lobbyists bought politicians who then provided this absurd benefit to the pharma companies.)

• The profit incentive often overrides the incentives to produce new cures.

• We need to reduce the cost/risk of basic pharmaceutical research.

• The patent exclusivity system allows drug companies to charge as much money as they want for life-saving drugs and the patient has virtually no alternative to paying the price – unless we consider pain and dying as viable alternatives.

• Gaming the patent exclusivity system keeps lower-priced generics off the market for years.

Sometime in the past, Big Pharma's research claim might have been partially true; but real basic research is a ridiculously small part of drug companies' budgets today, and what they call research has changed considerably. The industry average amount of their corporate budget spent on research, based on their own reporting is about 17%. A small part of this amount pays for people in white lab coats doing experiments – real, old-fashioned research.

If we accept that the cost of research drives up the cost of drugs, we still need an explanation for why Americans pay so much more than people in other countries do. Are Americans paying for the research while the rest of the world benefits? The answer is simple. Yes!

For several decades, the pharmaceutical industry was a miracle maker – continuously discovering new wonder drugs and devices for treating and curing a wide range of diseases and conditions. The prices for these cures and treatments were profitable for the drug companies and affordable for the consumer. Our tacit agreement as consumers was that we were willing to pay their prices in return for their continuing to bring us more miracles. Then, gradually, something changed. We have now reached the point where the drug companies' primary mission has shifted from finding cures to making money. The companies should be profitable, but not at the expense of reducing the investment in new cures. The CEOs admit that their goal is to make money for their investors. Moreover, the CEOs compensation is based on the profits, not the cures; and the compensation is very, very generous.

Individual patients have truly little bargaining power when buying prescription drugs, but that is not at all true of governments. Since many countries provide healthcare for their citizens, they have a tremendous advantage in purchasing drugs. These other governments find that pharmaceutical companies would rather lower prices significantly than simply not sell in that country. Therefore, other countries bargain with the pharmaceutical companies on behalf of their citizens. This bargaining significantly lowers the price of brand name medications in these countries.

The big exception is the US government. We are the single largest market for medications in the developed world. Therefore, our government is in the best possible position to bargain on our behalf.

Even though this strategy works for all the other governments, our government will not do it. Why? US law prohibits our government from taking any active role in negotiating the prices charged by pharmaceutical companies. That's right! Our elected representatives passed laws to prevent our government from bargaining for lower drug prices for us. That is the reason we pay more (much more) than anyone else in the world for drugs. Congress made that "bargain".

Many of the people most affected by rising drug prices are older patients on Medicare, who often live on modest incomes, are in poor health, and take four or more prescription drugs. One way to reduce drug costs for this population is to reverse the policy set by the 2003 Medicare Modernization Act, which created Medicare's prescription drug program. At Republican insistence, that law barred the federal government from negotiating with drug manufacturers. It relied on bargaining by private insurers that manage drug benefits for Medicare patients, like UnitedHealth, Aetna, and CVS Caremark, to wring discounts from the drug makers. That was not enough[216].Not mentioned in the article was the major role the lobbying efforts of big pharma played in the Republicans position. In 2015, pharma and healthcare spent over $250M on lobbying[217].

Look at this price disparity another way. Consider the following table comparing the price pharmacies in the U.S. pay[218] for some commonly prescribed medications to British Columbia's national insurance coverage[219] for the same medications.

---

216. http://www.nytimes.com/2015/09/21/opinion/use-medicares-muscle-to-lower-drug-prices.html?_r=0

217. https://www.opensecrets.org/lobby/indusclient.php?id=H04&year=a

218. https://medical.rossu.edu/about/blog/us-vs-canadian-healthcare

219. https://pcbl.hlth.gov.bc.ca/pharmacare/benefitslookup/

Medication and Dose	Price in the US	Price in Canada
Abilify 20 mg	$40.51 per pill	$4.33 per pill
Effient 10 mg	$12.59 per pill	$2.96 per pill
Humalog Insulin 100 units/ml	$12.47 per ml	$2.78 per ml
Pradaxa 150 mg	$5.64 per capsule	$1.78 per capsule
Spiriva 18 mcg	$10.98 per capsule	$2.34 per capsule
Xarelto 20 mg	$11.60 per pill	$3.06 per pill

Table 1: Comparison of brand name drug prices in the US and Canada.

The difference is even bigger than it looks. First, because the prices shown for Canada are in Canadian dollars, and second because the prices shown for the U.S. are the prices the pharmacies pay in the U.S. for these drugs. They mark them up when they sell them to consumers. Canadians have universal healthcare coverage, $750 to over $10,000 per year with no additional markup. Why the difference? Because even though pharmacies in other countries buy drugs from the same suppliers and pharmaceutical companies that our pharmacies use, they pay only a fraction of the price our pharmacies pay.

Humalog insulin, released 22 years ago, remains unchanged since its release, but its price has increased 200% during that time, from $21 a vial to $275. A one-year supply has gone from $750 to over $10,000 with no changes to the insulin.

The world's medical scientific community has made remarkable progress in the recent past, with the ability to work at the molecular and genetic code levels. America's universities and corporate research labs are among the best in the world – an advantage we could lose if we do not nurture and support them. We have to encourage basic research into all kinds of healthcare issues by reducing the risk and cost in the process. We need to start with the fundamentals – basic research – the high-risk/high-reward beginning step in the process.

How can we fix the problem? One way governments encourage basic research is through tax incentives. In today's financial world, quarterly profits are valued far more than long-term strategic research investments. To counter that, we need to provide tax incentives that reward long-term investments in basic research.

Research, by its very nature, is a risky business. It may require dozens or even hundreds of failed attempts before a single breakthrough. In the pharmaceutical industry, the process then runs into another potential barrier, clinical trials. Before the FDA approves a drug for sale for human use, it must successfully go through clinical trials. The trials can take years and cost millions of dollars.

To remain in business, let alone become profitable, a pharmaceutical company must regularly bring new drugs to market. Meanwhile, companies in other countries are making investments and developing new competing drugs with government backing. The challenge is to pick the right potential winners and invest in them to keep America's pharma companies competitive. What new model for the industry will result in investing in research for cures to the many health problems facing everyone? Centralizing the provision of medical and healthcare services (a National Health Program – NHP), would make it easier to coordinate and manage collaborative R&D efforts.

In the 1980s, major tech corporations had large internal research labs like IBM's Watson Labs, AT&T's Bell Labs, and Xerox's Palo Alto Research Center (PARC). Today, some of the best basic research is occurring at university research centers[220]. There are formal and informal interest-based networks and consortia working at all levels of the R&D continuum. It may be time to consider providing more incentives to encourage collaborative healthcare and pharmaceuticals basic research efforts.

In today's world, with international threats to America's pharma leadership, the FDA should consider establishing a National Drug Research Consortium (NDRC) to pursue basic pharmaceutical research – similar in mission and function to the MCC thirty-five years ago. It almost always helps to look back in history, find something that previously worked well, and adopt it or adapt it to

---

220. https://en.wikipedia.org/wiki/

Microelectronics_and_Computer_Technology_Corporation#History

the problem at hand. In 1982, America faced a threat to our world leadership in computers and microelectronics. Our response was to form a consortium of the major American hi-tech companies to collaboratively conduct basic research and share the results. Basic research resulted in the discovery of the transistor. Applied research identified things that could be done with them.

The multi company collaboration for basic research in computer technology was called the Microelectronics and Computer Consortium[221] (MCC), headed by retired Admiral Bobby Inman. Twelve companies, including DEC, Harris, Control Data, Sperry-Univac, RCA, NCR, Honeywell, National Semiconductor, Advanced Micro Devices, and Motorola, contributed money and personnel to get the effort underway. They located the new venture on the University of Texas campus in Austin, TX. The participating company representatives met regularly to identify topics of interest and direct the research. The consortium members funded the programs and placed their own employees on the research teams.

I was working in the Corporate Research division of Digital Equipment Corporation (DEC) at that time. We were one of the original participating companies in the program. One of my colleagues moved to Austin to serve as our liaison. Although the program received no direct federal dollars, the sponsoring companies received research tax credits for their support. The consortium members shared the results of all the projects. Their challenge and opportunity were to select potential gems and polish them into products. Everyone had access to the same research. The winning companies were the ones that made the best use of it. MCC produced countless products and several new companies. Declaring victory, the MCC program shut down in 2000. The R&D

---

221. https://en.wikipedia.org/wiki/

　　Microelectronics_and_Computer_Technology_Corporation#History

consortium model served our microelectronics industry very well. Let's do the same in medicine.

Because so many pharma companies are global organizations, it may not be practical to exclude them. In which case, we should still lead the effort and ensure we dedicate the best minds and resources to finding cures. America leads the world in the design and production of military equipment. We should also lead the way in the discovery and provision of healthcare/medical products. The worldwide market is enormous. Even with modest profits, the potential economic benefit would provide countless jobs and at the same time provide a better life to billions of people. Far more Americans die each year from diseases and severe medical conditions than from military attacks. Despite this fact, our government spends orders of magnitude more money on military defense R&D than on healthcare research.

When a company invents a new drug, it applies for a patent on it. If granted, the company has twenty years of exclusivity for the product. Sometimes the clinical trials and other steps in the process required to bring the drug to market can take up to eight years and cost billions of dollars. That leaves the company only about twelve years of exclusivity to make a profit before generic manufacturers can enter the market with a lower-priced competitive version of the drug. To retain their exclusivity advantage, the original inventor typically begins a series of legal maneuvers to extend the patent. It is good for the drug company, but not good for the consumer.

Generic Drugs: Don't Ask, Just Tell[222] Generic drugs have the potential to save the healthcare system billions of dollars. However, a few issues interfere with achieving these savings.

---

222. http://www.health.harvard.edu/blog/generic-drugs-dont-ask-just-tell-201301075766

• **Consumer Doubt:** Some consumers are not convinced that generics are as good as the brand name versions of the drug. In some cases, this doubt is a valid concern.

• **Doctors' Doubt:** Some doctors share the consumer doubt and are reluctant to prescribe generics.

• **Patient Preference:** Some doctors are willing to prescribe generics, but the patient insists on the brand name.

Eric G. Campbell, Ph.D., professor of medicine at Harvard Medical School and Massachusetts General Hospital led a study that determined prescribing a brand-name drug when a generic is available "is a huge source of wasteful spending that can be prevented".

A generic is a carefully regulated approximation of its brand-name equivalent. A knock-off is a counterfeit with no guarantee of its quality or effectiveness. If you are walking down the street and a street vendor offers to sell you a Gucci bag or a Rolex watch for a low price, chances are the product is a knock-off. It typically looks just like the product it pretends to be – right down to the label. However, the quality of the materials and the artisanship are typically inferior to the original brand product. That is quite different from a generic drug product. The generic product has its own brand name and a statement that it is a generic for a more expensive brand name drug.

Generics typically look different from the brand name, have different inactive ingredients and other differences not related to the drug's efficacy. The biggest difference is the cost, and your portion of the cost. Generic medications typically cost about 80% to 85% less than the same brand-name drug. The question that remains is, "How do generic drugs compare to the brand name equivalent for their effectiveness?" The FDA requires all generic drugs to:

- Contain the same active ingredients as the brand-name drug.

- Be identical in strength, dosage form, and administration.

- Work the same way in the body (be bioequivalent).

- Meet the same standards for identity, strength, purity, and quality.

- Be made by the same rules the FDA has set for the brand-name drug.

Are Generics Really the Same as Branded Drugs? [223] Drug manufacturers tell consumers that generics are just like their name-brand counterparts. Some medical professionals are starting to say that is not the case. Despite the list of FDA requirements, generic drugs are not as equivalent as the manufacturers portray them. When a drug manufacturer decides to produce a generic version of an existing brand name, it has access to the patent information plus the list of ingredients on the packaging. That's it! The company must reverse engineer the product and then figure out what process the original manufacturer used to combine the ingredients to meet the bioequivalence requirements. The result is more an approximation than a duplicate.

This point is where the regulations enter the picture. The required degree of bioequivalence is 20% below or 25% above the original. That is a 45% range or margin of allowable difference. Next, we need to consider the additional inactive ingredients; also known as

---

223. http://fortune.com/2013/01/10/are-generics-really-the-same-as-branded-drugs/

excipients. These can be different or of lower quality. These two factors can have a major impact on bioavailability – a measure of the actual amount of the drug available to be absorbed into the bloodstream. For drugs, whose dosage is critical, this variability can be problematic.

What is Delaying Some Generic Drugs from Coming to Market?[224]Reminder, in today's world, drug companies are in the business of making profits. Providing cures is a secondary goal. Big drug companies use a couple of strategies to delay the availability of a generic version of a profitable drug. The first is **"Pay for Delay"**. When the patent is expiring on a profitable drug, generic drug manufacturers can begin the process of bringing a generic version to market. To prevent it, the original manufacturer offers the generic manufacturer compensation[225] not to produce it.

> *In a recent case, "Cephalon offered payments and business deals worth around $300 million to four generic companies in exchange for a guarantee that no generic would come to market for another six years. The Federal Trade Commission's recent $1.2 billion settlement over the drug Provigil has brought so-called "pay for delay" deals for generic drugs back into the spotlight. Opponents say these deals delay generic medications getting to market, costing consumers billions. ... We've done a study of this back in 2010 where we really studied this very carefully and we estimated that it cost American consumers about $3.5 billion a year. ... Provigil did go generic in 2012, and the price fell from more than $700 to $16 for a three-month supply."*

---

224. http://www.pbs.org/newshour/bb/arent-generic-drugs-coming-market-sooner/

225. http://www.newsweek.com/ftc-reaches-record-12-billion-settlement-over-alertness-drug-provigil-336763

The second delaying strategy is **"Evergreening"**. In this case, when a profitable drug is approaching the end of its patent protection period, the drug company brings to market a 'new' drug for the same problem and raises the price of the older drug – forcing people to shift to the newer drug. There may be some discomfort in switching to the new drug, so when the generic of the old drug comes to market, people are reluctant to switch back. In fact, it is exceedingly rare for patients to switch back when the generic version of the old drug becomes available.

Big Pharma is relentless and insidious in its ongoing attempts to control the patent and pricing of drugs. One current illustration of this activity is their efforts to insert language in the Trans-Pacific Partnership (TPP) agreement that would make it more difficult to oppose or reject evergreening patents such as the one involved in the Novartis case. The language they want to insert would bar 'pre-grant opposition' that currently allows opposition to patent applications. Without this protection, the patent would have to be challenged in court – potentially tying up the ability to produce generic versions for years.

Big Pharma also plays a role in denying patients' access to the medical benefits of marijuana. Studies have shown why pharma is fighting it. When patients have access to Marijuana, they buy fewer pain, anti-seizure, and antidepressant medications. Jeff Sessions is in the pocket of big pharma as he fights to prevent legalization.

> *"One striking chart shows why pharma companies are fighting legal marijuana*[226]

---

226. *https://www.washingtonpost.com/news/wonk/wp/2016/07/13/one-striking-chart-shows-why-pharma-companies-are-fighting-legal-marijuana/?utm_term=.c1f8704edc5f*

They found that, in the 17 states with a medical-marijuana law in place by 2013, prescriptions for painkillers and other classes of drugs fell sharply compared with states that did not have a medical-marijuana law. The drops were quite significant: In medical-marijuana states, the average doctor prescribed 265 fewer doses of antidepressants each year, 486 fewer doses of seizure medication, 541 fewer anti-nausea doses and 562 fewer doses of anti-anxiety medication.

As with most things, if there are vast sums of money involved, then politics and greed will appear. Healthcare is a major portion of everyone's budget, and it is all connected to poverty and our current democratic process's inability to improve it.

Military – Defense

What does our military have to do with Poverty in the US?

• A disproportionate percentage of homeless people in the US are military veterans.

• We spend more on military defense than the next eight countries combined and most of them are our allies, leaving too little to spend on infrastructure and public service jobs.

• Our military is referred to as 'volunteers'. Many of the volunteers enlist to escape poverty.

• There is only so much money in the budget. Military spending has better lobbyists than infrastructure and public service sectors.

"A more serious challenge for the democracy that is America, however, is the ethical one. Today, more than 300 million Americans lay claim to rights, liberties, and security that not a single one of them is obligated to protect and defend. Apparently, only 1 percent of the population feels that obligation. That 1 percent is bleeding and dying for the other 99 percent.

Further, that 1 percent does not come primarily or even secondarily from the families of the Ivy Leagues, of Wall Street, of corporate leadership, from the Congress, or from affluent America; it comes from less well-to-do areas: West Virginia, Maine, Pennsylvania, Oklahoma, Arkansas, Mississippi, Alabama, and elsewhere. For example, the

Army now gets more soldiers from the state of Alabama, population 4.8 million, than it gets from New York, Chicago, and Los Angeles combined, aggregate metropolitan population more than 25 million. Similarly, 40 percent of the Army comes from seven states of the Old South[227]."

These numbers are driven more by poverty than patriotism.

Our economic and military strengths are the foundations of our way of life. All Americans support a strong and flexible military, ready to protect and defend us anytime and anywhere we need them. It is a proven fact that we have the biggest, best trained, and best-equipped military in the world. We have some 'hawks and doves' at the fringes who want more or less, but for the most part, Americans are proud of our military and want to support it. Having said that, surveys also show that most Americans want to reduce defense spending[228]. We want a world leading military, but not a wasteful one. In fact, many of us are angry about the lack of support of the military personnel and veterans while we spend money on unneeded hardware systems and expensive military contractors. We spend too much on Defense and not enough on relieving poverty and promoting Safety and Security.

---

227. *https://www.theamericanconservative.com/articles/the-deep-unfairness-of-americas-all-volunteer-force/*

228. http://time.com/4253842/defense-spending-obama-congress-poll-voters/

Issue #20 - We are spending too much on military defense.

It's "Cui bono?" time again. Regardless of what we are investigating, the first question that we need to ask is, "Cui bono?", or "Who benefits?" In this case, we are considering the issue of the greatly disproportionate amount of money the US spends on its military when compared with the rest of the world. General Dwight D. Eisenhower was one of America's greatest military leaders and the person chosen to be the Commanding Officer of the Supreme Headquarters of the Allied Powers in Europe (SHAPE) towards the end of WWII. He was later President of the US. At the conclusion of his Presidency, he had some chillingly prescient words for us all. Please read the following advice from President Eisenhower closely[229]. He accurately captures what used to be great about America and warns of the possibility of the conditions that we see today. In case you are not familiar with his background, President Eisenhower graduated from West Point. His background makes his cautionary tale even more powerful. He paints a picture of the dangers of not maintaining a social, political, and economic balance[230].

"Eisenhower's Farewell Address to the Nation

January 17, 1961

...

My own relations with Congress, which began on a remote and tenuous basis when, long ago, a member of the Senate appointed me to West Point, have since ranged to the intimate during the war and immediate post-war period, and finally to the mutually interdependent during these past eight years.

In this final relationship, the Congress and the Administration have, on most vital issues, cooperated well, to serve the nation well rather than mere partisanship, and so have assured that the business of the nation should go forward. So, my official relationship with Congress ends in a feeling on my part, of gratitude that we have been able to do so much together.

We now stand ten years past the midpoint of a century that has witnessed four major wars among great nations. Three of these involved our own country. Despite these holocausts,

---

229. http://mcadams.posc.mu.edu/ike.htm

230. https://www.youtube.com/watch?v=8yO6NSBBRtY

America is today the strongest, the most influential and most productive nation in the world. Understandably proud of this pre-eminence, we yet realize that America's leadership and prestige depend, not merely upon our unmatched material progress, riches, and military strength, but on how we use our power in the interests of world peace and human betterment.

Throughout America's adventure in free government, our basic purposes have been to keep the peace; to foster progress in human achievement, and to enhance liberty, dignity, and integrity among people and among nations. To strive for less would be unworthy of a free and religious people. Any failure traceable to arrogance, or our lack of comprehension or readiness to sacrifice would inflict upon us grievous hurt both at home and abroad.

Progress toward these noble goals is persistently threatened by the conflict now engulfing the world. It commands our whole attention, absorbs our very beings. We face a hostile ideology—global in scope, atheistic in character, ruthless in purpose, and insidious in method. Unhappily, the danger it poses promises to be of indefinite duration. To meet it successfully, there is a call for, not so much the emotional and transitory sacrifices of crisis, but rather those which enable us to carry forward steadily, surely, and without complaint the burdens of a prolonged and complex struggle—with liberty at stake. Only thus shall we remain, despite every provocation, on our charted course toward permanent peace and human betterment.

Crises there will continue to be. In meeting them, whether foreign or domestic, great, or small, there is a recurring temptation to feel that some spectacular and costly action could become the miraculous solution to all current difficulties. A huge increase in newer elements of our defense; development of unrealistic programs to cure every ill in agriculture; a dramatic expansion in basic and applied research—these and many other possibilities, each possibly promising in itself, may be suggested as the only way to the road we wish to travel.

But each proposal must be weighed in the light of a broader consideration: the need to maintain balance in and among national programs – balance between the private and the public economy, balance between cost and hoped for advantage – balance between the clearly necessary and the comfortably desirable; balance between our essential requirements as a nation and the duties imposed by the nation upon the individual; balance between actions of the moment and the national welfare of the future. Good judgment seeks balance and progress; lack of it eventually finds imbalance and frustration.

The record of many decades stands as proof that our people and their government have, in the main, understood these truths and have responded to them well, in the face of stress and threat. But threats, new in kind or degree, constantly arise. I will mention two only.

A vital element in keeping the peace is our military establishment. Our arms must be mighty, ready for instant action, so that no potential aggressor may be tempted to risk his own destruction.

Our military organization today bears little relation to that known by any of my predecessors in peacetime, or indeed by the fighting men of World War II or Korea.

Until the latest of our world conflicts, the United States had no armaments industry. American makers of plowshares could, with time and as required, make swords as well. But now we can no longer risk emergency improvisation of national defense; we have been compelled to create a permanent armaments industry of vast proportions. Added to this, three and a half million men and women are directly engaged in the defense establishment. We annually spend on military security more than the net income of all United States corporations.

This conjunction of an immense military establishment and a large arms industry is new in the American experience. The total influence—economic, political, even spiritual—is felt in every city, every State house, every office of the Federal government. We recognize the imperative need for this development. Yet we must not fail to comprehend its grave implications. Our toil, resources, and livelihood are all involved; so is the very structure of our society.

In the councils of government, we must guard against the acquisition of unwarranted influence, whether sought or unsought, by the military-industrial complex. The potential for the disastrous rise of misplaced power exists and will persist.

We must never let the weight of this combination endanger our liberties or democratic processes. We should take nothing for granted. Only an alert and knowledgeable citizenry can compel the proper meshing of the huge industrial and military machinery of defense with our peaceful methods and goals, so that security and liberty may prosper together."

Was Eisenhower right? According to CNBC[231]: Military Spending in 2014 was the biggest chunk of our tax dollar – 42.2 cents of every income-tax dollar go to fund the military. Over half of it, or 28.7 cents, go to pay for the current war and military, 10 cents go to interest payments on past and present military debt and 3.5 cents is allocated for Veterans' benefits. If we use the numbers from Whitehouse.gov, the percentage of our tax dollars is still nearly 40. We must spend more on personal security by spending less on national security. Far more people in the US are dying from poverty and its results than from hostile foreign attacks or Terrorism.

America has established a worldwide reputation for defending freedom and human rights, but domestically the rights are eroding. Many of our finest young people have given their lives or been seriously wounded or maimed in our military defense forces. However, the people making the sacrifices today come from a smaller and smaller demographic group – mostly people who have extremely limited options for other careers. We call it a 'volunteer' military, but most people with other realistic options are not volunteering. For the most part, the children of people with power or money are not going into the military. Once again, poverty plays a role. People living in poverty and unable to get a job 'volunteer' to serve in the military. It is not really volunteering if the only other option is poverty. At the same time, the battles we ask our military personnel to fight are more for political and economic reasons than military

---

231. https://www.cnbc.com/2008/09/29/How-Your-Tax-Dollars-Are-Spent.html?slide=2

defense. I am concerned that America's military has evolved from the Department of Defense to the Department of Offense.

During a presidential debate, Donald Trump said he would bomb the shit out of ISIS. Bomb ISIS – Great idea – Right? How has it worked so far? ISIS is not a place. In fact, ISIS is not even in one place. ISIS is an idea. So how do we bomb an idea? The only way to attack an idea is with a better idea. So, what is the better idea? The United States is based upon it. We have laws and people who enforce those laws. ISIS is not a military problem, it's a criminal one. Acts of terror are against the law – not just US law, but international law. Let's use these outrageous criminal acts (the bombings in Europe and the Middle East) to instigate a truly international police force tasked with solving the crimes, capturing, and punishing the perpetrators, not just for this incident, but for all crimes.

One of the things that nurtures an idea like ISIS is the seemingly indiscriminate bombing and occupying of Muslim countries. This statement is not speculation. It's a fact! Despite that, during the presidential debates then candidate Trump called for the US to respond with, "A bombing campaign that's not afraid to kill innocent civilians." Isn't that what terrorists do? We must be better than the terrorists are if we want to win the battle of ideas.

We have the United Nations, NATO, the European Union, and Interpol as a start. Let's improve and empower them to deal with these criminals.

News Flash – Al Qaeda Has Won! Did our mighty military protect us from an attack on September 11, 2001? Not at all. Who won that day? Who has been winning since that day? Al Qaeda won that day, and the conservatives are their biggest accomplice in their winning ever since! I can make a case that the US lost the war against

Al Qaeda – not militarily, but in terms of which side achieved its objectives.

Our country and the lifestyle it used to represent have changed dramatically since 9/11/2001 and most of those changes represent changes for the worse. It all started on that horrible day in September of 2001. Not September 11th, September 12th. On the 11th, we experienced a national tragedy resulting in the loss of far too many innocent lives. As tragic as that loss was, it pales when compared to what we have done to ourselves since then.

Immediately following the attacks, Carl Rove and his gang recognized the opportunity to use the fear of another attack to political advantage. By October 26, 2001, George Bush signed the Patriot Act – greatly reducing most American privacy expectations.

> *"The Act dramatically reduced restrictions on law enforcement agencies' ability to search telephone, e-mail communications, medical, financial, and other records; eased restrictions on foreign intelligence gathering within the United States; expanded the Secretary of the Treasury's authority to regulate financial transactions, particularly those involving foreign individuals and entities; and broadened the discretion of law enforcement and immigration authorities in detaining and deporting immigrants suspected of terrorism-related acts. The Act also expanded the definition of terrorism to include domestic terrorism, thus enlarging the number of activities to which the USA PATRIOT Act's expanded law enforcement powers could be applied."*

The Act represents a huge loss of freedom and privacy expectations for most Americans. **Score one for Al Qaeda.**

Next, came the creation of the Transportation Safety Administration (TSA) and color-coded travel danger levels. One former TSA executive subsequently referred to the organization as Transportation Safety Theater because all the inconveniences placed on passengers have a very minor impact on our safety, but they have a politically advantageous psychological impact on everyone. Former Bush administration senior officials admitted that they deliberately manipulated danger-level color codes for political advantage as we neared the 2004 elections. I was living in Atlanta at the time and there are many, many security gates available at Hartsfield Airport. Despite that, there were times when it took over 2 hours to get through security. Standing in line was a reminder of the constant vigilance it took to keep us safe – NOT! **Score another one for Al Qaeda.**

It was not enough to remind us of the dangers when we fly. Apparently, too many people in this country do not fly so they were not getting the "FEAR" message. Therefore, the Department of Homeland security upped the ante and installed metal detectors at the entrances to stadiums and other large gathering places to remind more people that we are in grave danger of another attack and the government is protecting us. Do we really believe that all those metal detectors deterred a single terrorist? Of course not! However, they did a great job of reminding everyone that the conservatives are the masters of protecting us from harm. Moreover, they got Bush a second term. **Score another one for the bad guys.** (I am not saying getting Bush re-elected was a victory for the terrorists. It was a victory for Al Qaeda who manipulated public opinion using fear of another attack.)

Nine years later, and into a new administration, the terrorists were still winning. The conservatives, heavily influenced by the religious right, raised a major objection to the building of a Muslim community center in the vicinity of Ground Zero. This country was founded on a set of principles embodied in the constitution. The Founding Fathers made religious freedom a part of the First Amendment to the Constitution. There is no room for debate about what they meant by freedom of religion. Many of the earliest settlers came to this country to escape state religions and to be free to practice whatever religion they chose. The phrase "separation of church and state" does not appear anywhere in the Constitution. Thomas Jefferson wrote that the first Amendment erected a "wall of separation" between the church and the state (James Madison said it "drew a line," but it is Jefferson's term that sticks with us today). The phrase is commonly thought to mean that the government should not establish, support, or otherwise involve itself in any religion.

A small subset of the Catholic Church carried out The Spanish Inquisition – a subset of Christianity. Should Spain ban all Christian churches from the country because of the actions of a few fringe zealots? Of course not! Doesn't a similar absurdity exist with the suggestion to ban a Muslim mosque from Manhattan because of the actions of a small lunatic fringe? More importantly, doesn't even suggesting that the government should interfere with a religious activity violate one of our country's basic values? If we start violating our own founding principles because of the actions of the terrorists (abetted by the religious right in this country), they win. **Score another one for Al Qaeda!**

Surely you remember the words," Give me your tired, your poor, your huddled masses yearning to breathe free." It's the invitation to immigrants on the Statue of Liberty. That invitation resulted in the arrival of people from literally all over the world. They came here because they believed in our dream and wanted to live it with us. It has served us very well for centuries. As we see the world becoming a more competitive global market, one of the ways we can continue our international innovation and economic leadership is by continuing to invite innovative, industrious, motivated people to join us. Look around you! The rich diverse mixture of cultures and ethnicities in our societies constitute one of our greatest strengths. Do we need to control immigration? Absolutely! However, it should not be a divisive partisan issue. Whether they are Muslim, Hindu, Buddhist, Jewish, Christian, Shinto, or any other religion should not make a difference. Our greatness comes from our diversity. Those among us who push for immigration reform to advance their own agendas are our enemies, not the people seeking to build a place of worship to improve their community. **Score another one for Al Qaeda!**

Finally, we must consider the wars in Iraq and Afghanistan. The 9/11 attack killed 2,995 innocent people. Since 9/11 in two wars justified by that terrible event, we have lost nearly 7,000 lives; and that does not count the much larger number of civilian casualties – many of them the direct result of our efforts to get the bad guys. In the nine years after 9/11, America spent more than $1.1 Trillion dollars on the wars, and the spending continues. "Estimates conclude that there are 150 full-time insurgent Taliban forces and we've spent $337.8 billion to date in Afghanistan. That's $2.2 billion per full-time Taliban insurgent. If we can't kill them with 150,000 troops, maybe we should try to buy them off by giving each Taliban insurgent the same net worth as Barron Hilton[232]." When we also consider the Abu Ghraib and Guantanamo prison situations, where we have again violated some of our basic human rights principals – not to mention broken international law – we have damaged our moral and human rights leadership reputation in ways that will take decades to repair.

Somewhere in a cave in some remote region of the Arab World, there is a group of Al Qaeda leaders smiling as we carry on their

---

232. https://www.huffingtonpost.com/michael-ford/perspective-on-war-costs_b_683069.html

work for them. They provided a spark that set off a chain reaction that continues to this day. It was a brilliant strategy. They saw the weaknesses in our system and exploited them masterfully.

Somewhere in a cave in some remote region of the Arab World, there is a group of Al Qaeda leaders smiling as we carry on their work for them.

It is time for a few strong leaders to step up and look beyond their own personal political future. What we need now are not politicians but statesmen, truly willing to put the good of the country first. Occasionally, we see flashes of it from both sides of the aisle. It is time for the media to stop encouraging the political squabbles that raise their ratings and instead to recognize and encourage bold statesmanship.

I have seen Tea Party members with signs saying, "I want my country back!" Ironically, I agree with their statement – if not their meaning. America is facing enough problems economically in this globally competitive environment. We need to all work together and focus on rebuilding the basic freedoms, moral foundations, and economic and industrial traditions that made this country great.

How many foreign countries have military bases on American soil? None! Did you know that the U.S. has 662 overseas bases in 38 foreign countries? In most cases, America pays at least 75% of the cost for operating the base. In some cases, we pay the full cost plus rent. A closer look at these bases and America's embassies across the globe reveals that in addition to their diplomatic and security value for relations with the host country, they also provide a base for espionage activities (both electronic and human intelligence).

We should be able to close many, if not most, of the military bases on foreign soil! Bring the troops home! We will not need most of them if we are truly teaming with other countries and treating international acts of aggression as crimes.

Seventy years after World War II and 62 years after the Korean War, there are still 174 US "base sites" in Germany, 113 in Japan, and 83 in South Korea, according to the Pentagon. Hundreds more dot the planet in around 80 countries, including Aruba and Australia, Bahrain and Bulgaria, Colombia, Kenya, and Qatar, among many other places. Although few Americans realize it, the United States likely has more bases in foreign lands than any other people, nation, or empire in history.

The article goes on to provide additional thought-provoking ideas. I encourage you to read the complete article. The point is that we maintain a global collection of nearly 800 military bases in foreign countries, at great economic, personal, and political cost. Citizens from other countries perceive us as an occupying force across the world. If you asked the average American if America intended to be a global occupying force, most would say, "Of course not!" Nevertheless, the facts are undeniable – we are!

I am not saying that we do not need any of our foreign bases. Many of our military personnel in foreign lands serve as excellent examples of what has made America a strong nation with a high standing in the world. I am simply saying that as a local citizen in a foreign land living near an American military base, the sight of foreign soldiers walking down the street, even in civilian clothes, would feel like living in an occupied country.

Rarely does anyone ask if we need hundreds of bases overseas or if, at an estimated annual cost of perhaps $156 billion or more, the United States can afford them. Rarely does anyone wonder how we would feel if China, Russia, or Iran built even a single base anywhere near our borders[233], let alone in the United States."

Aruba!?!

We need a military base in Aruba?

The next obvious questions are, "What are we getting for this investment of money and lives? What nation or city-state is a realistic threat to the US?" No country is going to attack us militarily. We do have threats, but they are not the traditional military version. We have economic, cyber, and religious fanatic threats. Spending over $150B on foreign bases has extraordinarily little effect in defending us from these threats. In fact, there is evidence to suggest that our military presence in some Middle Eastern countries serves as a recruiting tool for our religious fanatic enemies. However, the problem is worse than that. While we are spending over $600B on military defense, we are neglecting to maintain or upgrade our national infrastructure, cutting back on research and development that would create thousands of professional jobs. Instead, we are enduring a long-term decline in the prosperity of the average American family. We have American citizens here at home living in poverty while we pay billions of dollars into foreign economies supporting our bases there.

There is another major economic problem with maintaining all these foreign bases. Let's look at where the $150B goes. The obvious answer is that the money goes to the foreign bases – outside the US.

---

233. https://www.thenation.com/article/world/the-united-states-probably-has-more-foreign-military-bases-than-any-other-people-nation-or-empire-in-history/

It is where it goes from there that is interesting. A significant portion of the money goes to civilian/military contractors who provide services like construction, infrastructure, food services, etc. Military service members and civilian employees get paid nominal wages, while military contractor employees get paid significantly more for the same work. Some of the money pays the civilian contractor employees, and much of it goes to corporate operations and profits. Another major part of the money pays the military salaries. The next round in the cycle of spending is more impactful. The people living on the foreign base spend their money in the community and country where they are located. The result is a major injection of cash into the local economy. Bases are major sources of revenue for their host communities. Every foreign base means that those bases benefit local communities outside the US. If we take just half of the money the US is spending overseas and move those bases back onto US soil, that $75B could benefit communities in the US – without reducing the size of the military.

Finally, there is the personal or family cost. If you are a military person assigned to a base in the US, chances are your family (spouse and children) are with you. That is not always the case for foreign bases. Many of the military people assigned to foreign bases leave their families behind. The result is, as we would expect, stress on the family. Kids grow up without one of their parents for long stretches of time. Even if the base is in a peaceful country, where the personnel are in no physical danger, the separation from the family is stressful.

I would venture to say that the biggest reason we maintain military bases in foreign countries is that contractors are making huge profits. We frequently hear politicians urging us to support our troops. The best way to support our troops would be to bring many of them back to bases in the US. They make many sacrifices for their country.

Being separated from their families unnecessarily should not have to be one of them.

If we really want to honor our fallen troops, let's pledge to stop getting them killed for nothing! Just stop and think about it. Since 9/11, the US and the world have suffered thousands of casualties, both military and civilian; and for what? Are we freer? Are we more prosperous? Are we safer? No, no, and no!

In the name of The Patriot Act, we gave up some freedoms to allow our country to protect us better. Do you not see the irony in that last statement? We willingly gave up some of the very freedoms our brave warriors are supposed to be fighting to preserve.

More prosperous? Not by a lot! The only ones who are prospering are the people who are already rich or at the very top of the wealth and income pyramid. In another irony, the warriors who are fighting for us are poorly paid, must fight for their benefits, and are sacrificing their lives for nothing. America is in no imminent or even remote danger of being attacked! There is no military force anywhere in the world even one quarter the size of ours.

Just think about our recent "military" successes. Did they involve major troop activities, fleets of ships, and aircraft? No! They were accomplished by a highly trained and well-equipped elite group of people like Seal Team 6. They gathered intelligence, developed a tactical plan, executed that plan, and eliminated the threat. There was a minimum of casualties on our side, and very few civilian casualties. And the bad guys were eliminated. Sounds more like a SWAT team than a military action, doesn't it? Additionally, fewer children had to grow up with a parent deployed and far less money was spent; money that could be used for a wide range of domestic programs to fix infrastructure, improve the economy, create jobs, reduce poverty, and restore the middle class.

When I hear a presidential candidate talking cavalierly about war, it saddens me and angers me – mostly because his rabid supporters cheer his rhetoric, without realizing that if he does what he says, more people like them will suffer or die while he just gets richer. "I will bomb the shit out of them!" "I'll kill their families, their wives, and children!" President Trump actually said this! And people cheer for this?! Seriously?! Does that really make anyone proud to be an American? The America I am proud of stands for just the opposite. We should stand for the moral high ground. We used to be a global leader because of what we stood for – not just because we could and might "bomb the shit out of" people who threatened us. Other countries were proud to call themselves our allies – not just because of our military might, but also because of our moral positions. Leaders around the world are justifiably expressing concern about what they see happening during this current political season.

The Russian attack on Ukraine is an example for trying a justice versus military response to an attack. Thousands of innocent citizens and misled soldiers are dying and killing in Ukraine because of one megalomaniacal war criminal – Vladimir Putin. What is the world's response? Send more planes, tanks, bombs, and bullets for more killing and dying! History is clear. Nobody wins that type of war except the people who profit from the Military Industrial Complex – the people who make and sell the bombs and bullets.

We are at a unique point in history. There is overwhelming global sentiment and irrefutable evidence that Putin's actions are war crimes. Even other autocrats are less than enthusiastic in their support because they know that bombing women and children is indefensible. It is time for the United Nations to step up, take control over, and fix the problem by arresting, prosecuting, and punishing Putin and his inner circle of war criminals. Any other approach will place more innocent soldiers in a position of killing each other for nothing.

The UN should establish an international Tactical Team with the specific mission to bring Putin to justice at the World Court without fighting a traditional military action. It might start with a global information campaign that makes the Russian people aware of the true situation. The Russian and Ukrainian people should not be fighting. They are historically friends and family. The Russians have been deceived into believing that they need to attack Ukraine. Fixing this requires information, not weapons. The program must also include humanitarian programs to rescue and restore Ukraine using money seized from Russia and its oligarchs. Perhaps if the maniacs responsible for the war are made to pay for it, other oligarchs and autocrats will have less incentive to initiate future aggressions. We don't need war; we need justice. And we need it now!

On Memorial Day weekend, let us truly honor our brave, dedicated past and present military members and their families, not just with sincere words of thanks, but by committing to a path that puts fewer of them in harm's way in the future.

That wraps up my rambling thoughts on the topic of war and the military. I invite you to share these thoughts with others to get more people to think that war is not the best answer to anything. If we could get to that point, then there are countless other things we can work on here at home to truly become the great nation we were and could be again. In fact, we can be better than we ever were. We must start thinking of National Security as more than National Defense. Homeland Security is meaningless to people living in extreme poverty. We need to find a better balance. We need a war on poverty.

Issue #21 - Security must be more than merely being safe from military attack.

To be fair, we need to recognize that much of the military spending creates and maintains well-paying manufacturing jobs making armaments in states all over the country. We need to use that money to make fewer arms and more bridges and buildings.

The mission of the Department of Defense is to provide the military forces needed to deter war and to protect the security of our country. As I have grown older, I have realized that the country is very secure, but many of its citizens are not. Anyone living in poverty is not feeling secure. It's time to redefine National Security to include personal security. If people cannot safely walk through their neighborhood, then they are not feeling secure. If they are living in poverty, they are not feeling safe and secure.

In his 2018 9/11 column, 'Anonymous' Is Hiding in Plain Sight, NYTimes Op-ed columnist Thomas Friedman said[234],

> *"And don't get me started on the recently signed $716 billion defense budget for the 2019 fiscal year — a spending hike so dramatic, as defense analyst Lawrence Korb pointed out, that it means since Trump took office under two years ago, "the defense budget will have grown by $133 billion, or 23 percent." And there's no major war going on."*

---

234. https://www.nytimes.com/2018/09/11/opinion/anonymous-op-ed-republican-party-trump.html

The United States spends more on defense than the next eight countries combined

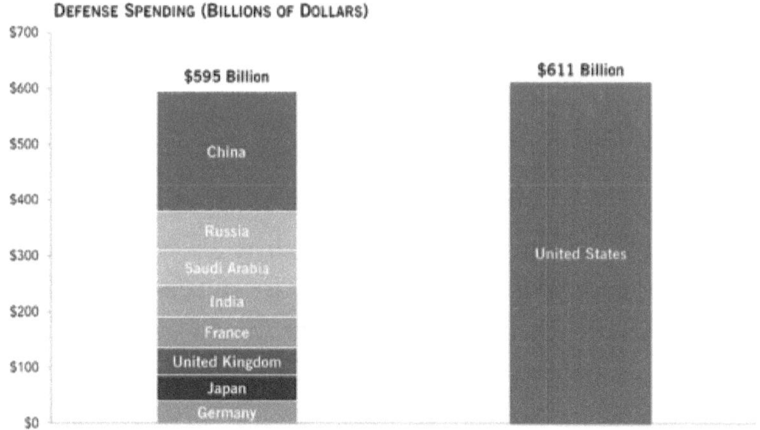

SOURCE: Stockholm International Peace Research Institute, SIPRI Military Expenditure Database, April 2017. Data are for 2016. Compiled by PGPF.
NOTE: Figures are in U.S. dollars, converted from local currencies using market exchange rates.

© 2017 Peter G. Peterson Foundation   PGPF.ORG

Every year we celebrate Pearl Harbor Day, Veterans' Day, Memorial Day, and other patriotic occasions; and pay tribute to the members of the military and their families who suffered and died in military service. In all cases, the recognition is richly deserved. I am proud to be a veteran who served during the Vietnam War. Many of my friends' and classmates' names are displayed on that shining black granite wall memorial on the National Mall. We can all be proud of the patriotism, bravery, and commitment that the members of our armed forces demonstrate every day. At the same time, we can be dismayed that most of the casualties from the current engagements are not gaining us anything. "Why Can't The World's Best Military Win Its Wars?[235]" provides a thorough analysis of our military 'failures' since WWII. In case you haven't heard, we haven't 'won' a war since 1945 (more about that later).

Many military and civilian leaders agree that there was no reasonable military solution to the situation in Afghanistan or other countries in the region. After all the human and economic costs from over ten years of fighting, within a year of our departure the only evidence we had been there is whatever survived from the infrastructure we built. Politically, economically, culturally, and educationally, they are gradually falling back to their old ways.

Now, consider an alternate universe. Instead of invading them militarily, we could have worked with our fellow members of the United Nations and formed an international police force and gone after the terrorist organization responsible for 9/11. Treat them like the organized criminals they are. They are not an army. They are a rag-tag bunch of zealots, thugs, and gangsters. At the same time, we could have saved about 80% of the money we spent on a military invasion and occupation (and thousands of civilian lives) and used a portion of it to send in people to assist the Afghani people in creating a modern economy with the complete infrastructure to support it.

We do not start with trying to convince them to give up several millennia of cultural and religious beliefs. If we do a good job of improving living conditions and providing a quality education system, gradually they will increase their level of interaction with more developed countries and realize that there may be room for modifying some of their traditional practices (e.g., the role of women in society). During this program of activities, the boots on the ground are not military. They are truly civilian advisors from all over the world. At first, there will be some danger, but nothing like an armed invasion force faces. A small international police force will protect both the locals and the advisors. Over time, the local people

---

235. https://www.huffingtonpost.com/entry/in-present-american-wars-repeating-past-

mistakes_us_5ae9ff86e4b081860d8ca158

will learn to value the presence and investment that the advisors are bringing and will actively protect them. As the local economy grows, the advisors will be able to leave. Unlike the previously described military pullout, when the advisors leave, there will be a lasting difference for the better in the lives of the Afghan people. Meanwhile, the international police force will benefit because of the civilian economic advisors' efforts. The locals will recognize that the police force is on their side and the terrorists are their enemies. The locals will make it easier to bring the terrorists to justice.

Why is it that whenever two countries go to war, the leaders, who make the policies that create the situation that leads to war, get to sit back in relative safety while the soldiers and civilians have to fight and die? When all is said and done, what have we really gained? How many people died in Iraq as a part of US retaliation? Classified US military documents released by WikiLeaks in October 2010, record Iraqi and Coalition military deaths between January 2004 and December 2009.The documents record 109,032 deaths broken down into "Civilian" (66,081 deaths), "Host Nation" (15,196 deaths),"Enemy" (23,984 deaths), and "Friendly" (3,771 deaths).

We can do the math if we want to, but we do not need to add up the totals to appreciate that an outrageously large number of people were killed because of the US military response to the acts of 12 religious fanatics on 9/11/2001. Now ask yourself, 'What have we gained?' Is America any safer than it would have been if no people had died because of our retaliation? There was no standing army of terrorists waiting to follow-up on the 9/11 attack, no armada of ships waiting to transport their forces to attack our shores, and no air force filled with bombs fueled and ready to attack.

From another perspective, if you were living in the Arab World, how would you perceive the US? When you walk to your neighbor's home and worry about being blown up by a drone-launched Hellfire missile, would you be thinking of America as a protector, or as a predator? Eliminating a specific terrorist leader is a 'targeted killing' according to the US. However, Britain's Reprieve human rights group calculated that it takes about 28 innocent lives to take out a single terrorist leader, often with multiple drone strikes[236]. Meanwhile, the US has spent trillions of dollars for "National Defense" and "National Security" while suffering at home with crumbling infrastructure, underfunded schools and social programs, and a disappearing American Middle Class. We must do better.

Let's look at why those 12 fanatics flew those four planes into their targets. Was it personal? Not at all. There is no indication that any of the fanatics knew any of the people they killed that day. Some zealous religious/political leaders convinced them they should do it. Note – the leader did not join them on their mission. He stayed behind to send more loyal followers to their death.

Why did the US attack Afghanistan? Our political leaders told us that it was because the country allowed the Al-Qaeda organization to exist and train terrorists. The Taliban and Al Qaeda were a hostile force occupying the country against the wishes of the people and we were going in to 'free' the people from these occupying forces. But wait, what did these occupying forces look like? They were a rag-tag bunch of hungry fanatics inspired by a charismatic leader. Their organization and weaponry were loose and primitive.

There is an old saying, "When the only tool you have is a hammer, everything looks like a nail." The US has tanks, Humvees, rockets, bombs, drones, etc.. Given these options, how should the US have fought the Taliban? In our typical fashion, we threw everything at them.

---

236. https://www.rt.com/news/208527-reaping-lives-drone-strikes/

It is now over a decade later. Did we win? In a larger sense, when was the last time America won a war? Don't get all patriotic about it. Consider the facts. How would you define winning? If we killed more of their people than they killed of our people, does that mean we won? Try telling the families of the Americans that were killed that they won. All they know is that they lost a loved one, and they hope and try to believe it was for something important.

At this point, we probably need to have a discussion of what it means to win in a war. One definition is that we preserved our freedoms. Our precious freedoms are worth preserving, but is going to war the best way to achieve that? Do we need to send our innocent sons and daughters off to kill innocent sons and daughters of another country to preserve our freedom?

The only way a war is ever won is if both sides stop killing each other. Everybody wins! Did we win the Vietnam War? In the sense that both sides stopped killing each other, yes. However, by any military or political standard, nobody won; or the North Vietnamese did. President Nixon's political label for the bombing of Hanoi was to achieve "peace with honor." To achieve that, in December of 1972, the US dropped over 20,000 tons of bombs, killing more than 1,600 civilians. The Vietnam War cost over 58,000 American lives, and hundreds of thousands of Vietnamese lives. The US Navy authorized me to wear the Vietnam Service medal. [I was technically in the "War Zone" for about a week and never in any danger.] However, I am not convinced that my service or their sacrifice gained our country anything.

What about the Korean War? Nobody won! Thousands of people died and then we stopped fighting. North Korea is still there, trampling on the human rights of its citizens. Look at Afghanistan and Iraq. Who won? Nobody. Some hawks say we should put more boots on the ground. Then we could win. We cannot win either of those wars – mainly because they are not our wars in the first place. All we are achieving in that part of the world is providing our enemies with minor victories by being there. Our presence and the collateral damage we have caused, and continue to cause, have created a major resentment towards the US – feeding the terrorist splinter groups with a steady stream of recruits. Not only that, but our internal response back here at home has been to change our way of life to protect ourselves from the terrorists. The bitter pill is that we gave up some of our freedoms and liberties in the name of homeland security.

In every war I can think of, we went to war because our leaders and their leaders chose to go to war. If another country commits what we consider an act of war, is the best response to retaliate with a military attack? Who is killed in a military battle? Not the people who decided to attack us. Innocent soldiers and civilians from the attacking country are killed (We're good at retaliation!) along with some of our troops.

Let's consider another option. If one country attacks another, consider the attack a crime – an international crime – and go after the people who really committed the crime – the leaders who ordered the attack. Treat it as a criminal action, not a military one. The police force must be a global international one that captures the suspects and brings them to trial in a world court. Instead of attacking their soldiers, we should selectively and surgically arrest and try the leaders who caused the attack.

Let's take a closer look at the US response to 9/11. What was the connection between the Afghanistan population and Al-Qaeda? Basically, the Afghan people were victims of the Taliban and AL Qaeda.

According to Encyclopedia Britannica,

[The] "Afghanistan War, [was an] international conflict in Afghanistan beginning in 2001 that was triggered by the September 11 attacks and consisted of three phases. The first phase—toppling the Taliban (the ultraconservative political and religious faction that ruled Afghanistan and provided sanctuary for al-Qaeda, perpetrators of the September 11 attacks)—was brief, lasting just two months. The second phase, from 2002 until 2008, was marked by a U.S. strategy of defeating the Taliban militarily and rebuilding core institutions of the Afghan state. The third phase, a turn to classic counterinsurgency doctrine, began in 2008 and accelerated with U.S. Pres. Barack Obama's 2009 decision to temporarily increase the U.S. troop presence in Afghanistan. The larger force was used to implement a strategy of protecting the population from Taliban attacks and supporting efforts to reintegrate insurgents into Afghan society."

How did we fight the "war"? The US brought its full military might to bear on the issue. We used sledgehammers to attempt to kill a few ants. The big problem with that approach is that the bad ants lived among the good ants, and a sledgehammer cannot tell the difference. As a result, we killed thousands of good ants along the way. We have become so callous about this effect we have created a euphemism for it. We call it "Collateral Damage." According to Wikipedia,

"Collateral damage is damage to things that are incidental to the intended target. It is frequently used as a military term where non-combatants are accidentally or unintentionally killed or wounded and/or non-combatant property damaged as result of the attack on legitimate military targets."

Check out the Getty image collection online[237]. This website is a collection of pictures of the homeland of the terrorists. Does this collection of images make you think of a country militarily prepared to attack the US? Of course not! And they didn't! A small bunch of fanatics did.

Their Military Our Military

Which side would you bet on?

● **What they did!**

o Killed 2,996 people on 9/11 including the 12 terrorists and all 4 planes' passengers.

---

237. http://www.gettyimages.com/photos/

taliban?sort=mostpopular&excludenudity=true&mediatype=photography&phrase=taliban

• **What we did** (In Pakistan, Afghanistan, and Iraq)!

o War and occupation directly and indirectly claimed the lives of about a half-million Iraqis from 2003 to 2011, according to a groundbreaking survey of 1,960 Iraqi households. The violence peaked in 2006 and 2007, say public health experts who were part of the study.

According to costofwar.org[238],

"The ongoing conflicts in Iraq, Afghanistan, and Pakistan have taken a tremendous toll on the people of those countries. At the very least, 174,000 civilians have been determined to have died violent deaths because of the war as of April 2014. The actual number of deaths, direct and indirect, as a result of the wars are many times higher than this figure."

The decades-long war in Afghanistan has continued to take lives with each passing year. As of February 2014, at least 21,000 civilians died violent deaths because of the war. The total number of civilians killed in Pakistan may be as high as or higher than the toll in Afghanistan, with NGO estimates ranging widely between 20,000 and 50,000 recorded deaths. In Iraq, over 70 percent of those who died of direct war violence have been civilians. Iraq Body Count conservatively estimates that at least 133,000 civilians died in direct violence due to war between the invasion and early May 2014. In

---

238. http://l.facebook.com/

l.php?u=http://costofwar.org/&h=RAQGPxrabAQHM1JogBVmF1scPouUzat4PoVTMX

MXAmD9o3Q&enc=AZOH7lRQ9uAgy0SC6Ie-jrFi_pha5-ptSeabj-tH9HeySdG-

9o19WBwiLdgVF26WiyFAp21Oe5E-

DPWAojLlGcHRrbxszJ9wTLmjniHSvoPO7pn0oCeSJCK7S-

eTs6k5bDgd6QRXNMATRYTo5DO9SGOWLCLgri2SNckrWKP-pxvf25R-

ux5bqhEaewHskYmLBdo&s=1

addition to the direct consequences of violence represented by these numbers, thousands more Iraqis, Afghans, and Pakistanis are falling victim to the dangers of a battered infrastructure and poor health conditions arising from wars. In the case of Iraq, excess deaths indirectly resulting from the war add several times the 133,000 civilians killed directly by violence.

Did we win? Remember, "Mission accomplished?" It was the huge banner on the aircraft carrier where President Bush prematurely declared victory. We did not win! Nobody won except for those who profited from the war. According to International Business Times,

> *"Private or publicly listed firms received at least $138 billion of U.S. taxpayer money for government contracts for services that included providing private security, building infrastructure, and feeding the troops."*

Ten contractors received 52 percent of the funds, according to an analysis by the Financial Times.

Who was the No. 1 recipient? Houston-based energy-focused engineering and construction firm KBR, Inc., which was spun off from its parent, oilfield services provider Halliburton Co. in 2007. The company was given $39.5 billion in Iraq-related contracts over the past decade, with many of the deals given without any bidding from competing firms, such as a $568-million contract renewal in 2010 to provide housing, meals, water, and bathroom services to soldiers, a deal that led to a Justice Department lawsuit over alleged kickbacks, as reported by Bloomberg[239].

> *That's right! The controversial former subsidiary of*
> *Halliburton, which was once run by Dick Cheney,*
> *vice-president to George W. Bush, was awarded at least*

---

239. https://www.ft.com/content/7f435f04-8c05-11e2-b001-00144feabdc0#ixzz3cVim0veA

> *$39.5bn in federal contracts related to the Iraq war over the*
> *"past decade*

Did Dick Cheney serve in the military? According to Bio.com[240],

> *"During his time as a student, Cheney applied for and*
> *received five draft deferments and thus avoided being drafted*
> *in the Vietnam War, stating that he "had other priorities in*
> *the 60's than military service."*

The US spent $138B just on contractors. Unfortunately, that is only the tip of the iceberg. According to the Congressional Research Office report, The Cost of Iraq, Afghanistan, and Other Global War on Terror Operations Since 9/11 is:

> *"With enactment of the FY2014 Consolidated*
> *Appropriations Act on January 1, 2014 (H.R.3547/P.L.*
> *113-73), Congress has approved appropriations for the past*
> *13 years of war that total $1.6 trillion for military*
> *operations, base support, weapons maintenance, training of*
> *Afghan and Iraq security forces, reconstruction, foreign aid,*
> *embassy costs, and veterans' health care for the war*
> *operations initiated since the 9/11 attacks."*

Because the following is purely hypothetical, I cannot provide you with any actual budgetary evidence, so just consider the following as a conceptual model. I think you will agree that there would be a much greater return on investment than we got for the $1.6T we

---

240. http://l.facebook.com/l.php?u=http://Bio.com/&h=6AQFGm_-wAQENU-

RTTJLK9lw73euguXv6IQjHOieszOlt4A&enc=AZP9H3NaLp2Y2uoFaulW5aXIp70w1rl

Lh2W9GofR82apKoLki7ZDxDWPhTUbb6D_F2wqH6pFeb6GqLKtrPSIYiQYhcoNXr

H5tqjo7ayUAT_Pi37VGppPv-5WwHq7JeqhchZL81MoGCPqcJri8r1cr-

CpUXazke2pYbvCqFo9IIUUpYnrdfD3QD5WrCUSwMn69Q4&s=1

spent on the wars. More importantly, if we had not attacked the countries, millions of people (theirs and ours) would still be alive and whole. Remember, our goal is to improve the safety and security of our American people, values, and way of life. If we had pursued the following hypothetical model before 9/11, the attacks on the twin towers might not have happened. In the following hypothetical, I assume we will maintain a reduced military posture as long as it is needed in parallel with the police force.

Let us, just for the sake of argument, assume that the world could be a peaceful place; and if instead of a focus on military might, we treat all acts of aggression as criminal acts. Instead of huge armies, we would need a truly international police force and court system. If a country commits an act of aggression, instead of attacking the aggressor country with military force – killing soldiers and civilians on both sides – we arrest and indict the individual(s) that caused the aggressive act, take him to court and punish him. (I say him, because since the beginning of the 20th century, I don't think there has been a female head of state that led her country to war.) The head of a country considering an aggressive act towards another nation might have a different perspective if instead of an army doing the fighting; the head of state ordering the aggression was charged with a crime and punished. The international court would be used to settle international disputes, not the military. If a peaceful country felt threatened, militarily, geographically, or economically, rather than ramping up their military preparedness, the threatened country could 'press charges' against the leader of the suspected potential aggressor in the world court.

We should begin by truly exercising international leadership and calling a meeting of all nations – not just our allies. The purpose of the meeting would be to announce to the world that the US would no longer be the military force for the international community.

Instead, we will team up with an international police force, treat any future international acts of aggression as crimes, and seek to identify, capture, and punish the people responsible for the aggressive acts – even if those people are heads of state.

We will invite all countries to contribute people and resources to the international police force and court system in proportion to their population and GDP. (We would need to work out some formula.) This international court will have authority over a short list of international crimes. We would start out with a focus on just acts of aggression in the former military sense. As the organization grows and learns how to work together, there will be a process for adding other areas of concern – like economic and cyber-attacks. The international court will have no authority over internal national activities. Each participating country will maintain its sovereignty for domestic policies and laws. At this point, it's just an idea, but one worth further consideration.

What if a country declared war but the soldiers and civilians decided they did not really want to fight? Maybe it already happened! The Iraqi army's willingness to let Ramadi fall to ISIS "surprised all of us," Deputy Prime Minister Saleh al-Mutlaq told CNN[241].

> *"It's not clear for us why such a unit, which was supposed to be trained by the Americans for years and supposed to be one of the best units in the army, would withdraw from Ramadi in such a way."*

> *"This is not the army that we are willing to see or we are expecting to see."*

---

241. https://news.vice.com/article/iraqi-soldiers-fleeing-isis-claim-they-were-abandoned-by-senior-officers

Al-Mutlaq, a Sunni who leads his own party and often criticizes Prime Minister Haider al-Abadi, spoke with CNN's Frederik Pleitgen on "Amanpour," a day after scathing criticism of the Iraqi military by U.S. Defense Secretary Ash Carter.

"They were not outnumbered," Carter told CNN's Barbara Starr in an exclusive interview. "In fact, they vastly outnumbered the opposing force. And yet they failed to fight; they withdrew from the site."

"The complete collapse of Iraqi forces in Mosul came as a shock to many observers, particularly as it was apparently at the hands of less than a thousand gunmen and they, along with the rest of the country's military had benefited from $25 billion worth of training and equipment provided by the US before it withdrew from Iraq at the end of 2011."

Maybe they just decided that it was not their fight to fight. Back in 1936, poet Carl Sandberg wrote an epic poem titled, "The People, Yes[242]." One line from that poem has been repeated many times throughout history.

*"In the 1960s, several variations of an anti-war slogan began appearing on posters, in print and in songs. The version that became most common (as shown by the comparatively huge number of Google hits it gets) is **"Suppose they gave a war, and nobody came."** [...]*

In the poem, the line is said by a little girl who sees a group of soldiers marching in a parade. It's from a part of the poem in

---

242. http://www.quotecounterquote.com/2011/12/suppose-they-gave-war-and-nobody-came.html

which Sandburg seems to foresee the potential devastation of a second and possibly a third world war:

"The first world war came and its cost was laid on the people.

The second world war — the third — what will be the cost.

And will it repay the people for what they pay?...

The little girl saw her first troop parade and asked,

'What are those?'

'Soldiers.'

'What are soldiers?'

'They are for war. They fight and each tries to kill as many of the other side as he can.'

The girl held still and studied.

'Do you know ... I know something?'

'Yes, what is it you know?'

'Sometime they'll give a war and nobody will come"

Maybe the Iraqi Army will start a trend.

Nobody wins a war – except those who sit at home and profit from it. We need to spend our defense and security dollars (not to mention our personnel) more wisely and effectively. Then we need to take the savings and invest them in infrastructure and public service programs that will reduce poverty and provide real security to millions of Americans.

Public Education

Allan is a lifelong educator, convinced of the importance of quality public education and committed to doing what he can to improve it. If you do not share his passion, you may want to skip this chapter. If you share his passion, we encourage you to give us feedback on our ideas. We have a website that provides information about his efforts to transform K-12 education at https://emaginos.com/ with an email link on the contact page.

With a few isolated exceptions, great public schools are located in affluent communities and poorly performing public schools are located in poverty-stricken communities. I do not need to cite research to convince the reader of this. You are consciously aware that the statement is true. At the same time, we all know that quality education is essential for an individual's success, and that the lack thereof is an anchor holding an individual back. Dedicated teachers in poverty-stricken community schools occasionally inspire some individual students to persevere and become successful, but many of the students are so downtrodden and discouraged by the world as they see it, that they give up and join another generation stuck in poverty.

Teachers are tirelessly doing all they can to provide the right mechanisms that will help the students be engaged. They are not 'bad kids' or 'lazy kids'. They are just realists. They look around and their world is not very inspiring. Any program aiming to eliminate poverty must ensure that every citizen has access to a quality public education. Society as a rule understands this and spends a lot of money on it. Due to the recent challenges with Covid-19, children were not able to go outside to go to school. They were taught online for three years. and became disengaged with school and the education being provided. Now that children are able to attend school, most go with the desire to learn, and the majority go to get out of their homes.

The following educational reforms are a sample of the well-intended programs that have subsequently been twisted from their original intent to benefit students and have instead become programs that take money from children and funnel it to company bottom lines.

Accountability started out as a good idea. Lew Gerstner, CEO of IBM Corporation, became interested in and frustrated with the state of K-12 public education in America. In 2009 Gerstner penned an article for the Wall Street Journal titled, "Lessons From 40 Years of Education 'Reform'[243]".

> *"It is most crucial for our political leaders to ask why we are at this point—why after millions of pages, in thousands of reports, from hundreds of commissions and task forces, financed by billions of dollars, have we failed to achieve any significant progress?*
>
> *Answering this question correctly is the key to finally remaking our public schools.*
>
> *This is a complex problem, but countless experiments and analyses have clearly indicated we need to do four straightforward things to bring fundamental changes to K-12 education:*
>
> *1) Set high academic standards for all of our kids, supported by a rigorous curriculum.*

---

243. http://online.wsj.com/news/articles/SB122809533452168067

2) Greatly improve the quality of teaching in our classrooms, supported by substantially higher compensation for our best teachers.

3) Measure student and teacher performance on a systematic basis, supported by tests and assessments.

4) Increase "time on task" for all students; this means more time in school each day, and a longer school year.

Everything else either does not matter (e.g., smaller class sizes) or is supportive of these four steps (e.g., vastly improve schools of education)."

Let me be clear; his heart was pure. He was not looking to make a buck for himself or IBM. He genuinely believed in the importance of K-12 public education and was sincerely concerned with the problems he had observed. The third recommendation on his list, *"Measure student and teacher performance on a systematic basis, supported by tests and assessments."* seemed reasonable and innocuous at the time. It was a continuation of a theme he had begun years earlier at an annual IBM K-12 education event he hosted where he introduced the need for 'accountability'. Who can argue with that? Of course we need accountability. The problem arises in how we implement the concept. Who could have anticipated that what started as a logical call for accountability would turn into a multi-billion-dollar testing program that takes money from teaching and moves it into testing? At the same time, it takes students from learning and saddles them with memorizing; boring students, and burning out teachers.

Another potentially positive step towards improving K-12 public education was the creation of a comprehensive, valid set of educational standards. Every school district and state in the country struggles with identifying what to teach to its students. The vast majority of what needs to be taught in one district needs to be taught in another district; so, it makes sense to invest in developing a set of Common Core State Standards (CCSS). If the CCSS were made available to districts, then the districts could build their local curriculum and student evaluation systems around them. Sounds excellent. However, the 'reformers' did not stop there. They used federal funding as a cudgel to force districts to buy into an intensive testing regime to determine if the students have mastered the CCSS. Time spent testing is time not spent learning. Once again, the problem is with the implementation.

There has been some concern expressed over the CCSS as a part of a vast national conspiracy to turn out generations of non-thinking worker-bees for America's large corporations. Not so! The CCSS is a list of things that a collection of well-meaning academics and state leaders believe are essential for people to know to be successful after they graduate from high school. They are intended to build a capability for and love of learning that the students will retain and use throughout their lives. The problem arises when we start high-stakes testing around the standards and threaten teachers, administrators, and schools with penalties for poor performance on the tests. The previously advisory standards are no longer advisory. They became mandatory.

Issue #22 – We put too much emphasis on testing and not enough emphasis on learning.

Milton Chen from the George Lucas Foundation[244] sums up America's flawed focus on testing with the following example.

---

244. http://www.edutopia.org/dont-weigh-elephant-feed-elephant

> *"I was at a meeting recently when a colleague told a story of being in India, where an educator there asked her, somewhat skeptically, "In America, you test your students a lot, don't you?" She replied, "Well, indeed, the United States has a national policy that requires testing of all students in certain grades." The Indian educator said,* **"Here when we want the elephant to grow, we feed the elephant. We don't weigh the elephant."**

In America, we not only put a lot of stock in frequently weighing the elephant, but we also think we can determine how good the trainer is by weighing the elephant.

All of these so-called education reforms started out with good intentions. Unfortunately, many of them have been caught up in the greed epidemic. Accountability has turned into a means of getting rid of higher-paid experienced teachers and replacing them with entry level teachers who cost less money and unfortunately provide a poorer education to their students. The Common Core State Standards have led to an intense focus on teaching to the test, thereby burning out teachers and boring students. On the greed side, testing has become a major source of revenue for testing companies. The most glaring recent example is the decision by the LAUSD to take $1B from a bond to build and renovate buildings and spend it on iPads and testing software from Pearson. There is no research-based evidence that this program will have any positive educational impact, and a lot of historical empirical experience says it will be academically harmful. In three years, the iPads will be obsolete, the Pearson contract will expire; and the buildings will not be built or renovated.

Remember the old saying, "Be careful what you wish for." For decades we have witnessed level or declining financial support for

K-12 public education. We have asked for more money to improve the learning environment in our children's schools. We got more money, but it never made it to the classrooms in any way that truly benefits the students. As soon as more money entered the system, corporate vultures swooped in and consumed it. They then decided they liked the taste of this new meat so much, they looked for more meat to eat out of the system.

In 2016, we elected a man who promised to Make America Great Again. Among the many related promises was one to improve public schools. President-elect Trump then delivered several bushels of lemons to America's K-12 public education system by appointing a billionaire who supports charter schools and vouchers and wants to make it easier for profiteers to suck money out of public education. Let's look at the numbers[245].

- There are 98,328 K-12 public schools

- Total public-school enrollment: 50,094,00

- Total public-school teachers: 3,109,101

- Total public-school expenditures: $607.8 billion

- Total funding of public education: $597,485,869.5 billion

  - Federal: $75.99 billion (12.7% of total)
  - State: $259.8 billion (43.5% of total)
  - Local: $261.7 billion (43.8% of total)

The percentages are a bit misleading in terms of the influence on policies. While the federal share is relatively small, it is significant to the point where the districts rely on having it. GOTCHA! If we

---

245. https://nces.ed.gov/

take the federal money for anything, we have to follow their rules for everything.

Seeing the big dollars America spends on education, it is easy to understand why profiteers want to get their hands on it. However, the numbers also tell another story. All those teachers and many parents from the schools do not want their local schools replaced by charter schools; and do not want a so-called choice to send their child to some school outside their local neighborhood. We do not need to guess about this. New Orleans is over 90% charter schools, with choice being a part of that equation. So given a choice, what do parents choose? A New Study Reveals Much About How Parents Really Choose Schools[246].

> *"It seems self-evident that parents, empowered by choice, will vote with their feet for academically stronger schools. As the argument goes, the overall effect should be to improve equity as well: Lower-income parents won't have to send their kids to an under-resourced and underperforming school just because it is the closest one to them geographically.*
>
> *But an intriguing new study from the Education Research Alliance for New Orleans suggests that parent choice doesn't always work that way. Parents, especially low-income parents, actually show strong preferences for other qualities like location and extracurriculars — preferences that can outweigh academics."*

The article goes on to point out many disadvantages of school choice. It turns out, people seeking choice are looking to escape a bad school, not go away from their neighborhood school. In fact, they will

---

246. https://www.npr.org/sections/ed/2015/01/15/376966406/a-new-study-reveals-much-about-how-parents-really-choose-schools

choose a slightly inferior neighborhood school over a slightly better school a greater distance from home. If offered a better neighborhood school, their choice is obvious. They will choose to transform their neighborhood school.

Remember, K-12 public education is under the local control of the 13,515 school districts. They receive about 13% of their funding from the feds, but 87% is state and local money. 13% is a significant amount of money, but the feds would have a tough time withholding that money because the local district is spending it to transform its schools, especially when the feds are promising to transform schools. Let's get busy, people. We have some lemonade to make!

Nine years ago (January of 2014) I wrote a book titled, <u>Unleashing America's Greatest Natural Resource</u>. The following is an excerpt from that book. It takes a metaphorical look at public education in America.

"America's Public Education Ship of State

Today's educational ship of state is loaded down with programs, dragging along additional responsibilities, and being pushed around by well-meaning forces. The result – making no headway!

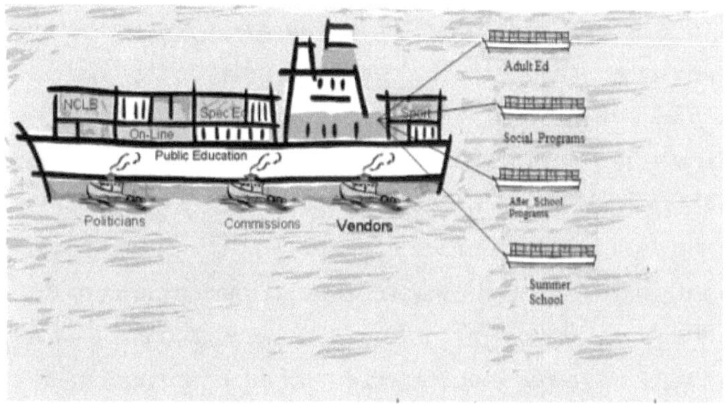

If we use a sleek ship as the metaphor for America's earlier education system, then that original sleek ship has been retrofitted into what we have today; a super-sized container ship with the holds filled with pallets of freight (buildings, vehicles, curriculum, staff, technology, etc.) and the decks stacked six-high with cargo containers (special education, alternative education, vocational education, preschool programs, free and reduced lunch programs, sports programs, etc.) However, it would not stop there. You would also see pods attached along the hull like a series of blisters (guidance counseling, parent/teacher organizations, booster clubs, internships, etc.). If you look astern, you will see a trail of barges being towed along (adult education, Title IX, NCLB, high-stakes tests, etc.). And alongside the ship would be a swarm of tugboats in an uncoordinated, frantic effort to change the direction of the whole affair. (The tugs represent the politicians, commissions, and reformers.) Not visible in the picture are the submarines owned by the companies seeking to make fortunes from education. They are launching torpedoes hoping to destroy the existing ship so they can be paid to rebuild it.

Many of the containers stacked on the deck are there to correct problems buried deep in the holds of the ship. The effect is that the ship has slowed nearly to a halt and there is no short-term way to trim it down and get it moving in the right direction. When I shared this metaphor with some friends, I heard back from Vint Cerf[47], "The boat is coated with barnacles, and we have some serious cleaning to do." After considering his comment, I decided the barnacles would represent the resistance to change inherent in any large established system, and yes, we definitely have some serious cleaning to do.

We do not need just another tugboat. In fact, we subscribe to the recent findings from several studies that the original ship is dysfunctional and beyond repair. What we must do is closely examine the entire existing ship and all its associated elements, then select those elements that are essential to having a ship that can efficiently and effectively get the passengers and all the cargo to the chosen destination. It should be designed, built, and tested as a completely new vessel. For each cargo container, we need to look at what it was meant to fix. Then we must look deep into the hold and examine the original issue to determine if it is still needed. If so, we must redesign the solution and integrate it into the blueprint for the new ship. The result of this overall systemic approach will be the creation of a new, sleek, efficient, and effective education vessel. By eliminating the need for the cargo containers, pods and barges the new ship gets to its destination more directly and economically. Along the way, we will be able to pay the crew more money and the passengers will enjoy the voyage more. Then we need to get

---

247. *https://www.nist.gov/director/vcat/biography-dr-vinton-g-cerf*

the tugboats to all push in the same direction! We're going to need everyone's help with the barnacles."

Seven years have passed since I wrote the book and K-12 public education is still not meeting the needs of many of our children. According to the PISA Report from OECD, the US is in the middle of the pack compared to other developed countries in student achievement in Math, Science, and Reading. Access to quality public education that creates an informed electorate is essential if we want to restore the democratic underpinnings of the country. The National Center for Education and the Economy (NCEE) produced a study examining the 2009 PISA report called "Standing on the Shoulders of Giants[248]". In their analysis, they noted several areas where the US used to provide an example to the world, but now we have fallen behind. Foreign countries have taken what used to be American innovations, adapted, and evolved them to produce far better results than we are getting. For example, in the countries that are ahead of us, poorly performing schools get more money than highly performing ones so they can improve. In the US, the opposite is true.

Xxx

Critics of the PISA Report and the NCEE analysis of the results question the rigor and reliability of the research. The critics point out that many of the developed countries ahead of the US in the report spend less money than we do and get better results. The following quote from NCEE Director, Mark Tucker[249], points out the fatal flaw in their criticism.

---

248. http://www.ncee.org/wp-content/uploads/2011/05/Standing-on-the-Shoulders-of-Giants-An-American-Agenda-for-Education-Reform.pdf

249. http://blogs.edweek.org/edweek/top_performers/2018/02/ the_us_education_system_is_very_inefficient_fact_or_fiction.html

"The most important cluster of these expenditures has to do with the services that governments provide to families with young children. The types and amounts of expenditure in this realm vary widely from country to country among the top performers. In some top performing countries, especially in Asia, these expenditures are not greater than in the United States. However, in others, they are far larger. I am speaking here of such things as child allowances, child bonuses, well-baby services, nutritional services, extensive paid family leave, high quality childcare and high-quality early childhood education. The extreme differences we now see between the incomes of our wealthiest families and our poorest combine with inequities in our school finance system and our demographics to produce a very large proportion of children entering our compulsory education system who may be homeless, malnourished, culturally deprived, ill, in need of dental care, and severely traumatized.

[...] For a long time, I have believed, on what is now overwhelming evidence, that the United States has one of the least efficient education systems in the industrialized world. I do not blame our teachers for that. Indeed, I think the record shows that the teachers are the victims of a rather dysfunctional system, not the creators of it."

Unlike the factors listed above that fall within the realm of school policy and can be changed by people who make school policy, these things do not fall in the realm of school policy, but they have a dramatic effect on the ability of the schools to do their job, as well as the cost of doing it.

Are teachers the most important factor in student success? Sounds like a simple question, doesn't it? However, the outside of school factors greatly outweigh what happens in school. So, to make the question relevant, let me rephrase it to ask, are teachers the most important in-school factor in student success? The answer, in my opinion, is they could and should be, but in most cases in today's K-12 classroom, they are not. How can that be? The simple answer is that they are not allowed to be.

Have you heard that US Army recruiting slogan, "Be all that you can be!"? In the typical classroom today, teachers are so tightly constrained that they are not allowed to be all that they can be. Under rules that tie teacher performance metrics to their students' scores on high-stakes tests (HST), teachers are forced to focus on preparing students for testing. Some brave and outstanding teachers have figured out that they can focus on learning and the students will still do well on the tests, but it is at their risk if the students don't measure up to the testing standards. The students will have received better education, but the metrics do not give credit for learning that cannot be measured by the tests.

Classrooms constrained by efforts to focus intensely on high-stakes test preparation are intellectually stifling. To pressure teachers to focus on test results, some districts are using student test results for measuring teacher effectiveness. They may achieve their test-results goals, but at what cost? I'll paraphrase an article I read several years ago in the LA Times to illustrate the point.

Assume there are two teachers in the same school with the same type of students in their classes. Teacher A dogmatically focuses on raising test scores. Therefore, she concentrates on topics that will be tested. She drills, practices, discusses, and tests with the fervor of a true believer. The students are glassy-eyed, but they become excellent test-takers and show major improvement in their test scores.

Teacher B is a believer in developing the whole child, so she takes her students on field trips, assigns projects, discusses current events, works on science experiments, etc., all selected to cover topics that are on the test. Her students love school and think learning is fun, and they show a reasonable improvement in test scores. (But less than teacher A's students)

From the test score differential and the NCLB testing perspective, Teacher A is the winner. But which classroom do you want your child to be in? I have always liked the Mark Twain quote, *"I never let my schooling interfere with my education."* In my example, teacher A focused on schooling, while teacher B was more dedicated to education.

Memorization and recall are valuable skills, but not anywhere close to the top of the list. We must change what we measure in schools to change the way we teach it.

"What we want is to see the child in pursuit of knowledge, and not knowledge in pursuit of the child."

~~ George Bernard Shaw ~~

What is the alternative? Empower and allow the teachers to make the decisions about what, when, and how to teach the material. I am not talking about total independence from all structures. Provide the teachers a set of standards, (Most states already have them.) and let the teachers collaborate to determine when and how to teach them to make sure the students acquire the core content for each discipline. If we empower the teachers at this level, they will be the most important factor in student success. Empowered teachers can collaborate across disciplines to coordinate the content for their students' learning in contexts that show the connections between the topics. For example, when the history class is learning about the Holocaust, the science teacher is covering genetics and eugenics. In literature, they read books like <u>Exodus</u> or <u>The Diary of Anne Frank</u>.

When I tell people that we should empower teachers, I mean totally. Give them the authority and responsibility to run the school. At this point, people typically react with some concern that the teachers will act in their own self-interest, not the students'. For the sake of illustrating the point that teachers look out for their students, let's consider a relevant anecdote from the Tracy Learning Center (TLC) schools that operate under an empowered teacher model that they developed. Several years ago, during budget discussions at the schools, the teachers preparing the budget reached a painful conclusion. Given California's severe economic conditions at that time, there was not enough money! They were going to have to select one of the following three options.

1. Cut a Program.
2. Cut a Teacher.
3. Take an across-the-board pay cut.

Bear in mind that the people preparing the budget were a group of empowered teachers. They run the schools. After some discussion about criteria for making the decision, they decided that the primary criterion was, "Which option will have the least negative impact on the students?" As a result, the committee recommended option #3. The full faculty overwhelmingly supported their recommendation. Empowered teachers make great decisions. The empowered teacher model is like a variation of the "Quality Circle" concept that originated in Japan following the work of Professor Kaoru Ishikawa in 1960. The simple concept behind the program is that the people closest to the work have the best understanding of the work and are in the best position to manage and improve it. The TLC teachers have created an outstanding program.

On the other hand, district, state, and national leaders are implementing mandated programs that are taking billions of dollars from the students' classroom learning opportunities and spending it on programs that have proven harmful to students – high-stakes testing is just one example. When teachers develop and administer their own tests, they get immediate relevant feedback about how well their students understand the materials presently being taught at a level of detail that can be used to refine and review the lessons. All they get from the high-stakes tests are periodic global measures of no real classroom learning value.

The medical metaphor is frequently used for education, so let's consider it here. Can you imagine a doctor waiting for a periodic test to provide global information about their patient? Of course not! Testing is a diagnostic tool in both education and medicine. Just as the doctor determines what and when to test and subsequently how to use the results of the test to shape the procedures to be followed, teachers should be empowered to determine what and when to test, and how to use the results.

We might say, "Teachers can and do give weekly tests and quizzes". Problem solved? Not so much! If the teachers are locked into the ultimate goal of students performing well on the HST, then the weekly and daily activities tend to serve that same master. Consequently, weekly quizzes tend to become practice activities for recalling memorized information. They are diagnostic only in the sense that they determine which facts need further memorization practice for the HST. The quizzes and tests are not intended to measure understanding, comprehension, or the ability to use information. Too much of education today is all about recall. However, learning is much more than recall. If we unlock the bonds that result from teachers' performance evaluations being tied to student HST performance and empower the teachers to construct lessons that emphasize using information, deeper comprehension, and understanding, then the students will get a more comprehensive and useful education.

Teachers are national heroes. There is overwhelming evidence that individual classroom teachers are not to blame for the poor performance of many schools. In most cases, the teachers are doing the best they can, given the system and conditions they are required to work in. Empower them and get out of their way.

Is There Really a Common Core? I Am Having Second Thoughts. I had a strange epiphany a couple of years ago. One of the joys of my life was the opportunity to tutor my granddaughters. As Elsa and I were practicing finding the square root of a series of expressions, I could not help thinking, "Why are we doing this?" It is a question that students ponder every day in many subjects, not just math. I can find examples where some people might have an occasion to use some of the things they are taught; but in general, I had to ask myself, "Is there really a Common Core?" I think the answer is, "Yes, but!" and the 'but' is huge compared to the 'yes'. Learning is a life-long endeavor. School is where we need to learn to learn. We have our whole life to learn stuff when we need it.

Issue #23 - We have to learn all this stuff while we are in school.

Part of the problem with the standards is they make an implicit assumption that learning stops when school stops, so we have to learn all this stuff while we are in school. WRONG! Up until recently, I had tacitly accepted having a set of academic standards while deploring the testing regimen attached to the standards. I based my earlier acceptance on the concept of standards, without thinking about the breadth and depth of the application. As I sat there with Elsa, I had time to reflect on the material she was studying in Algebra. I asked myself, "When did you last have to solve a quadratic equation? How often do you need to find the upper or lower limits of a parabola?" The list goes on…. The answer was almost never. Having said that, there are some valuable Algebra topics and principles, including:

- **Properties** – Associative, Commutative, Distributive, Identity, etc. (The names are not as important as their application.) In general, regardless of the subject area, fundamental principles and properties are good to know.

- **Abstract thinking** – Solving for 'x'. Working with unknowns and variables.

- **Estimating** and validating assumptions.

There is a longer list of items that will be useful to many people who pursue technical and professional careers. At the same time, many professions will never require any more algebra than those three topics. If you must take Algebra, then, by all means, learn as much algebra as you can. However, why so much Algebra? Moreover, it is not just Math subjects.

I did some volunteer work in a middle school science classroom. Looking back, students were learning about the periodic table, balancing chemical equations, and other interesting activities – to some of the students. Once again, there is much more material they are studying that they will never use than material that will be valuable to them later in life.

The standards have this lofty stated goal of getting the students 'college and career ready'. I have already pointed out that many careers require a minimum of Algebra and Science. Different careers or professions require different topical expertise. Accountants and architects both use math extensively in their work, but quite different elements of math. Do architects need to know about amortization and actuarial tables? Do accountants need to be able to apply differential equations to analyze stresses and force vectors? Most careers have their own set of knowledge standards that vary significantly from one profession to another.

There is also a body of knowledge needed to be a good citizen. I recognize that it is important to be an informed citizen on climate change, environmental, energy, social and other policy issues. You do not need to balance chemical equations or know what a covalent bond is to be a scientifically literate voter. If you do not need the knowledge for a career or to be a good citizen, what's left? College!

If you are planning to go to college, you need to take Algebra I & II and Geometry plus some other higher math courses in high school because you will not be able to pass the college math requirements without those fundamentals. Learning something simply to be prepared to learn more of the something you will never need does not make a lot of sense. Instead of having general math courses in college, they should offer math courses tailored to the professions.

With today's technologies and online resources, it is possible to customize education for every child. In education, we often refer to the 'teachable moment'. It is the moment when a student has expressed an interest in learning something that happens to coincide with the teacher's responsibility to teach that same thing to the student. In a traditional classroom full of students, those moments are few. There is an alternative.

The following idea comes from fascinating conversations with Roger Schank. The headline on his website reads, *"LEARNING OCCURS WHEN SOMEONE WANTS TO LEARN, NOT WHEN SOMEONE WANTS TO TEACH*[250]. Visualize a classroom where students begin by deciding what interests them. It might be becoming a musician or operating construction equipment. Literally, anything is fair game. After the students select something they are interested in learning about, the teacher asks all the students to start their learning by figuring out what they need to know or learn about their topic. As an example, she might pick some popular job, like being a Mom, and use it as a model. Walk the class through the process of learning how to be a mom. Tell them at the beginning that the most important thing they are learning is how to learn. In their lifetime, the students will typically have several different jobs or careers. They do not have to learn anything now about all those other possible jobs. In fact, if they learn it now, by the time they need it, much of what they learned will be obsolete. What they need to learn now is how to learn whatever they need to know whenever they need to know it.

At this point, she turns the students loose and becomes their learning guide. She is not the source of information. She is the guide to how to find and use information. Part of that guidance role is to review the learning needs the student identified and suggest additional topics that the student may have omitted. This coaching is done through a series of questions, not answers. Instead of saying, "You forgot to include politics.", she might ask, "What laws and regulations do you think might make it easier or more difficult for

---

250. *http://www.rogerschank.com/*

you?" She can then guide the students into expanding their learning list. As they proceed through their learning activities, students will find they need to know elements from math, science, language arts, social studies, etc. It will not be necessary to point out that their knowledge has traditionally been taught in discipline packages. It doesn't matter, and they don't care. What matters is that they are learning and enjoying it. Children are born with unlimited and nearly insatiable curiosity. Traditional classrooms squelch that curiosity before they leave elementary school. This model nurtures and builds upon their curiosity.

In this scenario, teachable moments fill the day. Students are continuously engaged in learning. She might require all students to produce a ten-minute presentation to the rest of the class describing what they learned that week. That's education, not schooling!

Shortly after his first State of the Union address (a year after his inauguration), I wrote the following letter to President Obama.

Dear President Obama

"I have been a big fan of yours for a long time. During the presidential campaign, I made phone calls on your behalf. I watched your State of the Union Address with great interest and hope. During the speech, you mentioned letters from ordinary citizens that helped you illustrate your points. I realize that those letters were selected by staffers and most of them never get in front of you. Hopefully, this one will reach you because I think you need to see it.

You and your administration have puzzled me with your approach to fixing the problems with Pre-K through 12 public education. You correctly state the importance of fixing the problems while systematically exacerbating them. For example, you say that every child should have an excellent education, but you support expanding choice and charter schools. Both choice and charter school programs make a better option available to some students while leaving a larger number of students behind in the schools from which they came. Race to the Top (RttT) basically picks winners and losers. We need a program that makes everyone winners. The groups that are benefiting most from the current round of reforms are the charter school operators and testing companies who are reaping huge windfall profits at the expense of our children; and the politicians who want to weaken the influence of the union workers. If that is your intention, (and I don't believe it is) you can stop reading here. If you genuinely care about providing quality education to every child in America, read on.

The Organization for Economic Cooperation and Development (OECD) Program for International Student Assessment (PISA) Report is correctly cited as proof that America needs to improve K-12 education. Unfortunately, the rest of the excellent information in the report goes largely unheeded. The National Center on Education and the Economy (NCEE) produced an analysis of the PISA report titled, <u>Standing on the Shoulders of Giants</u>, bench-marking America's programs, and practices with the countries ahead of us in the PISA rankings. I was present when your secretary of education, Arne Duncan, participated in the announcement of the report. The results of their analysis can best be summed up with the following brief quote.

"The Dog that Did Not Bark – "It turns out that neither the researchers whose work is reported on in this paper nor the

analysts of the OECD PISA data have found any evidence that any country that leads the world's education performance league tables has gotten there by implementing any of the major agenda items that dominate the education reform agenda in the United States."

Given that clear message, why do we continue to pursue the reforms that are not working? By the way, teachers' unions are a vital part of the excellent performance of schools in those countries that lead the US. According to the PISA Report, you don't need unions to help make it easier to fire 'bad teachers'. Instead, you need unions to help identify ineffective teachers and improve them.

Charter schools were conceived to allow passionate creative educators to test innovative learning programs. They worked! We have some excellent charter schools; but more importantly, we have some excellent proven educational innovations. Rather than create more charter schools, it's time to take the proven innovations and use them to transform existing public schools."

In her 1996 book It Takes a Village, Hillary Clinton quoted the old African saying, "It takes a village to raise a child." The inverse is also true, "It takes a good school to raise a community." There needs to be a carefully developed and maintained symbiotic relationship between a community and its schools. Instead of emphasizing and supporting the important roles of schools in their communities, the present national educational programs like RttT are identifying poorly performing schools and closing them down. While the intention is to put the students into better schools, the unintended consequence is the destruction of a vital community resource.

Schools are at the very heart of their communities. It begins in elementary schools and continues through high school – evidenced by the large numbers of people who attend Friday night football games to support their local teams. Go to a game and watch the social, cultural, political, educational, and economic (not to mention romantic) activity that occurs there – of course, there is also a football game. The neighborhood school is the gathering place for local businesses and service organizations. By eliminating 'poorly performing' schools, the NCLB and RttT programs are damaging their communities.

RttT starts off in the right direction by identifying the schools that are failing to meet the needs of the students and the community. However, after identifying them, the response should not be to close them but to improve them. It is time to stop experimenting with student lives. There are proven comprehensive transformational models. We need to be replicating these proven models, not trying to find another model that might work.

Under the RttT, after identifying poorly performing schools, the district then moves from that determination to a set of punitive and destructive options. Because of some long-term funding and other socioeconomic issues, the vast majority of these identified poorly performing schools will come from disadvantaged minority communities. Instead of punitive actions, the emphasis must be on investing in the resources and people needed to improve the disadvantaged schools and rebuild the communities based upon the proven models from the successful charter schools.

Race to the Top, in its present form, will not get us there!

You can't be in favor of a program that tacitly accepts some schools will be better than others and seeks equity by balancing access instead of raising quality. If you believe that everyone has the potential for greatness, then you must also want to ensure that every child is nurtured to achieve that greatness. And you should not only want it on moral or ethical grounds; you should also want it on economic grounds. There are many reports on the economic and social benefits of providing equitable access to quality K-12 education. America has some excellent public schools, but that is not enough. America's future is at risk as long as we continue to allow poor schools to exist.

In April of 2009, The McKinsey & Co. published, The Economic Impact of the Achievement Gap in America's Schools. The report summarized the issue as follows:

"This report finds that the underutilization of human potential in the United States is extremely costly. For individuals, our results show that:

• Avoidable shortfalls in academic achievement impose heavy and often tragic consequences, via lower earnings, poorer health, and higher rates of incarceration.

• For many students (but by no means all), lagging achievement evidenced as early as fourth grade appears to be a powerful predictor of rates of high school and college graduation, as well as lifetime earnings.

For the economy as a whole, our results show that:

• If the United States had in recent years closed the gap between its educational achievement levels and those of better-performing nations such as Finland and Korea, GDP in 2008 could have been $1.3 trillion to $2.3 trillion higher. This represents 9 to 16 percent of GDP.

• If the gap between black and Latino student performance and white student performance had been similarly narrowed, GDP in 2008 would have been between $310 billion and $525 billion higher, or 2 to 4 percent of GDP. The magnitude of this impact will rise in the years ahead as demographic shifts result in blacks and Latinos becoming a larger proportion of the population and workforce.

• If the gap between low-income students and the rest had been similarly narrowed, GDP in 2008 would have been $400 billion to $670 billion higher, or 3 to 5 percent of GDP.

• If the gap between America's low-performing states and the rest had been similarly narrowed, GDP in 2008 would have been $425 billion to $700 billion higher, or 3 to 5 percent of GDP

Put differently, the persistence of these educational achievement gaps imposes on the United States the economic equivalent of a permanent national recession. The recurring annual economic cost of the international achievement gap is substantially larger than the deep recession the United States is currently experiencing. The annual output cost of the racial, income, and regional or systems achievement gap is larger than the US recession of 1981–82."

There is a solution. You should look at the transformational model at the three schools at the Tracy Learning Center (TLC) in Tracy, California. By designing and building the solution as a new system, the solution can be delivered within existing budgets. The annual per-pupil cost at the TLC is less than $7,500. By empowering the teachers to manage the whole program, the system adapts daily in response to needs that arise. From the beginning, this school was built to be a model for transforming public schools – not building more similar charter schools.

In eleven years of operation, the school, with a diverse population, has had less than 1% dropouts! In the same timeframe, very few teachers have left their positions. In 2013, the TLC elementary school was ranked as the third best charter school in the state by the USC Rossier School of Education. (There are about 1,000 charter schools in California.) As good as the present model is, the program does not promote or include any radical new ideas. The system is a comprehensive integrated set of selected, proven, student-centered and organizational best-practices. If you would like to get a better idea of the program at the TLC, watch their video on YouTube[251].

The program at the TLC has been favorably reviewed by people from both sides of the political spectrum. Bill Brock, Secretary of Labor under President Reagan and Ed McElroy, President Emeritus of the American Federation of Teachers both endorse the TLC model and are both

---

251. *https://www.youtube.com/watch?v=Jg38Y60bX20*

supporters. Randi Weingarten (AFT) and Dennis Van Roekel (NEA) have both said that their unions recognize the TLC model as one they would support for transforming K-12 education. Raul Yzaguirre, former head of La Raza and US ambassador to the Dominican Republic is another supporter of the TLC model. During your first campaign for President, Linda Darling Hammond served as your education surrogate. She was and is fantastic. You need to read her book, The Flat World and Education, or call her in for a refresher course. Linda supports the model at the TLC. When I described what they are doing at the TLC to Vint Cerf, Google's Internet Ambassador, he commented, "That's the way we work at Google."

I live in nearby Haymarket, VA and would love to assist you in any way I can to improve America's schools. The following quote from my friend Jack Taub sums up the situation.

Together, we will create a national movement to unleash" America's largest, unlimited, and virtually untapped source !!!!of renewable energy: the minds of all of our children

Customizing education for every child will ensure that never again will our children's hopes, futures, and dreams be determined by the color of their skin, the quality of their healthcare, the poverty in their home and/or community and last but far from least the teachers' and students' ability to withstand the frustration and boredom inherent in today's public education systems."

The chorus from Whitney Houston's beautiful song, "The Greatest Love of All[252]", should inspire us all.

---

252. *https://www.youtube.com/watch?v=IYzlVDlE72w&index=7&list=RD3JWTaaS7LdU*

I believe the children are our future,

Teach them well and let them lead the way,

Show them all the beauty they possess inside,

Give them a sense of pride to make it easier,

Let the children's laughter remind us how we used to be."

I received a form-letter response to my letter to the President.

Educators, are you tired of playing defense yet? As I sat through countless football games over the holidays, I could not help but notice that the winning teams had a good defense, but more importantly, they had a great offense. I woke up one morning realizing that those of us who are playing this game of public education are allowing the other people to keep the ball and force educators to play defense. It's time to go on offense! For each of the areas where those who are destroying public education have been hammering teachers, it's time to turn things around.

Charters, Choice, and other Educational Options – Offense!

Let's stop arguing AGAINST charter schools and start arguing FOR public schools that outperform charters. Charter schools were conceived to test innovative ideas for improving teaching and learning. Some of them have succeeded. That is not an argument for more charter schools. It's an argument for taking those innovations and improving public schools. Instead of creating additional charter schools in their image, we must start transforming public schools using these successful models and practices. If we do that, we will save the money that is currently being sucked out of the schools for charter school administrative salaries and bogus facilities rental costs. These funds can be better used for directly supporting student learning. Let's stop fighting against charter schools and put our efforts into transforming public schools. Make the other side fight against making our public schools better. That is a tough position for them to defend.

The whole charter school concept was never intended to replace public schools. It was conceived as a way to allow dedicated creative teachers to test innovative ideas without some of the constraints they faced in a traditional classroom. The unintended consequence of this decision was that greedy entrepreneurs recognized the opportunity to make big profits – at the expense of the kids. The most frequently cited example is Eva Moskowitz, the CEO of the Success Academy in New York City, who paid herself a salary and bonuses of $567,500 in 2017 (and she has four assistants). The Success Academy network of schools has a total enrollment of less than 10,000 students. By comparison, the chancellor of NYC public schools, with an enrollment of more than 1.1 million students and a budget of over $25B, has a salary half that of Ms. Moskowitz.

The greedy edu-business charter school advocates found multiple ways to milk money from the students. In addition to paying outrageous executive salaries (while paying teachers less than their public-school counterparts), they pull off a real-estate scam. These profiteers buy potential school property under a separate company they own, and then lease it to their charter school for a huge profit.

After realizing the potential for pulling large sums of money out of the public school system, the next step was to create a demand for more charter schools. This push for more charter schools happened to coincide with the conservative political desire to weaken teachers' unions. The Perfect Storm! By reducing budgets for public schools and other policies designed to make the public schools look bad, they could close public schools with union teachers and replace them with charter schools without teachers' unions.

Charter schools are not the answer. According to the Stanford University CREDO Report[253], most charter schools are equal to or worse than the public schools in their communities.

> *"The group portrait shows wide variation in performance. The study reveals that a decent fraction of charter schools, 17 percent, provide superior education opportunities for their students. Nearly half of the charter schools nationwide have results that are no different from the local public-school options and over a third, 37 percent, deliver learning results that are significantly worse than their student would have realized had they remained in traditional public schools."*

How can we use this information? The healthcare industry is frequently cited as analogous to education, so let's consider a parallel instance in healthcare to create a metaphor for what this CREDO data means. We will consider the existing big-hospital healthcare provider infrastructure as analogous to the existing K-12 public schools; and privately run clinics (Doc-In-A-Box) as analogous to charter schools. If less than one-third of the time private clinics provide better results and two-thirds of the time the same or worse results, do you think there would be a national clamor to provide more private clinics? Of course not! So, why all this irrational demand to allow more charter schools? The answer is a simple one-word response. Money! There is a burgeoning, profitable industry in operating charter schools. Some people are ostensibly raising money to help students, but the real target of the severest critics of K-12 education is to make lots of money and break up or decrease the political importance and influence of teachers' unions.

---

253. https://credo.stanford.edu/wp-content/uploads/2021/08/ncss_2013_final_draft.pdf

Neither of these options is a positive step toward transforming the public schools and providing students with a better education.

Now consider the charter school option from another perspective. For the sake of this discussion, let us assume that we could wave a magic wand and it would ensure that every charter school would be better than the average public school. In that case, it would be unconscionable to allow less than 100% of the public schools to become charter schools. Does anyone believe that the total elimination of public schools as we have historically known them is a good idea? Of course not! We have over 13,000 autonomous school districts and about 132,000 K-12 public schools across the country. Our challenge is not to eliminate them and replace them all with charter schools. The challenge is to transform them into excellent student-centered neighborhood schools where every child receives a continuously engaging, customized learning opportunity.

School Choice – Offense!

According to edchoice.org[254], "*School choice allows public education funds to follow students to the schools or services that best fit their needs—whether that's to a public school, private school, charter school, home school or any other learning environment parents choose for their kids.*" Sounds like a good plan, but school choice does not work unless the parents are informed and involved. Basically, if you provide school choice, the students whose parents care and are involved will make the choice, while the students whose parents are working 2 or 3 jobs to put food on the table and a roof over their heads, don't have the time or luxury for getting involved in school issues. The competition that was predicted to drive improvement in all schools does not exist. School choice also introduces an additional transportation cost. Parents who choose a school out of

---

254. https://www.edchoice.org/school-choice/what-is-school-choice/

their neighborhood either must transport their children, or the district has to. Once again, this transportation requirement limits choices. The better option is to improve all the schools, so choice is not necessary.

The inequity of school funding driven by the local tax base is another major problem. The PISA (Programme for International Student Assessment) report, done by the OECD (Organization for Economic Cooperation and Development), periodically causes an uproar when it points out that American public education is far from a world leader. Inequity in school funding is one of the things it cites as a reason for the problem. In other countries, the administration identifies lower performing schools and directs additional funding to their improvement. In the US, just the opposite occurs. Lower performing schools enter a death spiral. The National Center on Education and the Economy wrote an excellent analysis of the PISA report with recommendations for responding called "Standing on the Shoulders of Giants[255]."

It is time to stop blaming and profiteering. Public education is too important to use as a pawn for political gain or corporate profit motives. We all need to stand behind truly transformational programs that engage all students and provide them with the knowledge and skills they will need to prosper in this global economy.

Common Core Curriculum – Offense!

Until we can eliminate it, we must embrace it as a guide and improve it. There are countless things wrong with the whole Common Core curriculum program, but at its roots are some good fundamental guidelines for what students need to learn. More importantly, its

---

255. http://www.ncee.org/wp-content/uploads/2011/05/Standing-on-the-Shoulders-of-Giants-An-American-Agenda-for-Education-Reform.pdf

proponents are well-funded and powerful. Rather than fight the program, embrace it for its good parts and immediately begin the process of improving it. Rather than fighting the whole concept, work to fix each piece of it. For example, the National Council of Teachers of Mathematics (NCTM) and National Association of Elementary School Principals (NAESP) could establish a joint task force to immediately work on revising the K-5 Common Core Math standards. Begin with a brief set of examples of existing inappropriate grade-level math standards and move immediately to the position of improving and adopting them.

It is hard for the general public to understand why educators are against rigorous academic standards. They are not! They are against some elements of these poorly conceived and implemented standards. While we are at it, let's expand the standards to cover learning skills, not just content. Our schools must produce lifelong learners, not good test-takers.

High-Stakes Tests – Offense!

We have let assessment and accountability become bad words. When used properly, assessments are a valuable tool for teachers to use in customizing the learning for each student. To be effective, they must be authentic and timely. Let's stop arguing against testing. Let's make it irrelevant by showing that timely, authentic, assessments produce much better outcomes. By the way, the money wasted on high-stakes testing can be better used for relevant learning resources.

At the same time, we must eliminate the mind-numbing teaching to the test classrooms that bore students and frustrate teachers. This change is going to take some strong leadership at the district and building level. The profiteers who promote high-stakes testing and sell the test-prep materials have created a false reality that causes teachers to focus on preparing students to do well on the tests. We do not need to teach to the test for the students to do well on tests. In fact, if you ignore the tests and focus on learning, the students will still do well on the tests. Doing well on high-stakes tests prepares students to be good Jeopardy! contestants – but not much else. Teaching students how to learn and use information prepares them for countless life challenges. Let's put the emphasis on learning, not testing.

Accountability – Offense!

Let's turn accountability in our favor. There is overwhelming evidence that the biggest factor in determining a student's academic achievement is poverty level, not teacher quality. Great teachers can do amazing things, but they can only do so much. Let's start forcing the accountability issue to focus on poverty. Schools can be centers of community economic development.

We need more equitable funding of schools across all communities. Until the local, state, and federal governments step up and seriously address poverty, we cannot hold teachers or schools accountable for academic performance. Accountability is a good thing, but it must be focused on the right issue.

Firing 'Bad Teachers' – Offense!

Nobody wants to have bad teachers in classrooms. We do not need to defend bad teachers. We need to identify, support, develop, and improve them. People do not become teachers to become financially wealthy. They do it because they care about kids and want to help them grow. If you have a teacher who cares, do not dismiss them without first attempting to improve them.

Value-Added Metrics (VAM) are a false measurement, but to the general public they can be sold as valid. At some gut level, they sound logical, and most people will not, and do not, bother to look closely at the mathematical model to see its flaws. Rather than fighting VAM, we need to put forward a valid set of metrics. We need to start with an analysis of what needs to be measured. Profiteers seeking to undermine confidence in public education created the current VAM to make teachers look bad. That sounds like an absurd statement, but given their design and use, what other motivation could there be? If we are going to have accountability, then there need to be metrics for measuring performance. We need to take a lead in defining what should be measured and how.

The metrics need to look at far more than just the teachers. The myth that administrators cannot fire bad teachers is both false and harmful, whether in a union or non-union setting. I repeat my earlier statement; nobody wants to have bad teachers in classrooms. Rather than defend a process that 'protects' teachers, change the narrative to a continuous improvement process that ensures we have great teachers. Both major teachers' unions have excellent programs for improving teacher quality. Let's stop defending unions and teachers. They don't need defending. Instead of being on the defensive, start emphasizing programs that ensure that every teacher in every classroom is good and getting better. One highly effective way to achieve this goal is to empower teachers and make them responsible for teacher quality. They will use mentoring, professional learning communities, peer-team support, and many other proven mechanisms for providing each individual teacher the right resources and means for becoming a great teacher.

Teachers are some of the most committed and dedicated public servants in the world. As a society, we need to get back to recognizing and appreciating that fact. Let's stop wasting time and resources defending them. They do not need to be defended. They need to be supported so they can become better.

Closing 'Bad Schools' – Offense!

Do you have a bad school in your community? For most people, the answer to this question is a resounding, "No!" Do we have some bad communities whose schools reflect their surrounding conditions? Unfortunately, yes. Is the solution to close the school? No! The school, as bad as it is, is probably the best thing in the community. Closing the school is treating the symptom. The cure is to treat the cause; and the neighborhood school can and must be a major part of the treatment. There is a wonderful old saying that is appropriate here, "If you are not part of the solution, you're part of the problem." In other words, get involved in your community schools. This includes volunteering in the school, attending school board meetings, and understanding what type of curriculum the school is teaching your children.

Let's Get Offensive!

I read several blogs, Facebook posts, tweets, and other social media. They are full of good and bad examples of what is currently happening in public education. Florida Governor Ron DeSantis has enforced into law the "Stop Woke Act" signed in 2022 that prohibits instructions or race relations diversity that imply a person's status as either privileged or oppressed is necessarily determined by his or her national origin, or sex. What does this mean? This creates a banning of Black studies and curriculum in high school and college level enrollment. Students won't be able to learn the history or cultural development of black people in American History. Recently, they have become more aggressive in attacking some of those who are denigrating and destroying public education. In a sense, they are taking the offensive in damaging K-12 public education. They are allowing people with bad intentions to make the rules of the game. It is time to change the game. We need to stop allowing the dark side to pick the small issues and wage battles over pieces of the problem. We need to elevate the level of discourse from individual issues to systemic transformation. Our elected officials are not serving the interests of our children or the country. It's time to change the game!

Getting Rid of Bad Teachers Is Not Enough - The book, <u>Special Interest Teacher America's Schools,</u> keeps repeating that we need to get rid of bad teachers and that would solve most of the problem. However, if we could wave a magic wand and have only wonderful teachers in every school, we would still not have truly transformed the schools in any significant way when it comes to preparing students for the new world that they will face after they graduate. As they are presently operated, many schools still prepare students for agriculture and manufacturing jobs – as those jobs existed 50 years ago. America's K-12 public schools are not adequately preparing students for the world they will enter when they graduate.

Issue #24 - Work Has Changed So The Preparation For Work Must Change.

Twenty-five years ago, noted Harvard social scientist Shoshanna Zuboff wrote a book titled, <u>In the Age of the Smart Machine</u>. High school algebra teachers should be particularly impressed with the example she gave of how technology was changing the workplace – and how education needed to change to prepare students for this new world. To illustrate her point, she described the roles of the workers in a paper mill. In the old mills, there were several stages in the process. A different worker monitored and operated each stage. The worker had a physical, sensory involvement in the process (sight, smell, touch, etc.). For example, the worker would smell the batch of molten paper pulp in the vat or squeeze it through his fingers to feel the sliminess and viscosity. At another stage, the next worker would slap the roll of paper before it went into the press to remove the liquid. The worker would listen to the sound or observe the depth of the depression made by the slap. Based upon these personal, physical observations, the worker would adjust the input of materials or the pace of the process. In short, each worker was responsible for a small, discrete part of the process and had a physical, sensory interaction with the process.

In the modern paper mill, the process is automated, with each stage being monitored by digital /electronic sensors that automatically adjust the inputs to keep the product within preset parameters. The worker is in a control room. Instead of being physically involved with the process, he/she is isolated from the process and only sees the process abstractly through a collection of dials and graphical representations. Instead of being responsible for only a discrete stage of the process, he/she is responsible for the whole continuum of the many stages in the process; they are remotely monitoring it through abstract graphical representations. How are America's schools preparing students for this changing world? Algebra is the place in schools where abstract thinking was first taught, but in most districts, algebra was only required for students on the college track. All students need to learn abstract and computational thinking.

It is now twenty-five years since Zuboff wrote her book and the nature of work has undergone another major shift. Tom Friedman captured its essence in his book, The World is Flat (In particular, in chapter 7, "The Quiet Crisis"). In the book Friedman quoted Shirley Ann Jackson, President of Rensselaer Polytechnic Institute, as saying,

> *"The sky is not falling today, but it might be in fifteen to twenty years if we don't change our ways, and all signs are that we are not changing, especially in our public schools. ... The American education system from kindergarten through twelfth grade just is not stimulating enough young people to want to go into science, math, and engineering (STEM)."*

Dr. Jackson could have stopped her caution with the words 'stimulating enough young people'. The problem goes beyond the STEM subjects. Schools are not stimulating for most students in many areas. The advancements in computing and telecommunications have empowered people in incredible ways. To be successful in a flat world, a person requires a completely different set of knowledge and skills than are being taught in today's traditional classrooms. The YouTube video called *"Did You Know*[256]*"* tells us,

> *"The top-10 in-demand jobs in 2010 did not exist in 2004. We are currently preparing students for jobs that don't yet exist, using technologies that haven't been invented, in order to solve problems we don't even know are problems yet"*

The recurring theme that is driving the need to improve our schools is an increasing recognition of the shift from an American centered economy[257] to a global economy."

The list is eye opening. It clearly demonstrates the need for major changes in what and how we teach our children. From another perspective, most of the information a person will need ten years after graduation did not exist when he or she was in high school. Craig Mundie, Microsoft technologist, said,

---

256. *https://www.youtube.com/watch?v=u06BXgWbGvA*

257. http://www.youtube.com/watch?NR=1&v=evAivHL2udk&feature=endscreen

"When the world gets this hyperconnected, the speed with which every job and industry changes also goes into hypermode. In the old days, it was assumed that your educational foundation would last your whole lifetime. That is no longer true. Because of the way every industry — from health care to manufacturing to education — is now being transformed by cheap, fast, connected computing power, the skill required for every decent job is rising as is the necessity of lifelong learning. More and more things you know and tools you use are being made obsolete faster. It's as if every aspect of our lives is now being driven by Moore's Law[258]. This is exacerbating our unemployment problem."

For anyone not familiar with Moore's law. Wikipedia defines it as:

"Moore's law is the observation that, over the history of computing hardware[259], the number of transistors[260] on integrated circuits[261] doubles approximately every two years. The law is named after Intel co-founder Gordon E. Moore[262], who described the trend in his 1965 paper."

In January of 2013, Thomas Friedman wrote a NY Times *column* titled, "It's P.Q. and C.Q. as Much as I.Q. Friedman closes his column[263] with:

---

258. http://en.wikipedia.org/wiki/History_of_computing_hardware

259. *http://en.wikipedia.org/wiki/History_of_computing_hardware*

260. *http://en.wikipedia.org/wiki/Transistor*

261. *http://en.wikipedia.org/wiki/Integrated_circuit*

262. *http://en.wikipedia.org/wiki/Gordon_Moore*

263. http://www.nytimes.com/2013/01/30/opinion/friedman-its-pq-and-cq-as-much-as-iq.html?nl=opinion&emc=edit_ty_20130130&_r=0

"The winners won't just be those with more I.Q. It will also be those with more P.Q. (passion quotient) and C.Q. (curiosity quotient) to leverage all the new digital tools to not just find a job, but to invent one or reinvent one, and to not just learn but to relearn for a lifetime. Government can and must help, but the president needs to explain that this won't just be an era of "Yes We Can." It will also be an era of "Yes You Can" and "Yes You Must."

Given these conditions, our emphasis on teaching, retention, and recall in the traditional classroom seems poorly targeted. Assume we could achieve perfection and that students could retain and recall 100% of what we teach in school. If we accept the futurists' estimate that 80% of what students will need to know ten years after graduation did not exist while they were in school, then ten years after they graduate, they will only have 20% of what they need. That is not to say that what they did learn will not be useful. It means that every day they need to be able to learn more. Our public schools spend far too much time teaching students to learn material represented by Curriculum Standards, and far too little time teaching the learning process. Ten years after they graduate their most important skill will be their ability to learn the new information they need.

Along with those learning skills, students must also acquire and practice using a set of high-performance skills like analysis, problem solving, teamwork, communications, responsibility, creativity, reliability, innovation, research, etc. This requires a structural transformation in the classrooms from teacher-centered to student-centered learning. Most teacher-union critics focus on reforming the traditional teacher-centered learning environment by simply changing the work rules in a teacher-centered learning environment. Instead, we need to empower our teachers to become more effective managers of a student-centered learning environment. The rules for this environment do not inhibit teaching and learning, they empower teacher creativity and innovation and student engagement and learning.

Issue #25 - We will not solve the poverty issue until we have equity and excellence in all our public schools.

Every child deserves an excellent education. An impressive collection of studies, reports, articles, and comments by national leaders supports this statement. The courts cannot fix the educational equity problem. The members of the Supreme Court are mostly well-intentioned and intelligent people. Therefore, it must be exceedingly difficult for them to participate in discussions about school integration and equity, knowing that nothing they can do will make any difference in the general quality of education that the children across the country will receive. They can approve all manner of programs for moving and shuffling students or money from school to school, but unless they make other significant changes in public education, the quality of education in the schools involved will not change, and they do not have the authority to make more substantive changes. As the recent discussions have illustrated yet again, all they can do is attempt to balance access to quality education across ethnic and racial groups. Unless the program results in all the poorly performing schools showing major improvements, there will still be too many students attending bad schools.

The whole concept of busing was an admission that the public education system was broken and that many neighborhoods had failing schools from which some students must be bussed to give them a chance to get a better education. Although 'bussing' in the traditional sense has largely ceased to exist, it has reared its head again in a new form. The latest version identifies poorly performing schools and puts them through a series of steps – potentially resulting in their closing. The students from the closed schools are assigned (bussed) to other, incrementally better, schools. For the most part, they are not put into great schools. Meanwhile, the community with the closed school has lost a valuable cultural, economic, and social resource – its neighborhood school.

If you believe that a person's intellectual capacity is racially, ethnically, or culturally predetermined, you may as well stop reading at this point. If you do not believe it, then you cannot be in favor of a program that tacitly accepts that some schools will be better than others and seeks equity by balancing access instead of raising quality. If you believe that everyone has the potential for greatness, then you must also want to ensure that schools nurture every child to achieve that greatness. In addition, you should not only want it on moral or ethical grounds; you should also want it on economic grounds. There are many reports on the economic and social benefits of providing equitable access to quality K-12 education. America has some excellent public schools, but that is not enough. America's future is at risk if we continue to allow poor schools to exist.

The disparity between the average income levels of the bottom 70% compared to the top 5% is growing at an exponential rate. If you look at wealth instead of income, the combined wealth of the top 1% exceeds the combined wealth of the bottom 95%. The result is the virtual destruction of the Middle Class in America. It is not a sustainable model for the future. The single most important means for re-establishing America's vibrant Middle Class is providing a quality public education to every child.

How important is it for America to have a strong middle class? The May 18, 2012, issue of Atlantic Magazine printed an article titled, "The 100% Economy: Why the U.S. Needs a Strong Middle Class to Thrive[264]".

> *"Widening income inequality helped drive us into the Great Recession and is holding back our recovery. It is tempting to view the stagnation of the middle class and the disappearance of middle-skill jobs as a problem for only some of us. That's simply untrue. Mounting economic evidence suggests strongly that Hanauer's argument is correct and is, in fact, fundamental to America's future. It's not a do-good argument. It is a selfish one, both for innovators and for every other American counting on the innovator class to power growth for decades to come.*
>
> *The evidence suggests that the United States needs a vibrant middle class. Not for any sentimental reasons, but because it's a very dangerous thing not to have."*

If you can travel, you should visit both developed and undeveloped countries. The most striking element of the third world or undeveloped countries you will see will be their lack of a middle class. There is a clear upper class and a massive lower class, but virtually no middle class. The resulting poverty and living conditions are frightening. You do not have to go far to see it. Try visiting a Caribbean island. The tourist areas on and near the beaches are surrounded by high security fences to keep the poor people away from the tourists. There are 'compounds' where the upper class live and shanty towns where the rest of the citizens live. There are virtually no middle-class neighborhoods. It is unpleasant to see.

---

264. http://www.theatlantic.com/business/archive/2012/05/the-100-economy-why-the-us-needs-a-strong-middle-class-to-thrive/257385/

More importantly, there is constant civil unrest and occasional outbreaks of violence. Frighteningly, there are signs of those distinctions in America with our gated communities and areas of abject poverty – and yes, occasional outbreaks of violence. We need to turn around the trend that is driving more people from the middle class to the lower class.

To strengthen our middle class, do we need 'integrated' schools, or do we need diverse schools? What is the difference? There are many forms of diversity, one of which is racial. One of the great strengths of this country is its diversity. However, even in a racially homogenous community, there is great diversity. We do not need forced integration to achieve diversity. Rather than relieving strife between communities, forced integration exacerbates it. People like the comfort and sense of belonging that comes with a community school and resent any program that disrupts that sense. This statement is not about a racial community. It's about a geographic community – the neighborhood school. Closing a school results in breaking up neighborhoods. It also creates tension and distrust. Despite this negative impact, some communities close schools or shift the boundaries between schools to achieve some well-intentioned equity goals. Many parents consider the quality of the schools as the major factor in purchasing a home. Imagine their dismay if they make the big step to move to a new home near a good school, only to have their child forced to enroll at another school to achieve some perceived needed balance. The solution is to ensure that every school is a quality school.

Every child must get a great education and we should not have to close neighborhood schools to provide it. The goal is to improve all the schools and provide equity through quality rather than closing schools. By making every school in every neighborhood an excellent school, there would be no need to close any of them. The focus should be on improving schools, not closing them.

Lack of equity is particularly a disaster for America's young black men. In his March 2006 article, Phillip Jackson, the executive Director of the Black Star Project, announced:

> *"Black Boys Become Black Men JUST IN CASE YOU HAVE NOT HEARD,*
>
> *America has lost a generation of Black boys"*

Jackson goes on to point out that in virtually every area from education and employment to health and housing, we have lost a full generation of black men. The critical question now is, "How many more generations will we lose before we correct the conditions that cause the problem?" One of the factors Jackson describes as creating the conditions leading to the problem is lack of quality education. He points out that less than half of the young black men in our major cities graduate from high school. Of those that graduate, a small number go to college, and only 22% of that small number finish college. Jackson continues:

> *"[...] Ironically, experts say that the solutions to the problems of young Black men are simple and inexpensive, but they are not easy or popular. It is not that we lack solutions as much as it is that we lack the will to implement these solutions to save Black boys. It seems that the government is willing to pay billions of dollars to lock up young Black men, rather than the millions it would take to prepare them to become viable contributors and valued members of our society.*
>
> *Please consider these simple goals that can lead to solutions for fixing the problems of young Black men:*

Short term

1) Teach all Black boys to read at grade level by the third grade and to embrace education.

2) Provide positive role models for Black boys.

3) Create a stable home environment for Black boys that includes contact with their fathers.

4) Ensure that Black boys have a strong spiritual base.

5) Control the negative media influences on Black boys.

6) Teach Black boys to respect all girls and women.

Long term

1) Invest as much money in educating Black boys as in locking up Black men.

2) Help connect Black boys to a positive vision of themselves in the future.

3) Create high expectations and help Black boys live up to those high expectations.

4) Build a positive peer culture for Black boys.

5) Teach Black boys self-discipline, culture, and history.

6) Teach Black boys and the communities in which they live to embrace education and life-long learning[265]."

---

265. *https://www.hbcusports.com/forums/threads/america-has-lost-a-generation-of-black-boys.64935/*

The above paper was written to describe the plight of young black men, but it applies to young black women as well. Moreover, the issue should be expanded to include all young people who live in disadvantaged families or communities. In reading the list, you quickly realize that many of the issues are more cultural than governmental. That is why the solution we describe in this book puts so much emphasis on the importance of the connections between schools and their communities.

Our Declaration of Independence states, "All men are created equal." This statement leads to a reasonable assumption that all men should be treated equally, and all men should have the same opportunities to achieve the American Dream. There is no denying that America has some diehard racist bigots, but most Americans are not racists or bigots. In fact, if you reduce the problem to a microcosm of looking at a single person, the outcome is very predictable. If the average American were presented with the story of a young child in the circumstances facing many of our disadvantaged minority population, that person would be outraged and want to get involved in finding a solution to the problem. Unfortunately, the problem is so big and pervasive the average American cannot grasp the magnitude of the problem, let alone conceive of a solution. This book describes such a solution. We must find a way to provide every American with quality education. No other solution will work.

The first step in fixing a problem is recognizing you have a problem. One of the reasons that America has been so slow to recognize the need to fix the problem is that we see ourselves as the best in the world already. In many ways, that is still true. So, as the old sayings go, "Don't mess with success!", or "If it ain't broke, don't fix it!" Even though we are still the best in many ways, the educational trend lines are heading in the wrong direction; and if we do nothing to change them, we are in serious trouble. Historically, America has produced a group of outstanding public-school graduates (the top 20%) whose talents and innovations provided opportunities that the rest of the country could take advantage of to be 'successful'. Realistically, the world is changing, and for everyone to be successful, everyone needs a better education. Low skilled jobs are vanishing, and global competition is rising. If we are to regain our global leadership, then we need to do a better job of educating all our students, not just the top 20%.

Emphasis of the critical nature of the equity issue was voiced in 2009 by Rev. Al Sharpton and former House Speaker Newt Gingrich[266] following a meeting with President Obama at the White House. Their coming together validates the point that fixing the issues of inequality in K-12 public education is at least a bi-partisan issue, if not a non-partisan issue. Speaker Gingrich became another of many national leaders to make the point that fixing this particular problem is potentially the first civil rights issue of the 21st century. The following quote from a 2008 interview with Bill and Melinda Gates[267] reinforces the equity point.

> It's "a paradox," he says in an exclusive interview with Fortune, that "America has been so successful with such terrible education." We've gotten away with it, he says, by pampering an elite 20% - those who attend top colleges and the best public high schools and private academies, as Gates did himself before famously dropping out of Harvard.
>
> But now that has to change, he insists. With low-skill jobs vanishing and global competition on the rise, "the imperative

---

266. http://www.washingtonpost.com/wp-dyn/content/article/2009/05/07/
AR2009050703969.html

267. http://money.cnn.com/2008/11/25/magazines/fortune/GatesFoundation_Wallis.fortune/
index.htm

is to not just do well for the top 20% but to do well for everyone."

Several studies and reports concluded that we cannot fix the problems of inequality in America's K-12 public education system by applying additional reforms on top of the broken system. The Gates foundation spent hundreds of millions of dollars on a program to reduce school size. It was helpful, but it did not solve the problem. Another Gates effort focused on improving the quality of teachers[268] in the classroom ("getting rid of bad teachers"). Once again, it was helpful, but it did not solve the problem. We cannot fix the equity problem by experimenting on a few schools. The problems are not new. Researchers have been seeking and trying solutions for decades. There are some excellent programs already in existence. The challenge is to select a few of the proven best-practices from existing excellent programs and then make it easier for school districts to adopt or adapt those programs for all their schools. We need to follow the counsel of Voltaire when he advised, "*The perfect is the enemy of good.*" There will never be a perfect model because the world is constantly changing. If Thomas Edison waited for the perfect light bulb, we would still be working by lamplight. We need to accept research as it exists and begin transforming schools to the existing best models. Over time, as new knowledge emerges, the models will evolve. However, we cannot wait for a perfect model. We must begin transforming schools now. If you want to learn more about transforming schools, go to the Emaginos website[269]. Implementing these concepts will ensure that all students and members of the community have equitable access to a quality education in their neighborhood school.

---

268. https://www.bloomberg.com/news/articles/2010-07-15/bill-gates-school-crusade

269. http://emaginos.com/

In a bi-partisan, well-intentioned effort, the No Child Left Behind (NCLB) Act promoted aggressive annual improvement requirements based on high-stakes testing results. Following the law of unintended consequences, previously engaging learning environments became 'drill and kill' centers emphasizing memorization to do well on the tests. In this tightly constrained NCLB setting, there is no time to teach or practice 21st century skills. In the YouTube video titled Education for Innovation – Teaching and Learning[270] the presenter, Dave Janosz, introduces his material with a short excerpt from a Wanda Sykes stand-up comedy routine. Wanda's piece is from the 16 – 58 second marks. She beautifully and humorously characterizes the impact of teaching-to-the-test on student learning. The rest of the 9:21 minute video provides excellent back-up material reinforcing Janosz's point regarding educational innovation. The link to the video is in the footnote.

If you have not seen Sir Ken Robinson's YouTube video on Creativity in Education[271]. Take the time to watch it. His 19-minute presentation is both humorous and thought provoking.

Nationally, the US has a major educational and digital equity problem (Digital Equity is the term coined to describe the need for equal access to technology between affluent and poor students). The Web-based resources required to transform to a nation of K-12 public school students thriving in Science, Technology Engineering, Arts, and Math (STEAM) already exist. Bridging the digital divide by providing the equipment and knowledge for tapping into these resources will result in a transformation that will be the foundation for a sustainable innovation-based economy and a robust middle class.

---

270. http://www.youtube.com/watch?v=AojlMZGip6E

271. https://www.youtube.com/watch?v=wX78iKhInsc

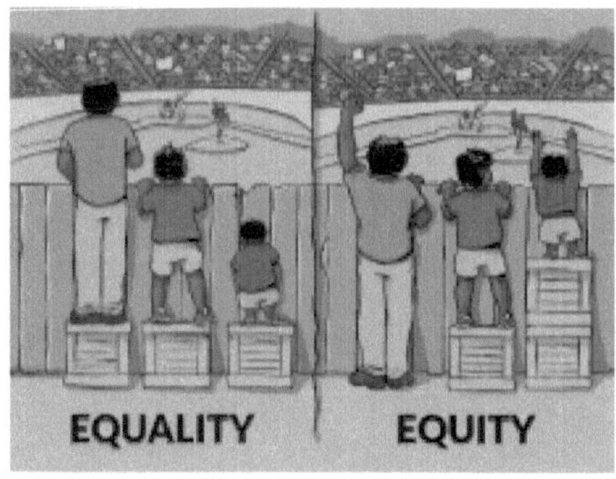

The Digital Divide Is Much More Than Just a Moral Issue. The 2016 presidential election campaigns shined a bright light on the glaring economic inequalities across the country. One of the biggest problems is the movement of the middle class towards poverty. The digital divide is a major manifestation and one of the many causes of this inequality. The digital divide is greatest in economically depressed communities and rural areas. It is a national economic issue. The digital divide leads directly to an unacceptable educational divide.

The US Bureau of Labor Statistics[272] reports that fifteen of the top twenty fastest growing industries in America are either healthcare or information technology related; and many of the healthcare jobs require extensive use of information technology tools and applications. How well is America preparing all its students to take advantage of the jobs in these sectors?

"Per an NTIA report, Falling Through the Net: Defining the Digital Divide[273], although black and Hispanic households are twice as likely to own computers today as

272. https://www.bls.gov/emp/tables/industries-fast-decline-employment.htm

273. *http://www.educationworld.com/a_tech/tech041.shtml*

they were in 1994, those households are still only 40 percent as likely to have home Internet access as white households are. In addition, whites are more likely to have access to the Internet from home than blacks or Hispanics are to have access from any location. A survey conducted by The Public Policy Institute of California found that even in California, a hotbed of technology, only 39 percent of the state's Hispanic people accessed the Internet compared to 65 percent of white people."

If America wants to compete successfully in a global marketplace, it must close the digital divide. We want students to harness the power derived from access to digital tools. The digital divide clearly affects students' academic performance, but it goes much deeper than that. It has a devastating and lasting impact on their earning potential. The lower their earnings, the more they require social safety-net programs. Closing the divide will reduce the need for safety net programs and ultimately cost less money than not closing it. America cannot afford to have a significant portion of its citizens unable to access or use digital tools.

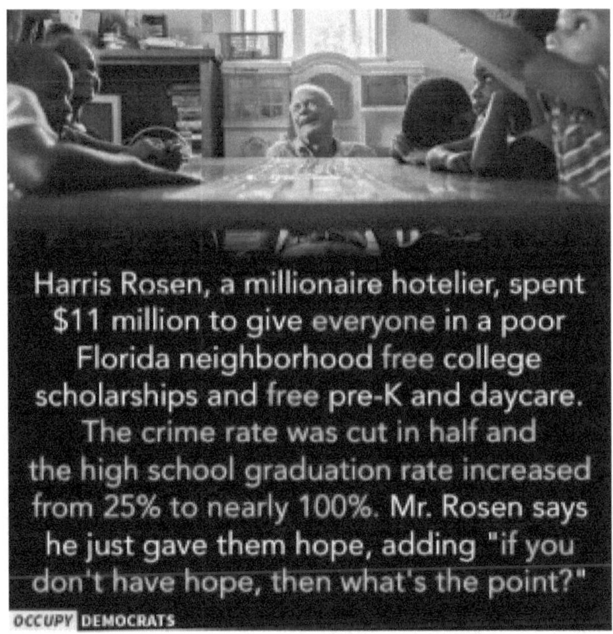
Harris Rosen, a millionaire hotelier, spent $11 million to give everyone in a poor Florida neighborhood free college scholarships and free pre-K and daycare. The crime rate was cut in half and the high school graduation rate increased from 25% to nearly 100%. Mr. Rosen says he just gave them hope, adding "if you don't have hope, then what's the point?"
OCCUPY DEMOCRATS

Conclusions and Solutions

Have we achieved our goal? Do you share our concern that our democratic principles are at risk? Do you agree that poverty is a major factor threatening our democracy? Are you ready to get involved in the fight to restore our democratic values? In this chapter we discuss some ways you can work with us to restore our country.

TWO THIRDS OF ELIGIBLE VOTERS DON'T VOTE

America does not have a problem. America has many problems, and they combine to threaten our democracy. Before we discuss a solution, let's review the issues.

- Poverty and its many symptoms and causes.

o Income and wealth inequality

o Homelessness

o Hunger and poor nutrition

● Minimum wage doesn't work – We need a Living wage.

● Lack of affordable healthcare

o High cost of prescription drugs

● Personal security and safety

o Terrorism – domestic and foreign

o Violence

▪ Mass shootings

▪ Lack of gun control

o Mass Incarceration and criminal justice

o Suicide

o Opioid crisis

● Crumbling national infrastructure

● Public education failing our children

● The world's best – and most costly – military

● Racism and discrimination

● Immigration

● Taxes

- Politicians who ignore the will of the people

As talked about in the previous chapters, we have discovered the orthodox cause of poverty and broken it down into categories. These are the issues that have allowed poverty to prosper. The orthodoxy correctly identifies the poor in contemporary society as those who fail to earn enough money to buy the things necessary for a minimally reasonable existence. The orthodox solution is therefore to raise the incomes of the poor. We've acknowledged low-income and the wealth gap, homelessness, scarcity, education, lack of affordable healthcare, restricted employment, security and safety, racism, immigration, and taxes. We also began to define the factors contributing to why there is so much lack in our community, state, region, country, and the world.

Poverty is manifested as a social problem. A social problem is any condition or behavior that has negative consequences for large numbers of people, and it is generally recognized that this condition or behavior needs to be addressed. Poverty appears to be hereditary. Homelessness, mental illness, unemployment, chemical abuse/dependency, domestic violence, foster care, pregnant youth, education, murders, lack of transportation and financial instability are all problems passed from generation to generation like some hereditary trait - all stemming from poverty. That is a frightening observation. The predominant cure for many hereditary conditions is Darwinian, those with the condition die off. Fortunately, it is not true. There are no genetic markers for poverty and its symptoms. Poverty is more like germ warfare, with some people deliberately spreading the germs. We know who they are. Our challenge is to stop them.

Fortunately, there are organizations already fighting the battles. Many organizations represent the same values and mission, use the same tools to operate, and take the same actions to help those in need. Unfortunately, they do not collaborate cross-sectionally with those who share identical goals and aspirations. Consequently, they do not perform as efficiently as they might if they worked more cooperatively. Organizations must ensure that they are partnering collaboratively, not competitively. There is an ancient business maxim that states, "The whole is greater than the sum of its parts." This is only true if the parts are organized and managed as a whole. Most cities, towns, and states have numerous agencies and organizations that focus on various selected issues in the list. I served several years on the Prince William County Continuum of Care (CoC) committee and some of its subcommittees - walking the walk. The function of the CoC was to coordinate the efforts of all of the agencies that served the populations listed above. I encourage you to learn about programs in your community and volunteer to assist in any way you can. If your community does not have a CoC, work with the county to form one to ensure your whole is greater than the sum of its parts.

Collaborating is about being able to share resources and services with those who are lacking those tools. Just as we stated in the first chapter, it takes:

1. **Opportunity**: having resources and key essentials that make their organizations valuable,
2. **Partnership**: collaborating with organizations to establish partnerships,
3. **Community connectivity**: referring and connecting organizations to clients and clients to organizations, and
4. **Success**: meeting the needs of clients and customers to provide benefits and produce ultimate success.

Without a foundation upon which to work with others, it is more difficult to make that change. This includes getting involved, learning, and understanding what is going on in the BIPOC (Black, Indigenous, and People of Color) communities. This final chapter, then, is a guideline for thinking and rethinking about how to deal with this situation in which we live. This plan is a proposal[274].

You may not agree with our perception of each of the issues, but we expect that you do agree that each of the issues we've raised is problematic and that under the existing conditions, there is not a clear path to fixing them. The intransigence of the problems on the list is daunting. Congress is apparently unable to make significant progress on any of the issues that produces a solution beneficial to most of the population. Witness the recent signature 'achievements' in healthcare and budget legislation. Congress fought along partisan lines, ultimately passing bills that nobody can be truly proud of. Our representatives must be willing to work across the aisles to produce, support, and pass universally beneficial bipartisan solutions.

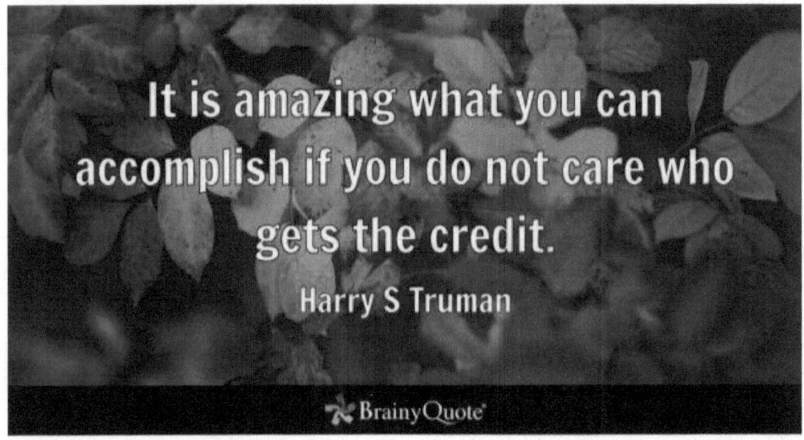

---

274. https://aalbc.com/authors/ebooks/master-plan-from-the-destruction-of-black-civilization-chancellor-williams.pdf

We Can Do This!

According to a 2022 Gallup survey[275] , the biggest issues threatening our democracy are:

economic issues, poor political leadership, poverty, crime and violence. It's time to show Congress how to do its job. To provide an example that progress is attainable, we will start by selecting a single issue that has popular bipartisan support among the voters and drive to get it done. Eliminating poverty is the place we should start. There is no established block of voters opposed to the idea. It is an umbrella issue that covers several included issues. There may be opposition to some of the previously tried solutions, but almost everyone agrees that eliminating poverty would be a good thing. A couple of possible first steps might include an infrastructure bill to stimulate the economy and reduce poverty and income inequality. We will include a living wage in the infrastructure bill. There is some partisan political opposition to this, but according to Pew Research[276], nearly two thirds of the voters favor a $15 minimum wage. They are our foot soldiers. The process will build momentum one issue at a time and demonstrate that, given the right incentives, Congress can work across the aisle to get important work done.

We will start with the economy/poverty followed by healthcare as the next issue to solve. We will be working directly on issues the voters care about and have expressed broad bipartisan support for. Indirectly we will be getting the government more productive. After fixing the healthcare issue, we will go to the next highest priority.

America's existing complex systems for electing people who will represent the citizens is badly broken. The recent elections were not

---

275. https://news.gallup.com/poll/1675/most-important-problem.aspx

276. https://www.pewresearch.org/short-reads/2019/07/30/two-thirds-of-americans-favor-

raising-federal-minimum-wage-to-15-an-hour/

stolen, but gaslighting and lying have created conspiracy theorists who are spreading the lies. Given all the voting obstacles mentioned earlier, it is no wonder that the government is not meeting the needs of the average citizen in either party. As we look back on the 2020 and 2022 elections, we are hearing more and more about efforts to corrupt the electoral process – particularly voter suppression and gerrymandering. We need to begin immediately to address it for 2024.

There is an enormous obstacle to passing any meaningful legislation. Without changing the incentives, we cannot count on the currently elected officials in their comfy political positions to go against the grain. The time has come to help our elected officials make better decisions. To achieve this goal, a group of philanthropists, political leaders, and statesmen, combined with citizen representatives from across society would need to team up to explore the options and propose a solution. For identification, we will refer to the team as the Democracy Defenders (DD) or the Poverty Fighters (PF) [We will have to do some research to come up with a name that is not already in use.] You may be wondering, "Who will empower this group to do anything?" Last time I checked, people do not need anyone to empower them to come together and solve problems.

Mikaya will organize and lead the DD teams, starting with small local teams that will grow and merge to form a national program.

Using infrastructure as an example, around the globe many developed countries have in place successful national infrastructure plans. The local DD teams will examine them, select, and combine the best elements from the existing proven programs to design their local programs. We will provide leadership and manage the cooperation that combines and integrates the local programs into a national plan. After the teams agree upon a national legislative infrastructure package that they believe will improve the current situation, they will present the concept to the American people. The citizens have the power! If the DD team does its job well, the resulting proposal will be appealing to people regardless of political party. Anyone running for election will need to back the plan if they want to win.

The next step is where the game profoundly changes. Historically, even though the people had the power of the vote, they failed to stand up to the power of the moneyed interests. The DD team will call upon the labor unions and other groups to assist in organizing and managing an unprecedented grass-roots effort to pressure their elected officials to support the proposed solution. Mark Zuckerberg and his company, Facebook (FB), should be feeling some embarrassment over revelations concerning Russia's use of FB to influence elections in the US and other elections around the world. FB might be eager to see its tools and platform used to strengthen democracy instead of subverting it.

The plan is not purely hypothetical. Idaho is in the middle of successfully implementing a similar plan when it comes to healthcare.

"In This Red State, Progressives Are Taking Matters Into Their Own Hands[277]

Amateur activists, sick of being ignored by the GOP, are fighting to cover the uninsured.

"To have hope, victory doesn't have to be certain. It doesn't even have to be probable. To have hope, victory just has to be possible." - Luke Mayville, Reclaim Idaho

---

277. https://www.huffingtonpost.com/entry/in-this-red-state-progressives-are-taking-matters-into-their-own-hands_us_5aadb598e4b0337adf8449fa

These activists, most of them new to politics, spoke of being inspired by the opportunity to make positive change in their communities. Some spoke of being driven to act by the election of President Donald Trump. But they all lamented the feeling that their government doesn't care what they want.

Like liberal activists mobilizing around the country on a variety of issues, acting is making these Idaho volunteers feel less alone and more empowered.

"I didn't think most of us realize how many out there feel the same way, and I found that knocking on doors," Pratt said. "I hope this spurs more throughout the state, I hope this spurs more throughout the country."

The national DD Team would be two groups – a small working group with a larger advisory team. We anticipate that one or more wealthy Americans will find the goals of the team worthy and provide some funding for the working group to do the administrative and operational work needed to advance the program. The members of the working group will be paid full-time professionals, while the advisory group will only come together periodically, as needed, to review progress and provide guidance for moving forward.

After the team agrees on the new model, it will use traditional and social media combined with good old-fashioned public political pressure to build grass-roots support for the model they developed. That pressure must be sustained through a couple of election cycles until the members of Congress realize who really controls their potential for re-election. After that lesson is taught, the rest of the issues on the list can be brought to the table – including making the changes required to ensure fair and democratic elections.

The Team Starts With You!

How do we begin? With whom? Where? How do we collaboratively get the funding? Or efforts to restore America's democratic greatness can be initiated with just one individual, you. Chancellor Williams gave us the book <u>Destruction of Black Civilization</u> that states, "*No great gathering or crowd starts a movement. Quite the contrary, when the many assemble it is because someone has already begun. One person has already thought matters through and resolved that a beginning must be made.*" Although Williams initially created his book specifically for black people to organize, we have found that the " Master Plan" is not only for one group of people, but for all groups and populations who may be oppressed and dealing with a barrier that seeks change. It is hard to organize without a firm foundation, and comprehension of what, where, how, when, and who needs fixing.

In order to make a change you have to look at yourself in the mirror and change you. Michael Jackson graciously sings *I'm starting with* " *the man in the mirror. I'm asking him to change his ways, and no message could've been any clearer, if you wanna make the world a* "*better place, take a look at yourself and then make a change* The song acknowledges that if you look at yourself and change who you are, you will be able to change the world. "*I see the kids in the street, without enough to eat. Who am I, to be blind pretending not to see their needs?*" Before we look at the world, let's look at ourselves.

Ask yourself "Am I eating healthy? Am I taking care of my body? Do I have the financial capabilities to feed myself and family for a week at a time?" If you are doing well, proceed to look at those who are malnourished and provide your service. If you answered, "No!", you may find yourself living in poverty. Either way, your understanding of the issues will move from hypothetical to very real; from theoretical to practical.

What classifies one as being in poverty? Someone who does not have enough money to meet basic needs including food, clothing, and shelter. You could have food and clothing but lack sufficient shelter. You could be living in a nice apartment, have enough food in your refrigerator, and good clothing; but you're living from paycheck to paycheck. You could have all of the above plus more, but still lack the knowledge of self. All of the listed choices are characteristics of poverty. Poverty insinuates oppression or being under unjust treatment and control. When you are absent from knowing thyself, you are conformed and confined to what the world wants you to believe about yourself.

Poverty is a national issue oppressing millions of people. But those millions are not one big mass of humanity. They are a collection of struggling individuals. At the same time, while it will take millions of people to fix poverty, it is not an amorphous mass. It is an organized collection of individuals, starting with someone like you knowing yourself and dedicating your energy to fixing the problem. Knowing thyself takes the courage to change the path that you're on. Using Mikaya's Kaya Kreatez method "Deeply Rooted: The Courage to Change Course " let me break it down for you on finding and acknowledging the essence of self.

1. **Truth:** speaking from an honest position and being vulnerable while telling your story.
2. **Getting To Yourself:** spending time asking yourself important questions that you've never had courage to ask about. Such as triggers and family trauma.

3. **Discovering Your Mission:** discovering and creating purpose, values, mission, and boundaries. This provides morals and acknowledges what you believe in from yourself and of others.

4. **Reflection:** Continuously reflecting on your progress. This doesn't mean you dwell in the past. This means you are evaluating your history of what you've been through and recognizing where you are is where you need to be.

5. **Gratitude:** Being appreciative of how far you've come, knowing you are blessed and abundant no matter where you are in life.

6. **Prayer:** Showing praises and appreciation as you are a reflection of the Divine. Even if you don't believe in a higher power, pray and praise yourself.

7. **Accountability:** Take responsibility for your own actions and be willing to acknowledge where you went wrong.

8. **Self-Awareness:** Discover your strengths and weaknesses. Because you are stronger than you think, anything that makes you weak, can make you strong. Anything that makes you strong, makes you secure.

9. **Self-Acceptance:** Accept where you've been and what you've been through. Your troubles are temporary. Accepting where you are and where you've been pushes you further to conquer more.

10. **Forgiveness:** Letting go and releasing the old. You've suffered pain long enough. Stop holding on to what no longer serves you. Forgive yourself, forgive the people who did you wrong, and grow from where you are.

11. **Growth, Wisdom, & Faith:** Change is often the most difficult part of achievement. When you change yourself, you grow. When you believe in yourself, you have more faith that everything will be okay in the process of where

you are. When you learn through the lessons you have gone through, you receive more wisdom.

12. **Manifest:** Co-creating and aligning because you are an alchemist. If you want things to change in the world, you have the power to see it flourish. Think it, write it, see it, believe it, manifest it, receive it. Receiving takes alignment.

13. **Freedom:** True authenticity and having authority over your life. You control your reality, no one else does. Freedom is a mindset that you can take advantage of; Don't hold yourself hostage to having a prosperous life.

Fighting poverty requires many dedicated individuals working as a team.

Forming the Dedicated Team!

Defeating poverty will require a dedicated team of people who are committed to restoring a functioning government. Mikaya will lead this activity, Forming a more perfect union, starts with establishing a dedicated group of individuals. This team does not have to start big nor have big names. Because poverty impacts everyone, although the effects may be different, it may be good for this group of people to be diversified—teachers, farmers, small business owners, healthcare professionals, military veterans, students, professionals, etc. This allows perspectives to be reached, ideas to be heard from all genres, and an opportunity for each member to specialize in their own category. Let's call them your planning committee. These will be your representatives. You will need a general name that everyone agrees to.

With these individuals, training, researching information, having statistics, and data produces an understanding of needs that need to be provided and met (just as we've discussed throughout this book). With outreach included to produce a large membership, by the second established meeting you should have 10-20 seekers who are willing to be a part of the movement.

You and Your Teams

Start with your team of one. As you read the book, you probably identified with some of the issues, some you are not interested in, while others made you passionately committed to getting involved in their solution.

- Make yourself a list of the latter issues and then capture your thoughts on the issue.

- Repeat this activity for each of the issues that raise your passions.

- Do this for each of the issues that fired your passions separately.

- Combine your separate issues, seeking common elements.

- Formulate a draft plan for your team of one to attack the issues.

- Look at your plan for one and you should discover places where one is not enough.

- Determine what additional resources you need.

- Identify and recruit additional resources/teams that improve your chances for success.

Outlining, Planning, and Organizing

1. Establish a general organization name, mission statement, and vision.
2. After recruiting your members, it's time to conduct and summarize an outline of the overall needs that are associated with poverty: what issues are we targeting and who are targeting them? With the statistical information obtained by members, broadcast and publicize your plan, mission, and goals to television companies, radio stations, print media, social medias and even commercials for:
    a. recognition, getting the word out, donations, more memberships, and establishing districts in other states.
3. Determine ways and means of funding the organizing activities and procedures[278].
    a. Procedures would be for building headquarters, establishing programs, creating services, and creating scholarships. (Through donations, fundraisers, festivals, and government grants.)
4. Determine the time and place for the first general assembly for the formal ratification and launching of an action-program.
5. Always provide accurate information when talking to a crowd. This means fact-based evidence and using credible resources. If you have a certain opinion or belief about an issue that you are passionate about, have data to support your thoughts. This contributes to your credibility.
6. The information and publicity committee maintain various media to keep constantly before the people the plans, purpose, or goals of the movement, who is doing what, and the progress being made.

---

278. https://aalbc.com/authors/ebooks/master-plan-from-the-destruction-of-black-civilization-chancellor-williams.pdf

    a. Adhere to your guiding principles of your organized movement.

Addressing Poverty Barriers

- Each city and state is affected differently from poverty. Identify the true needs of the community. Find organizations that correspond to the problem, and how they are solving problems.

- Whether you're going with a team or by yourself, come with an on-hand solution or idea that could benefit the organization. Partner with them. This creates a cross-sector collaborative connection.

- Know that for each person who is facing poverty, it is their choice and decision to make the change. It is not about holding their hand.

Opportunities

- The proportion of people who will support these changes is potentially many times larger than those who oppose it.

- New communications and collaboration technologies enable and allow us to build support for the new system and the plan for implementing it.

- You may be wondering why we included the 1%ers on the team. We need the 1%ers! In addition to their ability to fund the work, they are all very innovative and successful people. We need their creative minds and reputations in building the team and implementing the plan. We also do not want them to feel that the plan is against their interests. We want them with us, not against us. I do not know any of them personally, but from what I have read, most of them are strong supporters of the US in many ways. They appreciate that America allowed and enabled them to achieve what they have. They are not so insecure that they would be worried that the team would hurt their personal status. It is not the goal, and I can't imagine any scenario where that would be the outcome.

Evidence-Based Solutions

The Center for American Progress, a public policy research and advocacy organization, published an article on their website in June of 2021 titled, "The Top 12 Solutions To Cut Poverty in the United States[279]".

They took a different organizational approach to describing the issues, but they came to the same conclusions as we do in this book.

> *"Navigating through the current crisis and rebuilding better and stronger requires policymakers to take immediate action to provide equitable economic relief to all. Equitable rebuilding not only addresses systemic and institutional racism of past policy decisions but also focuses on inclusive economic transformation that can strengthen the U.S. economy and resilience in the long run. When the government invests in meeting peoples' basic needs and economic security through a robust safety net and jobs that help build financial security, children, families, and other vulnerable populations see improved outcomes in both the short and long term. The good news is that policymakers*

---

279. https://www.americanprogress.org/article/top-12-solutions-cut-poverty-united-states/

already have a range of tools that can prevent further increases in poverty and put all people on a pathway to economic mobility and resilience.

1. *Expand safety net programs to benefit all in need.*
2. *Create good-paying jobs that meet family needs.*
3. *Raise the minimum wage to ensure economic stability for all.*
4. *Provide permanent paid family and medical leave and paid sick days.*
5. *Increase worker power to rebalance the labor market.*
6. *Make permanent increases to the child tax credit and earned income tax credit.*
7. *Support pay equity to create a fair labor market.*
8. *Invest in affordable, high-quality childcare and early childhood education.*
9. *Expand access to health care.*
10. *Reform the criminal justice system and enact policies that support successful reentry.*
11. *Invest in affordable, accessible housing.*
12. *Modernize the Supplemental Security Insurance program."*

We have solutions, but where do we start? It starts with being a VISIONART! We have many organizations that ultimately do the same thing (have the same goals, mission, actions) that involves community change. Bringing these organizations together in protest, will allow political change. Every social problem needs time, effort, space, participants, and investment. Seeking monetary funds in regard to social programs will differ in size and quantity. The people have the ability to cause action in our own communities, states, and cities. It starts with our voices! How much are we willing to sacrifice to create the alteration and modification we want to see?

Will the America we know and love become a boiled frog? Will we continue to turn our backs and ignore the fact that millions of us are living and dying in abject poverty? Will the deaths of our innocent children in their schools be enough of a shock to force all of us to work together to change things? I have given it my best shot. If you have read this far, I must have struck some chords with you. The next steps are up to you.

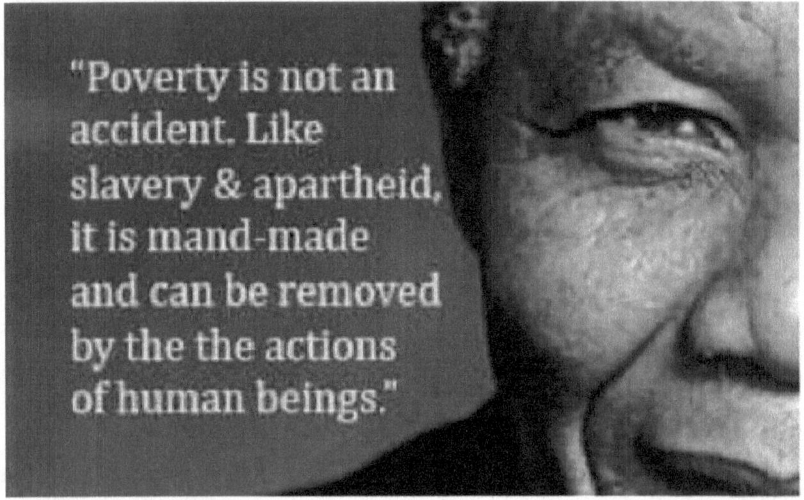

About the Author Mikaya L. Gent Mills

My grandmother always told me that when I came into this world, I came in fighting. She says, "Now, you don't have to fight"; however, I am fighting for another purpose and cause. That is fighting for social injustice, reducing poverty, and everything that stems from them. Since I was little, I have always had a passion for giving back, service, and helping my community. I learned this from my grandmother, "Giving is not just about receiving. It's about putting a smile on someone's face."

I became an advocate and activist because I saw the need within my own neighborhood that I grew up in and in my family. I am a native of Texas, specifically the Dallas part of "Oak Cliff, that's my hood!" In my childhood, I went through and saw a lot of traumatic events that initially seemed like it was supposed to hinder where I wanted to be, but it became the story that pushed me into becoming who I am. From domestic violence, to molestation, rape, bullying; you name it.

Right after high school, I received a scholarship to attend Philander Smith College, a Historically Black College/ University in Little Rock Arkansas. This school specializes in social justice, and career readiness. This school was for me as it taught me to shift my paradigm.

I started out with a major in Psychology, because I wanted to work with and understand the minds of people who look like me. Then, I got introduced to Social Work, and I fell in love with it. Just the fact that social work is broader and works with the micro (individual), macro (family), and mezzo (community) population; I knew that this route was for me. In March of 2020, I was told that I had to leave my school and go back home to Dallas. This is where I saw the need and effect of Covid-19. This is also where I was able to first-handedly use the knowledge I gained to help my community. Once I got home, I immediately got to work and created Kaya Kreatez! In 2021, I graduated Cum Laude with a Bachelor of Arts in Social Work with a minor in Psychology.

Essentially, the events that I went through and saw, are what prepared me to create my own company Kaya Kreatez LLC. that specializes in advocacy, self-love, life-coaching, and creating a comfortable and loving space for you to get through your traumatic experiences and flourish. If you read the final chapter of this book, you will see categories in what it takes to heal yourself. I have my own workbook entitled "Work Through, Grow Through Self-Love Workbook". This book goes into detail ways you can heal yourself through journal work, prayer, etc. I also hold workshops, bootcamps, and seminars that cater to categories such as (1) Wiz Theory: Know ThySelf, (2) Unpacking Your Baggage: Courage to Change Course, (3) Hacking Life On and Off The Court (for youth athletes).

My life purpose and goal is to bridge the gap between people that want to help those who are in need by providing services, but also pushing them to live a life of self-sufficiency. We find time and time again that those who are wanting help, are looking to be independent, but lack direction. Giving them an opportunity to be directed while making sure you don't manage them completely. Provide support but do not hinder them by "babying" their movements. The problem stems from not listening or hearing what their problem is, we just give them what we think they need.

About the Author Allan C. Jones

I have written from my personal perspective. To be fair to you, the reader, I want to tell you what my values are, so you can fairly assess my opinions. My goal with this book is to provide a broad range of information to anyone who will take the time to read it, and hopefully to motivate many of you to get involved with fixing the problems. The following paragraphs give you an insight into who I am.

When I wake up in the morning, I have two goals.

1. Learn something.
2. Make the world a better place.

I grew up in Portland, Maine. Mom and Dad were working-class parents. My father, Charlie Jones - a typewriter repairman, was a second generation American – his dad emigrated from England. My mom's family (Marjorie Jones) also came from Great Britain, but in the early colonial days. Mom was a Republican, a secretary to the State Attorney general, and an active Congregationalist Christian. Dad was a great human being who loved helping others. I do not fit into any political partisan or religious group. If I had to select a label, it would be Humanitarian. I have a simple but challenging goal. I want to leave the world a better place than I found it. The following points summarize the lessons Mom and Dad taught us. Those lessons guide me to this day.

The Golden Rule – While Mom taught the traditional Christian version, we learned it as a practical and valuable way to live. In its simplest form, it is still, "Do unto others as you would have them do unto you." In today's terms that translates to, "Treat other people the way you would like other people to treat you." It is such a simple and easily applied rule that you can apply it in any situation.

This leads directly to a slight variation in the rule – **Always play fair**. This one was a little more difficult to accept, but over time, it has made better people of those who learned from her. The hard part of this rule was that others may not be fair to us, but we were not allowed to use their unfairness as an excuse for us not to be fair.

Mom also taught us to take great pleasure from **doing things for others**. She was way ahead of her time. Have you seen the movie, "Pay it forward", with Haley Joel Osment? Mom was teaching that lesson over 70 years ago. She had an interesting variation. Her way of looking at it was, "**Don't keep score.**" If you can do something for somebody, just do it; without any expectation of them paying you back. If you enjoy doing things for others, then the payback is in the pleasure you get from helping them.

Her love was unconditional. She used to teach us that she may not love what we did, but she would always love us.

Good marriages and families take lots of effort, but they are worth it – so just do it! There is no expiration date on the positions of parent, sibling, or spouse. They are all lifetime commitments, so you need to do whatever it takes to ensure that you are the best parent, sibling, or spouse you can be.

Always tell the truth. In our home, there was a difference between kidding and lying; and the line was very clear. If you were pulling a practical joke and the joke required telling a 'white' lie, it was okay – up to a point. If the person caught on and asked you directly if you were kidding, you had to stop and tell the truth. Truthfulness and the trust that you earn with it were more valuable and important than the joke.

Be reasonable. From an early age, Mom would always take the time to tell us why we should do something; and the reason was never,

"Because I said to do it." She was very clear that in some emergencies we should just do what she told us to do and expect that the reason would come later. By always taking the time to teach us to be reasonable, she prepared us to make good decisions on our own.

Do not make excuses – Take personal responsibility. Everyone makes mistakes. The secret to success is to learn from mistakes and not repeat them. If you deny your personal responsibility when things do not work out right, then you miss the opportunity to learn and improve yourself.

Do the right thing – The culminating lesson was that you should do all these things not because you had to, but because they were **the right thing to do**. Doing what is right is not about reward or punishment. It's the right thing to do – so just do it.

My dad was a major influence in my development. If you asked most people to provide you a list of the great men of the past 100 years, my dad probably would not make the list. However, if you asked a group of people who knew him well, few would leave him off the list. Dad gave those who knew him a unique understanding of a special kind of greatness. His greatness came from serving, not leading. Dad took his greatest pleasure in helping others. He had a gentleness and caring about him that made him a pleasure to know and be with. To know Dad was to love him.

If you can measure a person's greatness by his impact on the people he knew, Dad was one of the greatest. If you knew Dad, you would become a better person. He taught not by preaching, but by his own example. He was the most honest and ethical person I ever met. He exuded a calmness and serenity that taught us how to deal with difficult or unpleasant times. In his last years, Dad constantly required oxygen and was frequently in the hospital with his lungs full of fluid. Anyone who asked him how he was doing during that period probably heard an answer like, "I'm doing fine. I just can't breathe." As though that were a minor annoyance.

Another remarkable aspect of his personality was that he could be an example of all these good qualities without ever giving the impression that he felt that he was better than the next person. He had a great sense of humor and was fun to be around. He had that rare ability to tease people without making them feel uncomfortable. He wasn't the life of the party, but he gave life to the party.

Dad was a great dancer. When we were young, he would stand my sister, Leslie, on his toes, and sing and dance with her. If he heard that good beat, he would soft-shoe or tap his way across the floor. When Mom and Dad danced at Leslie's wedding, they stole the show! They didn't take dancing lessons; they just had fun dancing and moved beautifully together. My brother Brad's son Spencer inherited Dad's love of dancing and occasionally provides us a reminder of Dad's light-footed whimsies.

Dad was the consummate handyman. He taught us all the confidence to try to fix anything. Unfortunately, we also learned never to throw anything away because you never know when it (or one of its parts) might come in handy.

The values that he and Mom taught their children, (and we have tried to pass on to our children) have resulted in a family that made him immensely proud. We all share his sense of service and commitment to our friends and community.

Dad gave us a new definition of "macho". He was gentle, kind, honest, funny, caring, open, family oriented, loving, warm, sweet, and polite. In addition, he managed to be all of that and still be a strong and masculine example of the best man we ever met. He touched many of our lives deeply. He was a genuinely great man. May we all carry on his greatness by following the example he set for us.

Many years ago, I read the following poem on the cover of the program for a DeMolay Conclave. It still sticks with me.

The Man in the Glass

Dale Wimbrow (c) 1934

1895-1954

When you get what you want in your struggle for self

And the world makes you king for a day,

Just go to a mirror and look at yourself,

And see what that man has to say.

For it isn't your father or mother or wife,

Whose judgment upon you must pass.

The fellow whose verdict counts most in your life

Is the one staring back from the glass.

He's the fellow to please, never mind all the rest.

For he's with you clear up to the end,

And you've passed the most dangerous, difficult test

If the man in the glass is your friend.

You may be like Jack Horner and "chisel" a plum,

And think you're a wonderful guy,

But the man in the glass says you're only a bum

If you can't look him straight in the eye.

You may fool the whole world down the pathway of years.

And get pats on the back as you pass,

But your final reward will be the heartaches and tears

If you've cheated the man in the glass.

I had the honor of attending the United States Naval Academy. I recently attended my 50th reunion with many of my classmates. What an incredible group of people! In 1971, I got out of the Navy and went into education. I subsequently earned a Master of Arts in Education and a certificate in computer technology. For the past fifty years, I have served this country as a naval officer or an educator. Now you know who I am, and why I wrote this book. I hope you enjoy it, but more importantly, I hope it motivates you to become actively involved in working to continue America's greatness.

Acknowledgements

This is a simple list of the people who shaped me into the person I am and inspired me to dedicate my life to making the world a better place. That lesson began early in life – taught by Mom and Dad (Margie and Charlie Jones)

The rest of the list must start with my immediate family, Cheri Jones, Heather Cleary, and Kim Scott. Each of them is amazing and loving. They are followed closely by Kim's family, Peter, Elsa, Carolyn, and Sally Scott, Talia Makarov, and Jason Cleary and his family – Sandra, Jim, and Sarah. Extending the family brings a large and loving group that starts with my sister, Leslie, and brother, Brad, and their sons, daughters, and grandsons and granddaughters. I love them all and am proud to call them family.

On the professional side, I have been truly fortunate to have met, worked with, and learned from some remarkable people. When I first started on this journey called 'education', I had the honor and pleasure of working for Irwin Pottle, the principal of Oxford High School. School Superintendent Dr. Frank Driscoll taught me about innovation and leadership. John Phillipo gave me many opportunities to learn and make a difference at the same time. Thanks to the reach of Facebook, I am still in touch with and encouraged by many of my former students and fellow teachers. One of them in particular, Mike Powers, has become a friend and advisor.

Jack Taub took me under his considerable wing and inspired me to shoot for the stars in transforming K-12 public education. Scott Taub picked up Jack's vision and continues to encourage me to pursue the dream. In pursuit of the dream, I had the honor of becoming friends with a couple of great Americans, Mort Bahr, and

Bill Brock. Mort was the President Emeritus of the Communications Workers of America, and Bill is a former US Senator from Tennessee and Secretary of Labor under Ronald Reagan.

My current collaborators and fellow dreamers are Winfred Payne, Bob James, Dr. Keith Larick, Bonnie, and Vic Sutton. They inspire and encourage me and together we will change the world. Without naming individuals, there are many dedicated public servants here in Prince William County, VA, who encourage me and allow me to be a part of their efforts.